# POEMS TO THE CHILD-GOD

*This volume is sponsored by the*
CENTER FOR SOUTH AND SOUTHEAST ASIA STUDIES,
*University of California, Berkeley*

The Center for South and Southeast Asia Studies of the University of California is the coordinating center for research, teaching programs, and special projects relating to the South and Southeast Asia areas on the nine campuses of the University. The Center is the largest such research and teaching organization in the United States, with more than 150 related faculty representing all disciplines within the social sciences, languages, and humanities.

The Center publishes a Monograph Series, an Occasional Papers Series, and sponsors a series of books published by the University of California Press. Manuscripts for these publications have been selected with the highest standards of academic excellence, with emphasis on those studies and literary works that are pioneers in their fields, and that provide fresh insights into the life and culture of the great civilizations of South and Southeast Asia.

RECENT PUBLICATIONS OF THE
CENTER FOR SOUTH AND SOUTHEAST ASIA STUDIES:

FRANK F. CONLON
*A Caste in a Changing World:*
*The Chitrapur Saraswat Brahmans*

KENNETH JONES
*Arya Dharm:*
*Hindu Consciousness in 19th-Century Punjab*

KAREN B. LEONARD
*Social History of an Indian Caste:*
*The Kayasths of Hyderabad*

LEONARD NATHAN
*The Transport of Love:*
*The Meghadūta of Kālidāsa*

M. N. SRINIVAS
*The Remembered Village*

# POEMS TO THE CHILD-GOD

## *Structures and Strategies in the Poetry of Sūrdās*

KENNETH E. BRYANT

University of California Press
Berkeley · Los Angeles · London

With sincere thanks to Ashok Aklujkar, Vinayaka Bhatta, Lee Ann Bryant, John Gage, Robert Goldman, Linda Hess, Eugene Irschick, Kathy Merken, Leonard Nathan, Bruce Pray, George Saliba, Jan Walls

and to the memory of Gordon Roadarmel

ISBN: 978-0-520-30285-3 (pbk. : alk. paper)

University of California Press
Berkeley and Los Angeles, California

University of California Press, Ltd.
London, England



Library of Congress Catalog Card Number: 77-80467

# CONTENTS


Preface .................................... vii
1. *The poet as tradition* .................... vii
2. *On the perils of translation* ................ xiii

Acknowledgments ........................... xv

Abbreviations ............................. xvi

Introduction ................................ 1
1. *The cowherd and the emperor* ............... 1
2. *The life and līlā of Kṛṣṇa* ................. 6
3. *Wytte and wundyr* ........................ 12

**Part One:** *Structures and Strategies in the Poetry of Sūrdās* ..................... 19

Chapter I: *Sūr-līlā* and *Kṛṣṇa-līlā* .............. 21
1. *Rasa and rhetoric* ......................... 21
2. *Censorship and the courteous critic* .......... 26
3. *Vātsalya-bhāva and the forgetful audience* .... 35
4. *The poem as event* ........................ 40

Chapter II: Narrative Strategies ................ 43
1. *Contract, closure, and the omniscient audience* . 43
2. *The eighth coming* ........................ 51
3. *Bowman and butterthief* .................... 60

Chapter III: The Verbal Icon ................... 72
1. *Signs and tokens* .......................... 72
2. *Figures of deceit* ......................... 75
3. *Frames for the icon: paratactic, sequential* ..... 90
4. *The irony of it All* ....................... 105

Chapter IV: Strategy and the Forms of Language ..... 113
1. *The hand that ropes the wind: figures of contiguity* ..... 113
2. *The union of sound and sense* ..... 124

Chapter V: Misers of Sound and Syllable: Summing Up ..... 134

**Part Two:** *Poems to the Child-God* ..... 143

*A word on the poems* ..... 145
*Maṅgalācaraṇa: Benediction* ..... 147
I. *Nandanandana: Nanda's Son* ..... 149
II. *Mākhancor: the Butterthief* ..... 166
III. *Giridhara: the Mountainbearer* ..... 181
IV. *Muralīdhara: the Flutebearer* ..... 193
V. *Sūraprabhu: Sūr's Lord* ..... 205
*Epilogue: the Last Poem* ..... 209

Notes to Part Two ..... 211

Glossary ..... 221

Bibliography ..... 235

Index ..... 239

# PREFACE

## 1. *The poet as tradition*

"Whatever looks like invention is theft."
—Ozick[1]

This is a book of and about the poems of the *Sūrsāgar*. It is not a literary history, nor is it a literary biography; historian and biographer will find the *Sūrsāgar*, its author, and its milieu to be most uncooperative subjects.

"I think that it is not at all impossible," confessed one exasperated Orientalist, "that no such person . . . ever existed, and that his name is a mere cover to the innovations of some freethinker amongst the Hindus."[2] The person in question was the poet Kabīr (fifteenth century? sixteenth century?); the Orientalist was the eminent H. H. Wilson (decidedly nineteenth century); but the exasperation remains an inseparable companion on any scholarly foray into the chaos of medieval Hindi literature. This is true for the student of the *Sūrsāgar* no less than for the student of Kabīr; yet, for the former at least, there are some things that may be said with confidence: the work is an immensely popular collection of several thousand devotional lyrics, existing in a number of different recensions, addressed to the god Kṛṣṇa, composed in the Braj-bhāṣā dialect of Hindi, currently employed for liturgical purposes by the Vallabha sect, and attributed to a blind sixteenth-century poet named Sūrdās.

Now I think it very likely (to reverse Wilson's pessimism) that such a person as Sūrdās (or Sūr, as he is commonly

1. Cynthia Ozick, "Usurpation (Other People's Stories)," in *Bloodshed and Three Novellas* (New York, 1976), p. 161.
2. H.H. Wilson, *Religious Sects of the Hindus* (Calcutta, 1958), p. 36, n. 25. Quoted in Charlotte Vaudeville, *Kabīr* (Oxford, 1974), vol. I, p. 9.

known) did indeed exist. Certainly, the sources for a biography of Sūr are far more numerous than for Kabīr. Here, in fact, lies part of the dilemma: there is ample evidence to support at least two radically different versions of the poet's life. The arguments for both have been discussed at length by Charlotte Vaudeville. Much, she stresses, depends upon whether one accepts Hindu sources or Muslim. The former consist chiefly of Vallabhite sectarian hagiographies, notably the *Caurāsī vaiṣṇavan kī vārtā*, in which Sūr is claimed as a disciple of Vallabha himself, and as a poet and musician attached to the Vallabhite temple of Śrīnāthjī at Govardhana. I have sketched the outlines of this, the most widely accepted tradition of Sūr's life, in the Introduction. Vaudeville, however, is more persuaded by Muslim accounts, and in particular by the *Āīn-i-Akbarī*, on the basis of which she portrays Sūr as a poet and musician *at the court of Akbar*, the Mughal emperor. Vaudeville goes so far as to suggest that the poet's association with the sect of Vallabha may have been, at best, peripheral:

> De fait, l'absence de toute référence à Vallabha, au *Poushti-mârga* et au temple de Shrî Nâthjî dans l'oeuvre de Soûr-Dâs semble bien indiquer que le poète ne se considéra jamais comme membre de la secte et qu'il n'avait pas de dévotion particulière à Shrî Nâthjî.[3]

Are we then to view Sūr as court poet (and a Muslim court at that), or temple poet, or both at once, or at different times—or, simply, as a composite of two different individuals altogether? For my part, I am inclined to accept the Vallabhite accounts; but in any case, I have no intention of reopening a debate that is unlikely ever to be resolved, barring the emergence of new documentary evidence.

Biography is the lesser of our problems: the uncertainty surrounding the poet's life is more than matched by that

3. Charlotte Vaudeville, trans. and intro., *Pastorales par Soûr-Dâs* (Paris, 1971), p. 38.

surrounding his actual writings. At least three attempts at completing a critical edition of the *Sūrsāgar* have been interrupted by the deaths of the supervising scholars: Jagannāth Dās "Ratnākar"; M. P. Gupta; and most recently, Jawāharlāl Caturvedī. The task is indeed gargantuan. Tradition ascribes to Sūrdās the composition of 125,000 *padas*; and while nothing like that number are to be found today, the thousands of surviving verses are contained in a large number of manuscripts, scattered across the whole of North and Central India, with many (including some purported to be the oldest) in jealously guarded private collections.[4] Of the extant manuscripts, all appear to have been written after the poet's death.

Indeed, I think it not impossible that much of Sūr's poetry was never written down during the poet's life. Sūr, it must be remembered, was heir to a largely oral tradition; in medieval India, themes, phrases, even whole poems were very much in the public domain. The genius of an individual poet often lay, not in composing a new piece out of whole cloth, but rather in retailoring a time-honored piece to fit the occasion of a particular performance. We may best view Sūr as a "Singer of Tales," rather than as a writer in the usual sense of that word; and if we imagine him so, it is not difficult to imagine as well a time, a generation after Sūr had died and passed into legend, when the sect that had adopted him undertook the task of setting down in writing those thousands of songs, by now sung and improvised by scores of poet-performers, which tradition ascribed to the magical name of a single blind poet.

Conjecture aside, one certain fact remains: there is and has long been a Sūr tradition. It is manifested in the body of poems known as the *Sūrsāgar*; the authorship may be in doubt, but the cohesion is unquestionable. Sūr may remain an unknown quantity; the Sūr tradition is readily accessible.

4. The most complete discussion of the extant manuscripts of the *Sūrsāgar* is Jawāharlāl Caturvedī. *Sūradāsa: adhyayanasāmagrī* (Mathura, 1959).

In an early draft, I attempted to make scrupulously explicit mention of this fact at every opportunity. "In the Sūr tradition," I would say; or, "we may then generalize that in poems from the tradition associated with the name Sūrdās . . . ." It proved cumbersome, and worse: it rang false. It implied that Sūr was a fictive character, and he is not; he is a *mythic* character, bigger than life, not smaller. Sūr lives for the North Indian audience as surely as Shakespeare lives for the English. To prove *Othello* written by Bacon or Marlowe would in no way change the fact that generations of schoolboys, scholars, and playgoers have enjoyed the play as a creation of The Bard, the same who left his "secondbest bed" to Ann Hathaway. The myth in all its detail inevitably conditions our experience of the work. And so I give fair warning: while I shall mean "the Sūr tradition," I shall say simply, "Sūr."

In textual terms, the Sūr tradition has come increasingly to mean the printed edition of the *Sūrsāgar*, containing some 5,000 *padas*, published by the Nāgarī Pracāriṇī Sabhā. While representing a mighty labor of collection and sifting, the text is by no means a critical edition in the strict sense of the term; it has, however, become the standard edition, in that it forms the basis for almost all modern scholarship on Sūr, both in India and abroad. Since it is the best-known "Sūr," it is one of two editions employed in the present study. The second is that of the late Jawāharlāl Caturvedī, which, while a critical edition, is incomplete. Where available, I have throughout given citations from both editions, and have noted any significant variations.

I have said little about the performance of the poems, and for two reasons. First, to describe the present contexts of performance would require a book in itself. Sūr's poems are employed for liturgical purposes in Vallabhite ritual; they also constitute a part of the repertoire of many a classical vocalist, and of many a village singer; read, recited, or sung, they are enjoyed daily by millions. And as regards the original, intended context of performance, for any individual poem or for the corpus as a whole, we dare not even speculate: here again we are up against the uncertainties of biography as well as those of text.

What, then, can we say about these poems? A great deal, I think. Whatever the uncertainties concerning their original intended audience, we may assume that it was a North Indian audience, of the sixteenth century or later; that it was an audience, then, who were familiar with the story of Kṛṣṇa and with the tradition of Kṛṣṇaite verse. And whatever the uncertainties concerning the original style of performance, we may safely assume that the poems were intended for oral performance. These few assumptions are central to the present study. I intend to approach the individual poem as something like a score for performance, a potential event, subject to a wide but not unrestricted range of individual interpretation. This might be characterized as a study of style and structure; I prefer the term *strategy*. The significance of the term will become apparent as the study unfolds. For the moment, suffice it to note that it is a term particularly applicable to the set of poems chosen for analysis in Part One of the book.

Finally, then, a word is necessary on the structure of this book itself, and on the corpus of poems chosen here for analysis and translation. It is the intention of Part Two merely to introduce the reader to a broad sampling of poems from the *Sūrsāgar*, in English translation, accompanied by a brief set of explanatory notes. The poems selected for Part Two are intended to present a cross-section of Sūr's work; they are weighted rather heavily toward poems on the child Kṛṣṇa, but this bias will surprise no one familiar with Sūr and his work; while the child-poems constitute only about a fifth of the five thousand poems in the standard editions, they are indisputably the poems for which Sūr is best known.

The intention of Part One is somewhat different. Rather than dealing with Sūr's creation in all its breadth, Part One examines a small, but significant portion of that creation in considerable detail. This narrowing of focus is motivated in part by simple considerations of space. The method of analysis employed requires that we savor each poem, that we linger. We cannot linger over 5,000 *padas*, or even over the 1,000 or so child-poems. What is needed is a manageable corpus; that selected here consists of the approximately 300 poems that I have labeled the "epiphanies": poems of revelation and ironic contrast, poems that play the child against the god. To a certain extent this particular choice reflects a desire to redress what I perceive as an imbalance in previous studies, which have rather uniformly stressed the "cute" aspect of the child-poems. What has been missing from most anthologies is the power of Sūr's verse; what must be restored is, to paraphrase Tagore, "the vitamins."

But there is yet another reason for lingering over the epiphanies: they are the most structurally complex of Sūr's poems, and thus afford us the greatest opportunity for examining the ways in which Sūr crafted his verse. For in Part One it is above all the poet's craft with which we shall be concerned: not so much *what* the poet says (that we may see in the poems themselves), but *how* he says what he does; how the poems employ the tools of language, myth, and convention to move their audience to feel and think in certain ways.

The two parts of the book may, of course, be read separately; with this in mind, I have provided a general introduction which should serve equally well for either. But for the reader interested in the whole, there is a reason behind the ordering of the parts. What I shall propose is a way of approaching Sūr's poetry—not a way that excludes other ways, but one that I hope will complement them. The test of Part One will be the extent to which its observations make clearer the poems of Part Two.

## 2. *On the perils of translation*

> "We danced . . . like *gajagāminīs*."
> —*The Sūrsāgar*[5]
>
> "*Gajagāminī*: a woman blessed with a graceful carefree gait like that of an elephant." —*A Practical Hindi-English Dictionary*[6]

A literal translation is a bad poem; an impressionistic translation is bad scholarship. Like all translators, I have attempted to strike a compromise. Like all translators, I owe my reader an explanation of the terms of that compromise.

My approach has in general been less "literal" than "linear." That is, I have for the most part (and in Part One, scrupulously) maintained the ordering of material from line to line, while taking some liberties with the ordering of material within the line. This approach is particularly appropriate for Hindi, where enjambment is a thing unknown; the line-unit is, in all but a very few cases, the syntactic unit as well.

I have tipped the balance toward the literal in those poems (particularly in the later chapters) where my analysis has looked most closely at individual words, their sounds, and their syntactic relationships. I have tipped the balance the other way when analysis has treated the subtleties of human relationships, or the sweep and suspense of narrative. In the poems translated for analysis in Part One, I have numbered the lines so that my translation may be compared, line by line, with the original—for it is the original, after all, on which my arguments are based, and on which they must

5. *Sabhā* 1666.

6. Mahendra Chaturvedi and B.N. Tiwari, *A Practical Hindi-English Dictionary* (Delhi, 1975), p. 166. For the epigraph, I have taken the liberty of removing parentheses placed by the authors around the words "a woman" and "like that of an elephant." The first is implied in the gender of the noun, and the second is explicit in the compound itself: *gaja*, "elephant," plus *gāminī*, "one (fem.) who moves."

stand or fall. In Part Two, I have taken somewhat greater liberties with lineation when these seemed justified in the pursuit of readable English.

Throughout I have used rhyme sparingly; the English-speaking audience of today is unaccustomed to verse that rhymes with as much regularity as does that of Sūr (or that of Pope, for that matter). With alliteration I have been less restrained, although English verse will not, alas, permit anything like the virtuoso alliteration of the original. I have not hesitated to replace an obscure epithet with one better known, unless the less-known epithet is itself of importance for understanding the verse; and I have not hesitated to alternate between *tatsama* and *tadbhava* spellings of certain words (e.g., "Syām" and "Śyāma"). The latter "inconsistency" is in fact thoroughly consistent with Sūr's own practise: like him, I have taken advantage of the Hindi poet's option to choose between Sanskrit and colloquial forms, for reasons of sound as well as sense.

# ACKNOWLEDGMENTS

Excerpt from *Kavitāvalī*, translated by F. R. Allchin. Reprinted by permission of George Allen & Unwin, Ltd.

Excerpt from *In Praise of Krishna: Songs from the Bengali*, translated by Edward C. Dimock, Jr., and Denise Levertov. Copyright © 1967 by The Asia Society Inc. Used by permission of Doubleday & Company, Inc.

Excerpt from "Marina" in *Collected Poems* 1909–1962 by T. S. Eliot, copyright, 1936, by Harcourt Brace Jovanovich, Inc.; copyright © 1963, 1964 by T. S. Eliot. Reprinted by permission of Harcourt Brace Jovanovich, Inc., and Faber and Faber Limited.

Excerpt from *Sanskrit Poetry from Vidyākara's "Treasury,"* translated by Daniel H. H. Ingalls, copyright 1965, 1968 by the President and Fellows of Harvard College. Reprinted by permission of Harvard University Press.

Excerpts from *Speaking of Śiva*, translated by A. K. Ramanujan (Penguin Classics, 1973), copyright reserved by A. K. Ramanujan, 1973. Reprinted by permission of Penguin Books Ltd.

"How Annandale Went Out" by Edwin Arlington Robinson is reprinted from *The Town Down the River* with the permission of Charles Scribner's Sons.

"The force that through the green fuse drives the flower" from *The Poems of Dylan Thomas*, copyright 1939 by New Directions Publishing Corporation. Reprinted by permission of New Directions Publishing Corporation and J M Dent & Sons Ltd., and the Trustees for the Copyrights of the late Dylan Thomas.

Excerpt from *The Love of Krishna: The Kṛṣṇakarṇāmṛta of Līlāśuka Bilvamaṅgala*, edited by Frances Wilson, copyright 1975 by The University of Pennsylvania Press. Reprinted by permission of The University of Pennsylvania Press.

Excerpt from "The Second Coming," from *The Collected Poems of William Butler Yeats*, copyright 1924 by Macmillan Publishing Co., Inc., renewed 1952 by Bertha Georgia Yeats. Reprinted by permission of M. B. Yeats; Miss Anne Yeats; The Macmillan Co. of London & Basingstoke; and Macmillan Publishing Co., Inc.

# ABBREVIATIONS

*: This symbol will be used to indicate epithets of Kṛṣṇa, with the exception of the two most common in Sūr's verse: Hari and Śyāma.

Caturvedī: Jawāharlāl Caturvedī, ed., *Sūra-sāgara* (Calcutta, 1965).

*Sabhā*: Jagannāth Dās "Ratnākar" et al., eds., *Sūrasāgara* (Varanasi: Nāgarī Pracāriṇī Sabhā, 4th ed., *saṃvat* 2029).

# INTRODUCTION

## 1. *The cowherd and the emperor*

Nobody asks
your caste or your class
at the court of the Lord of Śrī.
—Sūrdās[1]

In a seventeenth-century text on the lives of the Vaiṣṇava saints,[2] it is told that the Emperor Akbar once called before him a certain blind poet. Akbar had been impressed by the poet's verse; he was now to be astounded by his audacity, for the poet refused to sing the praises of Akbar, Muslim Emperor of India, preferring instead to sing of Kṛṣṇa, a cowherd's son and an infidel's god.

Yet the Emperor, known for his ecumenical views, was satisfied in all respects but one: if the poet had no eyes, how then could he describe so vividly the scenes of Kṛṣṇa's life? The Emperor posed the question; the poet remained silent.

Now Akbar was himself a man of considerable vision, a fact that our narrowly sectarian text finds it necessary to explain. The Emperor, we are told, had spent his former birth as a brahmin ascetic named Bālmukund; and it was only an unfortunate accident, involving a cow's hair and some unstrained milk, that damned him to rebirth as a merely Muslim ruler. But his powers of discernment had not been curtailed by his fall from brahminhood to the Mughal throne, and he perceived at once the answer to his own question:

He does have eyes; but they are with God,
and it is there that he sees.[3]

1. *Sabhā* 231.
2. The *Caurāsī vaiṣṇavan kī vārtā*. Portions cited here are from *Sūrdās kī vārtā*, ed. Premnārāyaṇ Ṭaṇḍan (Lucknow, 1968).
3. *Sūrdas kī vārtā*, p. 58. The explanation of Akbar's karmic ancestry

The tale echoes a common belief: that poets possess a power of vision denied to other men. For the devotees of Kṛṣṇa, it is in part this vision that gives the poet access to the *līlā*—the divine Play, the Sport, of Kṛṣṇa in the land of Braj. Once, long ago, the *līlā* was played on earth for all to see: the Lord took human form as a cowherd, and roamed the woods and villages that border the River Yamunā. Now this same *līlā* is played and replayed eternally, but a step removed from the plane of human existence, in a land accessible only to the chosen.

For these, participation in the *līlā* involves, not some ineffable mystic communion, but the acceptance of an active role in the day-to-day (and night-to-night) activities of that dusty, rustic world of cowherds into which Kṛṣṇa descends to spend his youth. During the day, Kṛṣṇa herds the cattle; and the poet who would know him, who would sing of him, must make a spiritual journey as cowherd himself. But at night, when the women of the village leave their husbands' beds at the first notes of Kṛṣṇa's flute, no man but Kṛṣṇa may join them on the banks of the Yamunā; a poet, if he dare follow at all, must follow as a woman.

Hence each poet must have three names, one for each role. The blind poet who had performed before the imperial court, we are told, herded cattle with Kṛṣṇa under the name Kṛṣṇa-sakhā. He—or rather, she—spent her nights enjoying Kṛṣṇa's love under the name Campak-latā. Finally, she—or rather, he—returned to tell the tale in five thousand poems, at the end of each affixing his third name: Sūrdās.[4]

It is probable that Sūr's *sakhā* and *sakhī* names were the invention of later chroniclers: "Kṛṣṇasakhā" and "Campaklatā" appear nowhere in his verse. It is probable that the

is given as the answer to a question that obviously bothered the commentator: how could Akbar, a *mleccha*, possibly be *vivekī*, "discerning"?

4. For a discussion of the *sakhā* and *sakhī* names, see Prabhu Dayāl Mītal, *Aṣṭachāpa paricaya* (Mathura, 1949), pp. 68–69. A similar development in the Caitanya movement is discussed in Kaṇikā Tomar, *Brajabhāṣā aura Brajabuli sāhitya* (Varanasi, 1964), pp. 594–597.

tale of his meeting with Akbar is equally apocryphal. Yet if we ignore the improbable, if we refuse to listen to the myth, there is little left to say about the man; and the otherworldly figure portrayed in the tales is mirrored in the poet's own work. "His eyes are with god," Akbar is made to say; and indeed Sūr's verse, opening inward to a vision of the timeless, turned a blind eye on the temporal. His poems tell us nothing of the emperor or his empire, although its busy center was a scant hundred miles from the poet's home. The poems are silent on the fall of the Delhi Sultanate and the ascendancy of the Mughals, yet these events occurred within the span of the poet's life. Absent too is all comment on the progress of a fragile peace between Muslim rulers and Hindu populace. Only once in five thousand verses does the poet allude to the fact of Muslim rule, and then obliquely: boasting himself the greatest sinner in history (and hence the most deserving of salvation), he compares his rivals to minor Hindu *rājās*:

> The rest are today's petty princelings;
> I am the *Sultān*![5]

If Sūr had nothing to say on the subject of his contemporaries, his contemporaries had next to nothing to say about Sūr: his life was not to be recorded until nearly a century after his death, and by then all was rumor. It would appear that he was born late in the fifteenth century and died in the second half of the sixteenth. The name of his village is traditionally given as Sīhī, but no-one really knows where Sīhī was. Presumably it was in the *Braj-maṇḍal,* that sacred strip of land along the Yamunā River, containing the earthly sites of Kṛṣṇa's līlā: the city of Mathurā; the village of Gokul; the forest of Brindāban; the hill called Govardhan. Certainly it was here that he spent his later life; and it was the dialect of this region, Braj-bhāṣā, that he employed in his poetry.

Both Sūr and his language profited greatly from the restoration of Mathurā and Brindāban as major pilgrimage sites,

5. *Sabhā* 145.

after a hiatus of several troubled centuries during which, as Growse writes, "the history of Mathurā is almost a total blank."[6] This "Braj renaissance" was in part the consequence of a change in political climate: in the second half of the sixteenth century, Mughal rule brought a stability that encouraged new construction. Yet the renewal was well begun a full three decades before Akbar ascended to the throne. Ultimately it is to the charisma of a Hindu revivalist, more than to the tolerance of a Muslim ruler, that we must credit the rebirth of the land and language of Braj. As early as 1520, Caitanya—the "Golden One" of Bengal, leader of a great movement of ecstatic devotion to Kṛṣṇa—dispatched emissaries westward to restore the sacred sites of the Kṛṣṇa cult. Soon the temples and seminaries of a dozen sects echoed with theological debate and devotional song; and while the former was still conducted largely in Sanskrit, a language of priestly prerogative, the latter came increasingly to employ the common speech of Kṛṣṇa's birthplace. Almost overnight the status of Braj-bhāṣā rose from obscure local dialect to major literary language, a status that it was to retain until well into the twentieth century.

The emergence of Braj-bhāṣā literature was by no means an isolated phenomenon. All over India, poets writing in the regional languages had begun to challenge Sanskrit's traditional supremacy as the medium of religious and literary expression; and, as in the Braj region, the ascendancy of local dialects was everywhere linked to the devotional movement known as *bhakti.* The *bhakti* movement appears to have begun in the far south of India, probably before the eighth century; by the sixteenth, it had spread to every corner of the subcontinent. It addressed itself to different gods in different regions: Kṛṣṇa shared the stage with Rāma, Śiva, and the goddess Kālī, as well as a variety of local deities. Equally various were the movement's targets for reform: it attacked the caste system, the Buddhists, the Muslims, the Jains. But

6. F.S. Growse, *Mathura: A District Memoir* (Allahabad, 1883), p. 33.

for all their variety, the sects of *bhakti* joined in a loud-sung denial of recondite brahmanical paths to salvation.

Orthodox brahmanical systems had long placed a high value on asceticism. They regarded man's passions as shackles binding him to the dreary round of birth, and death, and rebirth. The proponents of *bhakti* protested that man's salvation lay not in the suppression of passion, but rather in its redirection: the goal of *bhakti* was to bring man into a loving relationship with a personal god. And whereas the orthodox systems insisted on the authority of a fixed canon, the language of which was Sanskrit, the *bhakti* sects insisted as well on the authority of individual experience; the gods of *bhakti* understood any language a man might choose to speak.

Thus it was not surprising that when the *Kṛṣṇa-bhakti* sects of Caitanya and others arrived in the land of Braj, erecting temples in whose ritual song played a central role, Braj poets found themselves in great demand. Sūr himself was "discovered" in the ensuing talent search by Vallabha, founder of one of the new orders. There exists no contemporary record of the encounter; but if we may believe Vallabhite sectarian accounts, it wrought a crucial transformation in the poet and his verse.

Sūr had not always lived apart, withdrawn into the world of the *līlā*. Long before his meeting with Vallabha he had established a local reputation as a bard; and the verse attributed to those early years is surprisingly personal in tone, with the poet characteristically adopting the stance of a brazen, boasting, and eminently clever sinner, taunting God to test his powers of salvation, threatening Kṛṣṇa with disgrace unless he can redeem this sinner Sūr. It was just such poetry, we are told, which Vallabha first heard the blind poet singing as he sat in the dust of a village called Gāoghāṭ. While Vallabha was impressed by Sūr's art, he was dismayed by his choice of subject. He persuaded Sūr to abandon this self-denigration, to turn instead to hymning the wonders of the *līlā*.

The *līlā* Vallabha asked to hear was that which in later years would become Sūr's hallmark: the *bālalīlā*, the *līlā* of Kṛṣṇa's childhood in the house of Nanda. Thus, the tale continues, Sūr sang the first of his many poems to the child-god:

> So he sang before Vallabha the poem beginning:
>
> "When I heard that a son
> is born in Braj to Nanda. . . ."
>
> . . . Then Vallabha was very pleased; and he said, It was as if Sūrdās stood very near to the *līlā* of Nanda's house.[7]

Sūr seems always to have stood "very near to the *līlā* of Nanda's house." While he composed strong, well-crafted verse on Kṛṣṇa's other *līlās*, his enduring stature as a poet rests almost entirely on those thousand poems that portray the childhood of Kṛṣṇa. They return constantly to a single irony, inherent in the figure of the child-god: a child who never stops growing, beyond manhood and into godhood, glimpsing but seldom the still more awesome truth: that he is, has always been, source and substance of the universe.

## 2. *The life and līlā of Kṛṣṇa*

> There is no end
> to the telling of the tale
> of the *līlā* of the Lord of Sūrdās.
> —Sūrdās[8]

When the women of Braj assembled for their nightly trysts with Kṛṣṇa, it was only by his magic, his *māyā*, that the Lord could satisfy them all. As they formed the *rāsamaṇḍala*, the great circle-dance that served as prelude to their couplings, Kṛṣṇa divided himself into as many bodies as there were women who sought his love. And the most subtle aspect of the illusion was this: each woman thought that Kṛṣṇa danced with her and her alone.

7. *Sūrdās kī vārtā*, pp. 30–38.
8. *Sabhā* 762; Caturvedī p. 253.

If the women of Braj were enchanted by Kṛṣṇa's talent for multiplication, the same talent can be exasperating for the scholar. Just as there was a Kṛṣṇa for each woman in the dance, so is there a different Kṛṣṇa for each text in the Vaiṣṇavite canon. To a great extent, the differences represent stages in a process of development: between the stern, sermonizing charioteer of the *Bhagavad Gītā* and the impish cowherd of Sūr's verse stands a millennium and a half of syncretic growth.[9] But this is not to say that the charioteer ever wholly disappeared. It is a characteristic of the Hindu pantheon that the addition of new layers to a god's identity seldom wholly obscures the earlier strata; the forging of new relationships between god and god seldom severs ties of longer standing. By Sūr's time, the deities of Hinduism were related to one another by a marvellous web of mythological and metaphysical strands; no one god's identity could be fully explained without reference to a great many others. Yet even by the standards of such a system, Kṛṣṇa was a figure of uncommon complexity, an aggregate of often contradictory personalities. The contradictions were in no way a source of embarrassment for our poet. As we shall see, it is precisely the complexity of Kṛṣṇa's character—more, it is the very inconsistencies, the incongruities, in that character—which provide both the form and the substance of a great many of Sūr's poems.

The most straightforward of Kṛṣṇa's roles is that defined by his position in the *trimūrti*, the three gods among whom Hindu tradition distributes responsibility for the major processes of the universe. Between cycles of creation there exists nothing but a dark, infinite, undifferentiated sea. At the beginning of each cycle, the god Brahmā creates from this sea the world of name and form; at the end of each cycle,

9. The Kṛṣṇa mythos and its development have been discussed at length in a great many works. Among the best known are J. Gonda, *Aspects of Early Viṣṇuism* (Utrecht, 1954); and W.G. Archer, *The Loves of Krishna in Indian Painting and Poetry* (New York, 1957).

the god Śiva opens his third eye and burns the world to ashes, the ashes are immersed in a great flood, and the ordered world sinks once more into the chaos of the sea. In the interval between these acts—the creation by Brahmā, the destruction by Śiva—it is the task of the third god, Viṣṇu, to preserve the universal order against the threats of demonic forces. Time and again powerful demons arise to challenge the powers of the gods; time and again Viṣṇu, taking on human or animal form, descends to earth to thwart the demons, by force or by trickery, and to restore the stability of the cosmos. Tradition recognizes ten such incarnations, or *avatāras*, of Viṣṇu. Nine have come; one is yet to come; Kṛṣṇa is number eight.

The story of the Kṛṣṇa-incarnation begins with an evil king named Kaṃsa, who seizes the throne of the Yādavas. From his palace in Mathurā, Kaṃsa subjects the land of Vraja (Hindi *Braj*) to a reign of such cruelty that the very Earth rebels. Earth takes the form of a cow, and enlists the support of Brahmā; together they approach Viṣṇu with a plea for the destruction of Kaṃsa. Viṣṇu replies by plucking from his head a black hair and a white. From the white hair, he announces, will be born Balarāma, an incarnation of the cosmic serpent Śeṣa, Viṣṇu's eternal companion. From the black hair will be born Kṛṣṇa, incarnation of Viṣṇu himself. The two hairs will be implanted in the womb of Devakī, Kaṃsa's cousin but a righteous woman of royal birth. The white hair, Balarāma, will be Devakī's seventh son, and the black hair, Kṛṣṇa, her eighth; these two, Viṣṇu promises, will bring an end to Kaṃsa's tyranny.

But Kaṃsa is warned. As he rides one day in a chariot, with his cousin Devakī seated beside him, a voice from heaven announces that he will be slain by Devakī's eighth son. On the point of killing his cousin, the king is persuaded to imprison her instead, along with her husband Vasudeva. While in prison, Devakī gives birth to six sons, one after another; one after another, Kaṃsa orders them killed. But as the end of the seventh pregnancy approaches—the pregnancy conceived by the white hair of Viṣṇu—Kaṃsa suddenly receives word that there will be no seventh son. Devakī has miscarried.

What has actually occurred is far more complex: it has been not a miscarriage, but a transplant. The white hair of Viṣṇu was magically transplanted from Devakī's womb into the womb of a woman named Rohiṇī. Rohiṇī is the second wife of Vasudeva, and thus co-wife to Devakī herself; but unlike Devakī, she lives in hiding outside the city of Mathurā, across the Yamunā, in the cowherds' village of Gokula. The child Balarāma is born safely beyond Kaṃsa's grasp.

When word comes to Kaṃsa that Devakī is pregnant for the eighth time, the evil king becomes frantic; the prophesied moment has arrived. He orders Devakī and Vasudeva bound in shackles, has a lock placed upon their door, and posts a strong guard. But the precautions prove useless. On the night of Kṛṣṇa's birth, a hypnotic spell enshrouds the land of Braj. The shackles fall away, the lock opens, the guards sink into a deep sleep; even the River Yamunā conspires to still its current, permitting Vasudeva, with the child in his arms, to cross, unobserved, to Gokula.

Vasudeva goes to the house of his friend Nanda, chief of the cowherds. It is Nanda's house which already shelters Vasudeva's second wife, Rohiṇī, together with the child Balarāma. On this eventful night, Nanda's wife Yaśodā has also given birth—to a daughter; but gripped by the same spell that enshrouds Mathurā, Yaśodā is unaware of the sex of her newborn child. Vasudeva switches the children: leaving Devakī's son beside the sleeping Yaśodā, he takes Yaśodā's daughter and slips back across the river, to Mathurā, and to prison.

The fate of Yaśodā's daughter is a tale in itself; suffice it to say that the child was more than she seemed. But now events in Mathurā are far less important than those occurring among the cowherds. On the morning following the exchange, Yaśodā wakes from the trance and is delighted to find beside her a healthy son. He is black, like the hair of Viṣṇu, and so he is named Kṛṣṇa: "the Black."

Thus Kṛṣṇa and Balarāma, the black and the white, grow up among the cowherds; indeed, to the eyes of the world they are nothing but cowherds themselves, living in a dusty backwoods village. Soon even this haven must be abandoned, for Kaṃsa has learned that the child Kṛṣṇa has escaped him; his demon-armies scour the countryside, compelling Nanda to lead his villagers and their herds into the relative safety of the forest of Vṛndāvana. It is here that the years of Kṛṣṇa's childhood and youth are spent, in exile.

It is a gentle exile. Kṛṣṇa, a god who descended to be born a prince, now lives as cowherd—and is content. Instead of statesmanship, he learns herdsmanship; instead of the refined arts of courtly life, he learns to play a simple bamboo flute; instead of the manly arts of war, as would befit his royal birth, he learns (as we shall see) the manly arts of love.

Upon reaching adulthood, the brothers take up once more the duties of their incarnation: they return to Mathurā, slay Kaṃsa, and accept their rightful positions as noblemen among the Yādavas. The idyl has ended. Kṛṣṇa never returns to Gokula or Vṛndāvana, never returns to the women of Vraja. Even Mathurā is soon abandoned, as Kṛṣṇa relocates the Yādava capital in Dwārakā, far to the west; and while he now marries 16,108 wives, he never again takes a mistress; while he battles great demons, he no longer plays the flute. Mischievous cowherd has been wholly transformed to mighty warrior. It is in the latter guise that Kṛṣṇa participates in the great war of the Mahābhārata, where he serves as adviser to the Pāṇḍavas and as charioteer to Arjuna, and where he delivers at last his famous battlefield sermon, the *Bhagavad Gītā*.[10]

10. The version of the tale summarized here is one that appears to have been widely accepted by Sūr's time. Most features of the tale may be found in one or more of three major classical texts: the *Harivaṃśa*, the *Viṣṇu Purāṇa*, and the *Bhāgavata Purāṇa*. Certain features of the medieval

Told thus in outline, the Kṛṣṇa story is a heroic tale; but while the martial exploits of other gods captured the popular imagination, Kṛṣṇa's did not. The poets of Sūr's time all but ignored Kṛṣṇa's dealings with Kaṃsa, as well as the episodes of his later life in Dwārakā, treating these rather as a frame, almost an excuse, for that part of Kṛṣṇa's life which most singularly defined his character: his exile among the cowherds; his coming of age as herdsman to their cattle, companion to their sons, and as lover to their wives and daughters.

For Sūr and his sectarian fellows, the tale was far more than the story of a long-ago incarnation. It was something happening now, at each instant, forever; it was the *līlā*. The world, they claimed, is indeed a stage, but with a difference: Kṛṣṇa *is* the stage, and Kṛṣṇa is all the players, and the play and the playwright and the audience.[11] He is no mere *avatāra*, of Viṣṇu or of any other god; rather, he is the "true form" of that awesome abstraction, the *parabrahma*, the Absolute Being. All that is, is an extension of Kṛṣṇa's personality; all that exists, exists solely for Kṛṣṇa's amusement; and that which amuses Kṛṣṇa most, is the *Braj-līlā*.

Within this system, the ultimate goal of man—who is, in his normal state, an unwitting extension of Kṛṣṇa—is to gain admission to the innermost stage, to play a conscious role

---

version (notably the character of Rādhā) are later developments, the origins of which are perennial subjects for debate. "Speculation about Rādhā's ancestry," notes Edward C. Dimock, "is one of the favorite amusements of scholars who concern themselves with the religious history of Bengal" (*The Place of the Hidden Moon: Erotic Mysticism in the Vaiṣṇava-Sahajiyā Cult of Bengal*, Chicago, 1966, p. 34). There are also a few episodes (that of Śrīdhara, for example) which are to be found only in the *Sūrsāgar*, and which may well have originated with Sūr himself. For a detailed discussion of Sūr's narrative sources, see Jagdīś Gupta, *Braja-bhāṣā Kṛṣṇa-bhakti Kāvya* (Allahabad, 1968).

11. "Lila—the play, the game, a cosmic game, an amusement of the Divine Being. The child's joy, the poet's joy, the actor's joy, the mechanician's joy of the Soul of things eternally young, perpetually inexhaustible, creating and recreating Himself in Himself for the sheer bliss of that self creation, of that self representation—Himself the Play, Himself the player, Himself the play-ground" (Aurobindo, *A Glossary of Sanskrit Terms in the Life Divine*, quoted in Bhāradvāj, *Kṛṣṇa-Kavya*, p. 7n).

in the innermost play. Poetry is a means to this end. Through singing, or hearing, verses that depict episodes from the *līlā*, the devotee seeks to transform his own, private passion for Kṛṣṇa into the infinitely greater passion experienced by one of those whom the Lord most favored. Through the love felt for Kṛṣṇa by Kṛṣṇa's parents, companions, or lovers, the devotee aspires to realize himself as the parent, companion, or lover of God.

For Sūr, a favorite role was that of Yaśodā, Kṛṣṇa's mortal foster-mother, who believed the deity to be her own and ordinary son. Perhaps Sūr the devotee found in their relationship a paradigm for selfless love between human soul and divine. Certainly Sūr the poet found above all a fine irony in the figure of a woman who treats God like a child—teasing him, bribing, threatening, like any son's mother—and in the figure of Kṛṣṇa, a god who chooses to obey (and rebel) like any mother's son:

The mother says, "Dance!
  Kṛṣṇa, dance and I'll give you butter!"
His tiny feet pound and stamp upon the earth,
  his anklebells ring;

Sūr sings the praises of his name,
  earth and heaven resound with his fame,
    but the Lord of the Three Worlds dances
      for his butter.[12]

## 3. *Wytte and wundyr*

Wytte hath wondyr þat Reson tell ne can,
Houh a mayde bare a chylde both god & man;
Therfore leve wytte & take to the wundyr—
ffeyth goth a-bove, & Reson goth vndyr.
—Bishop Pecok[13]

Sūr was by no means the first Indian poet to discover the ironic aspects of "a chylde both god & man"; behind him

12. *Sabhā* 764; Caturvedī p. 256.
13. Carleton Brown, *Religious Lyrics of the Fifteenth Century* (Oxford, 1939), p. 186.

lay a long tradition of Sanskrit devotional and benedictory verse. Implicit in much of this earlier poetry is an awareness that irony is inherent in the very concept of incarnation, and that its proper measure is the distance between cosmic reality and earthly form. Indeed, there were poets who found in Viṣṇu's animal incarnations still greater scope for exploiting the paradox; for if the gap between "chylde & god" is great, that between god and beast must be wider yet:

> May the three worlds find in Keśava° protection,
> who when embodied in a fish did burst
> the horizon's limits with the scraping of his sides
> and whose belly was not filled by all the sea;
> who, having cut a potstand for the cosmic sphere
> in the toughened scales of his jumping back,
> did then with difficulty curb within his limbs
> the love of leaping.[14]

Nearer both in time and texture to Sūr's verse was the Sanskrit *Kṛṣṇakarṇāmṛta* of Līlāśuka Bilvamaṅgala, which treats the child-Kṛṣṇa theme in several terse poems of extraordinary cleverness. Some of these add yet another dimension to the irony, by portraying Kṛṣṇa's child-body as concealing, not only the powers of a god, but a most precocious sexuality as well:

> Kissed by the milkmaids, who thought him a child,
> he enjoyed their lips.
> Closely held by them, he reddened their neck with
> his embrace.
> Placed on their laps, he touched their private
> parts with his hand.
> May this foremost person of the wicked, the baby
> Kṛṣṇa, take our sins far away.[15]

But the poet-devotees of the popular *bhakti* sects tended, with conspicuous exceptions, to approach their deities with

14. Daniel H.H. Ingalls, trans., *Sanskrit Poetry from Vidyākara's "Treasury"* (Cambridge, Mass., 1968), p. 83.

15. Frances Wilson, ed. and trans., *The Love of Krishna: The Kṛṣṇakarṇāmṛta of Līlāśuka Bilvamaṅgala* (Philadelphia, 1975), p. 164.

a shade less levity than that permitted by the Sanskrit tradition; and this earnest piety was nowhere more conspicuous than in those regions speaking Hindi, a language that counts Sūr's own Braj-bhāṣā among its dialects. Thus that same love of irony which placed Sūr solidly in the classical tradition of Indian verse, served to set him apart from his immediate peers. An appreciation of the difference requires that we take a brief look at a fundamental dichotomy in Hindi *bhakti* poetry.

All but a few of the Hindi poets addressed themselves to one of two deities: Kṛṣṇa and Rāma.[16] The cults of the two gods, while nominally united under the broad umbrella of Vaiṣṇavism, attracted very different sorts of devotees, and inspired very different sorts of literature. For the followers of Kṛṣṇa, piety did not necessarily preclude sensuality; with few exceptions, the poets of *Kṛṣṇa-bhakti* aspired to reach Kṛṣṇa through the role of Rādhā, his favorite mistress. They held that the strongest human passion, and the passion most pleasing to god, was the erotic; the highest goal of man was to become woman—to become Rādhā. But the consequences of this transformation were more awesome still: for to realize the self as Rādhā meant to realize the self as Kṛṣṇa. At the very center of the *līlā*, Kṛṣṇa becomes at once himself and his mistress, Kṛṣṇa *and* Rādhā; and each enjoys the ecstasy of each enjoying the other:

As the mirror to my hand,
the flowers to my hair,
kohl to my eyes,
*tāmbul* to my mouth,
musk to my breast,
necklace to my throat,
ecstasy to my flesh,
heart to my home—

16. The major exceptions are the *sant* poets, notably Kabīr, who, while often addressing the divine by the name Rāma, nonetheless insist on his *nirguṇa* nature, and thus deny the validity of the Vaiṣṇavite mythos. For a discussion of the literary consequences of this schism, see K. Bryant, "*Sant* and *Vaiṣṇava* Poetry: Some Observations on Method" in *Sikh Studies: Working Papers from the Berkeley Conference*, ed. Gerald Barrier and Mark Juergensmeyer (monograph of the Graduate Theological Union, Berkeley; 1978).

as wing to bird,
water to fish,
life to the living—
so you to me.

But tell me,
Mādhava,* beloved,
who are you?
Who are you really?

*Vidyāpati says, they are one another.*[17]

Given such an immensely attractive conception of the mystic experience, it is hardly surprising that the great majority of *Kṛṣṇa-bhakti* poets concentrated on Kṛṣṇa's erotic *līlās*; indeed, much of what is commonly called *Kṛṣṇa-kāvya* might better be described as the poetry of Rādhā.

For the second major group of Vaiṣṇavite poets, however, eros and irony were equally inappropriate to the worship of god. These were poets who scorned the Kṛṣṇa incarnation entirely, favoring the sterner stuff of *Rāma-bhakti*. By far the greatest of these was a poet whose name is often linked with Sūr's: Tulsīdās, author of the *Rāmcaritmānas*, a work that some have hailed as "the Bible of Northern India."[18]

A well-known bon mot has it that "Sūr is the sun, Tulsī the moon, and Keśav Dās all the stars; the poets of today are like fireflies, flickering here and there."[19] This particular ordering of the heavens derives largely from a pun on Sūr's name,[20] but few, I suspect, would dispute the claim that Sūr and Tulsī are the major luminaries in the firmament of Hindi poetry. As to which of the two is greater, no agreement is ever likely to be reached; for they are religious poets, and few critics seem able or inclined to avoid taking sides, on the basis of religious criteria as much as literary. But the comparison

17. Edward C. Dimock and Denise Levertov, eds. and trans., *In Praise of Krishna: Songs from the Bengali* (New York, 1967), p. 15.
18. J.M. Macfie, *The Ramayan of Tulsidas; or, The Bible of Northern India* (Edinburgh, 1930).
19. "*Sūra sūra Tulasī sasi uḍugana Kesaba Dāsa/aba ke kavi khadyota sama jahaṃ-tahaṃ karata prakāsa.*" The lines are cited in almost every work on Sūrdās; see for example Janardan Misra, *The Religious Poetry of Sūrdās* (doctoral dissertation, Königsberg, 1939), p. 145; Charlotte Vaudeville, *Pastorales par Soûr-Dâs* (Paris, 1971), p. 40. I have yet to see the quote ascribed.
20. One of the meanings of *Sūr* is "sun" (Sanskrit *sūrya*, Hindi *sūraj*).

is perennial, and perhaps inescapable; the work of each provides a context within which to view the other.

The subject of Tulsī's epic *Rāmcaritmānas* is the life and deeds of Rāma. The tales of the two incarnations—Rāma, the seventh, and Kṛṣṇa, the eighth—are not entirely dissimilar in structure. Rāma's purpose, like Kṛṣṇa's, is to destroy a demon-king—in this instance Rāvaṇa, the ten-headed ruler of Ceylon. Rāma, like Kṛṣṇa, is of royal birth; like Kṛṣṇa, he is exiled from his kingdom; and like Kṛṣṇa he spends his exile in a forest. But here the similarity ends: for unlike Kṛṣṇa, Rāma carries with him into exile his princely identity and demeanor. His life in the forest is no idyl on a riverbank, but the austere existence of a hermit, passed in the company of none but Sītā (his *wedded* wife) and Lakṣmaṇa, his devoted brother. The exile culminates in Sītā's abduction by Rāvaṇa, and finally in war.

If Viṣṇu's early incarnations—Fish, Tortoise, Boar, and Dwarf[21]—are the most susceptible to ironic treatment, that of Rāma is the least so. While Rāma is a god in a man's body, his body is that of a king; the slender gap between earthly ruler and divine leaves scant space for the pursuit of irony. A mood of awe, and a sense of enormous decorum, dominate the texture of the *Rāmcaritmānas.* Even in Tulsī's shorter verse, his characters move in a world of epic proportions. We sit in a massive arena, watching the agonies of kings, the breaking of magic bows, the battles of heroes and demons; the air is filled with arrows, and with showers of blossoms thrown in homage by an admiring pantheon of petty gods. Tulsī is ever careful to ensure that our sympathies are not divided: his Rāma is a figure of aloof perfection; his Sītā an idealized, submissive wife; and his demons are properly demonic:

21. In the case of the one other "pre-human" *avatāra*—Narasiṃha, the Man-lion—the particular nature of the beast lends itself to treatment of the horrific, rather than the ironic, aspects of incarnation.

The demon's soldiers struck,
showering spears, darts and arrows;
From this side palm and *tamāl* trees flew
and rough sharp chunks of mountains.

Tulsī, the soldiers sparred with lion-like roars,
the brave were reft with swords while cowards
slipped away;
With tooth and nail they griped off arms,
while severed heads in myriads rolled down.[22]

The demons are there in Sūr's verse as well, but as Pundit Rāmcandra Śukla protests, they are hardly all one could ask for in the way of true enemies of the people. Tulsī's demons, Śukla tells us, "chew up Brāhmaṇs and make piles of their bones";[23] Sūr's are made of milder stuff, with a tendency toward the comic. For the rest, Sūr's world is inhabited by ordinary people reacting in carefully ordinary ways. Their love for Kṛṣṇa is predicated not on a sense of divine perfection which commands that love, but rather upon the usual complex of human emotions which governs relations between parent and child, boy and brother, youth and comrade, woman and lover. When there is conflict between Kṛṣṇa and another character, we are often led to find Kṛṣṇa at fault—an unthinkable occurrence in Tulsī. If an occasional poem leads us to watch the gods in their councils, we are called back again and again to watch a human, volatile, mischievous child grow to be a rebellious enemy of traditional religion. And yet even this rebellion is never a matter of great seriousness; Sūr's protest takes the form of a rather casual attitude toward social norms, and a positive contempt for structured philosophies. It is not the angry rhetoric of a prophet, nor a frontal assault on social constraints, but rather an amused tolerance for the folly of men, gods, demons, and even Kṛṣṇa himself, in a world that was, after all, created in jest.

22. *Kavitāvalī*, Laṅka 34. The translation is from F.R. Allchin, trans., *Kavitāvalī* (London, 1964), p. 121.

23. Rāmcandra Śukla, *Sūradāsa* (Vārāṇasī, 1948), p. 156.

Jest lies at the core of Sūr's poetry: the concept of creation as a child's game provided him not only with a theme, but with a principle of structure as well. There is in a sense a *Sūr-līlā* to parallel the *Kṛṣṇa-līlā*: the poet plays with his audience no less sportively than the god with his creation. The chapters that follow constitute an inquiry into the workings of this *Sūr-līlā*. So far, we have worked at establishing a context for the poet's work, and at conveying a sense of its texture. In Part One we shall turn from texture to structure, to a study of how the words of common speech can be so uncommonly arranged. In Part Two we shall turn again, from an examination of the poet's craft, to a sampling of the poet's art.

PART ONE

# *Structures and Strategies in the Poetry of Sūrdās*

CHAPTER I

# *SŪR-LĪLĀ* AND *KṚṢṆA-LĪLĀ*

## 1. *Rasa and rhetoric*

Maker, how do you make your song?
I listen, speechless; I only listen.
Maker, how do you make your song?
—Rabindranath Tagore[1]

The poet of Kṛṣṇa-*bhakti* must participate in the *līlā* if his poetry is to be true; if it is to be *effective,* he must lead his audience to participate as well. The first is a demand made by theology; the second, by rhetoric. Seldom have these two disciplines known a happier marriage than in the writings of Rūpa Goswāmin, a contemporary, neighbor, and possibly an acquaintance of Sūrdās. The intent of Rūpa's two great works, the *Bhakti-rasāmṛta-sindhu* and the *Ujjvala-nīlamaṇi,* is summarized by Sushil Kumar De:

> His two works, embodying what may be called the Bhakti-rasaśāstra, constitute a kind of Rhetoric of Bhakti, with all its psychology, conceit and imagery. If the mediaeval Troubadours of France and Italy conceived the love of Christ as an aspect of the Law and wrote a grammar of the amorous sentiment, the mediaeval Vaiṣṇavas of Bengal conceived the love of Kṛṣṇa as an aspect of Psychology, and wrote a Rhetoric of the erotic sentiment.[2]

The entire system was based on an ingenious adaptation of the *rasa* theory of classical Sanskrit poetics:

> A drama, and by extension poetry, arouses in the listener a mental state such as love, grief, anger, or fear. Such states reflect the fundamental mood of the work of art. . . . No single element must be allowed to mar or disturb this basic mood. All must be harmony.

1. Rabindranath Tagore, *Ravīndra racanāvalī* (Calcutta, 1961), vol. 4, p. 4.

2. Sushil Kumar De, *Early History of the Vaiṣṇava Faith and Movement in Bengal* (Calcutta, 1942), pp. 123–124.

> The emotional state into which the audience is thus put is called *sthāyi-bhāva*. . . .[3]

The classical scheme identified nine such *bhāvas*; Rūpa's theological emendation of the system described five;[4] since this study will treat primarily poetry of the child-Kṛṣṇa, we may limit our concern to two: the *vātsalya* (parental), and to a lesser degree the *sakhya* (comradely). Dimock defines them most concisely:

> *Sākhya*: a state in which the worshipper considers Kṛṣṇa his friend, as did the cowherds of Vṛndāvana. . . .
>
> *Vātsālya*: a state in which the worshipper considers Kṛṣṇa a child and himself the parent, as did Kṛṣṇa's foster parents in Vṛndāvana.[5]

These two terms loom large in Sūr criticism, and the results have not always been positive. Rūpa Goswāmin's system was undeniably brilliant; unfortunately, as with so many great works of scholarship, its very brilliance tended to stifle further exploration. In the case of Hindi scholarship on Sūr (and almost all scholarship on Sūr has been in Hindi),[6] the majority of studies place *bhāva* or *rasa* at the center of their critical apparatus;[7] and of these, the great majority exhibit two im-

3. Edward C. Dimock, *The Place of the Hidden Moon: Erotic Mysticism in the Vaiṣṇava-Sahajiyā Cult of Bengal* (Chicago, 1966), pp. 20–21.

4. For a discussion of the system of the *bhāvas* and *rasas* of *bhakti*, and its classical antecedents, see De, Chapter IV, "The Devotional Sentiments."

5. Dimock, *The Place of the Hidden Moon*, p. 23.

6. Notable exceptions have been Charlotte Vaudeville, *Pastorales par Soûr-Dâs* (Paris, 1971); Janardan Misra, *The Religious Poetry of Sūrdās* (doctoral dissertation, Königsberg, 1939); S.M. Pandey and Norman Zide, "Sūrdās and His Krishna-*bhakti*," in *Krishna: Myths, Rites, and Attitudes*, ed. Milton Singer (Chicago, 1966), pp. 173–199; and Charles S.J. White, "Kṛṣṇa as Divine Child," *History of Religions* 10:2 (1970): 156–177.

7. Munśīrām Śarmā claims that "In spite of all these '-isms' almost everyone has accepted *rasa* as the soul of poetry." *Sūradāsa kā kāvya-vaibhava* (Kanpur, 1965), p. 211. Equally revealing is the organization of the table of contents to Śaśi Tivārī's *Sūra ke kṛṣṇa: eka anuśīlana* (Hyderabad, 1969): Chapter 2, entitled "Bālaka Kṛṣṇa" ("Child Kṛṣṇa"), is divided into two sections: *saṃyoga-vātsalya* and *viyoga-vātsalya*.

plicit assumptions concerning the child-poems. First, it is assumed that each such poem must be either a poem of *vātsalya*, or a poem of *sakhya*. Second, it is assumed that the constraint described by Dimock for the classical system will hold true for Sūr as well: "No single element must be allowed to mar or disturb this basic mood. All must be harmony."

It must be admitted that both assumptions are justified for some of Sūr's poetry, and unalloyed *vātsalya* is unappetizing fare, heavy and cloying, for the Western audience. Nor does Sūr command the textural brilliance of Tulsī, or the solemn rhetoric of Kabīr, or the compactness of Bihārī. In fact, if there were truly "no single element" to disturb the mood of *vātsalya*, I would have to agree with Ram Avadh Dwivedi:

> Surdas' poetry is limited in its scope, since it does not comprehend life in all its variety. . . . We enjoy our trip into this little world of sweet dreams but are conscious all the time of the limitations and lack of reality which characterize it.[8]

Fortunately, "harmony" was not Sūr's intention at all. His intention was rather to enable his audience to participate in the *Kṛṣṇa-līlā*, by leading them through an experience paralleling that of the characters in the *līlā* itself. It is this audience experience, this "meta-*līlā*," that I have called the *Sūr-līlā*: for just as Kṛṣṇa creates a universe for his own sport, and puts his created characters through their paces, so does Sūr manipulate his audience in a parallel universe of poetry.

To say this is not to reject the neoclassical system of the *bhāvas* of *bhakti*. On the contrary, that system is a healthful restorative in its unflinching insistence that the locus of a poem is its *audience*, an approach made unfashionable to the point of heresy in Western criticism by the famous "fallacies" of Wimsatt and Beardsley.[9] Sūr most certainly intends us to

8. Ram Avadh Dwivedi, *A Critical Survey of Hindi Literature* (Varanasi, 1966), p. 69.

9. See W.K. Wimsatt, Jr., and Monroe C. Beardsley, "The Affective Fallacy" and "The Intentional Fallacy," in *The Verbal Icon: Studies in the Meaning of Poetry* (Lexington, Ky., 1954). For a rebuttal see Stanley

identify with Yásodā, or the cowherds, or Rādhā, and to experience as closely as possible what they experienced in their relations with Kṛṣṇa; and this is precisely what Rūpa Goswāmin's *bhāvas* are all about. Yet the experience of the characters in the *Kṛṣṇa-līlā* is not always in harmony with the mood of *vātsalya; their* moods are disturbed with great frequency. When Dwivedi speaks of Sūr's "little world of sweet dreams," he has passed over a great many nightmares inhabiting that same world; when another critic, Jindal, lauds Sūr's description of "a toddling child's attempts to cross the doorstep," he chooses to delete from his example a line which depicts that same child destroying the universe.[10]

In short, I am arguing that Sūr is a far more complex poet than has commonly been supposed. This complexity is most conspicuous in a set of poems which I shall refer to as "epiphanies": poems in which the divine facet of Kṛṣṇa's dual nature is revealed *against the background of the human.*

The term "epiphany" is one that received a good deal of wear during one brief era of Western criticism. and which has since more or less submerged. There are those who are quick to note that even Joyce, who first extended its sense from the realm of religion into that of aesthetics, ultimately abandoned the concept.[11] But critical fads aside, the term has a special applicability to the poems discussed here; indeed, it is tempting to suggest that "epiphany" is more aptly applied to Sūr's world than ever it was to that of Joyce.

First, it is apt in that it implies a relationship, currently unfashionable in the West but never so in India, between the

---

Fish, "The Affective Fallacy Fallacy," in *Self-Consuming Artifacts: The Experience of Seventeenth-Century Literature* (Berkeley, 1972), pp. 400–410.

10. K.B. Jindal, *A History of Hindi Literature* (Allahabad, 1955), pp. 109–110.

11. See for example Jackson I. Cope, "The Rhythmic Gesture: Image and Aesthetic in Joyce's *Ulysses,*" *English Literary History* 29 (1962): 67: "it is . . . not in the elaborations of an abortive theory of epiphanies, that we must recognize the origin of the aesthetic theory which was to be both form and cause of *Ulysses.*"

religious and aesthetic; more specifically, it implies that the artist's experience is a mystic one, and might well be extended (as it has been in Indian poetics)[12] to imply the converse: that the mystic's experience is also aesthetic. Rūpa Goswāmin borrowed the term *bhāva* from secular aesthetics and applied it to an experience of the sacred; Joyce borrowed "epiphany" from the language of the sacred and applied it to an experience of the profane, or more precisely, to a moment's revelation of that sacred which underlies every *thing,* no matter how commonplace. He took the *claritas* of Aquinas and rendered it *quiditas*—the "whatness" of the thing, which "leaps to us from the vestment of its appearance."[13]

But then Sūr works from the sacred to begin with; his poems of revelation are epiphanies not only in the Joycean, aesthetic sense (a showing forth of the *quiditas*) but in the original, religious sense as well (a showing forth of the divine). Joyce's Daedalus speaks of the artist's spiritual eye which "seeks to adjust its vision to an exact focus. The moment the focus is reached the object is epiphanized."[14] But while Joyce's artist must persuade his audience that there is indeed a sacred substratum to the commonplace, Sūr's audience needed no persuasion to see a god concealed by child's flesh. Sūr must work not so much to adjust our vision "to an exact focus," but rather (as we shall see), to *blur* that focus for a moment; to mask for a moment the sacred behind the ordinary, so that he may then part again that carefully constructed curtain, allowing Kṛṣṇa to "epiphanize" in both senses, religious as well as aesthetic.

The epiphanies, then, are essentially poems of ironic contrast, drawn between the poles of child and god. The ironic aspect of Sūr's poetry has not figured prominently in traditional criticism; the extent to which the present volume is

12. Writings on Sanskrit literary criticism are replete with speculations on the relationship between *rasāsvāda* and *brahmāsvāda.* See for example Sushil Kumar De, *History of Sanskrit Poetics* (Calcutta, 1960).
13. James Joyce, *Stephen Hero* (New York, 1944), p. 213.
14. *Stephen Hero,* p. 211.

revisionist may best be measured by a brief look at how Sūr is read by other critics. Ultimately, I shall argue, they are perceiving the same phenomena, but valuing them differently. Perhaps some among them are, with great courtesy, turning an intentionally blind eye to what they view as a great poet's occasional lapses; I suggest that it is in part those lapses that make the poet great.

## 2. *Censorship and the courteous critic*

> He told Cranly that the clock of the Ballast Office was capable of an epiphany. Cranly questioned the inscrutable dial. . . .
>
> —Joyce, *Stephen Hero*[15]

If one were to essay a brief illustration of critical approaches to a well-known English poet, the first step at least would be relatively simple: to select one or two poems which have been commented upon by a representative number of respectable critics. In the case of Sūrdās, the first step is complicated by, among other things, the magnitude of his work. There are 4,927 *padas*[16] in the *Sabhā* edition of the *Sūrsāgar*; it is thus not surprising that a great many have never found their way into the critical literature at all, and that only a very few appear with a frequency that would permit comparison.

When we find one poem, then, appearing in study after study (and invariably drawing nothing but the highest acclaim) we may reasonably assume it to be, by the criteria

15. *Stephen Hero*, p. 211.

16. *Pada* is the term usually applied to the genre of short lyric verse employed by Sūr. S.M. Pandey says of the genre: "The literal meaning of *pada* in Sanskrit is 'step,' 'mark,' 'trace,' or 'position.' It appears that among the musicians of the Middle Ages this word was also used to mean 'a description of a hero (*nāyak*).' Another meaning for the term is 'word' or language itself. The name *pada* was also given, for unknown reasons, to a musical form of short lyric poetry. This *pada* form was the most popular style for the singing of devotional songs in the medieval period" ("Mīrābāī and Her Contributions to the Bhakti Movement," *History of Religions* 5:1 [1965]: 59–60).

informing twentieth-century Hindi criticism, a masterpiece. Such a verse is *jasumati mana abhilāṣa karai*:

1 Yaśodā daydreams:
2 "When will my little one crawl upon his knees,
   when will he plant his two feet upon the earth?
3 When will I see his first two teeth,
   when will he lisp his first word?
4 When will he call Nanda 'Father,'
   when will he call me 'Mother'?
5 When will he catch at my skirt
   and babble angry words at me?
6 When will he first feed himself
   with his own two tiny hands?
7 When will he laugh and talk with me,
   his beauty dissolving my sorrows?"
8 She left Śyāma alone in the courtyard,
   busied herself in the house;
9 And a whirlwind arose,
   and the clouds began to growl.
10 Sūr says: The people of Braj heard this sound
   and froze in fear where they stood.[17]

The *Sabhā* text places the poem in a section entitled *tṛṇāvartavadha*, "the slaying of Tṛṇāvarta." Briefly, Tṛṇāvarta is a demon who stormed into Gokul in the form of an enormous whirlwind. His mission was to slay the infant Kṛṣṇa, whom Yaśodā had most conveniently left alone in the courtyard.[18] The sky darkened, the *Brajvāsīs* were blinded with dust and terrified by the roar of the wind; and Kṛṣṇa was plucked aloft and spun into the midst of the obscuring cloud of dust. (Kṛṣṇa, of course, speedily disposed of the demon; that dénouement, however, is conspicuously absent in the present poem.)

17. *Sabhā* 694; Caturvedī p. 142. For the Caturvedī version, the first half of line 8 should read instead: ". . . so saying, she left him in the courtyard."

18. In the classical version (*Bhāgavata Purāṇa* X:vii:18–19), Kṛṣṇa becomes miraculously heavy, so that Yásodā is forced to remove him from her lap. This supernatural explanation is totally absent from Sūr's version, as pointed out by Jagdīś Gupta, *Braja-bhāṣā Kṛṣṇa-bhakti kāvya* (Allahabad, 1968), p. 57.

Jagdīś Bhāradvāj is one of the very few critics to have discussed the poem *in its entirety.*[19] Bhāradvāj first lauds Sūr's description of Yaśodā's feelings of "maternal love" (*vātsalya*), "impatience," and "possessiveness," which precede the attack of Tṛṇāvarta. After paraphrasing Yaśodā's reverie (lines 1–7), he comments upon the effect of the closing lines:

> Against the particular background of Yaśodā's mental state, lost as she is in such joyful hopes and ambitions, what a tremendous sense of conflict [*virodhātmakatā*] is presented by the sudden emergence of the whirlwind! On one side, sweet, tiny ripples of emotion arise in the mother's heart; and on the other, a terrible storm has erupted.[20]

Bhāradvāj concludes by judging the poem a fine example of Sūr's *kavitvacāturī*—his "poetic skill," but also in a sense his "poetic cunning."

My own reading of the poem is very close to Bhāradvāj's. Clearly, the first line promises a poem of *vātsalya*; equally clearly, lines 2 through 7 seem to fulfill this promise. They do so by a sequence of repetitive, syntactically parallel descriptions of rather unextraordinary childhood behavior. The hypnotic drone of questions—"When, when, when?"—soon becomes self-sustaining, each repetition increasing our expectation of the next. The litany is scarcely calculated to arouse intense curiosity; by line 7, the course of the poem seems set: it will be cozy, domestic, perhaps a bit cloying.

Those first seven lines serve another, related function: they lead us to generalize the child. The very banality of the questions, the commonplace nature of the actions described, leads us away from Kṛṣṇa's godhood; it places Kṛṣṇa in a class with all children everywhere, and Sūr is careful not to break

19. The only other exception I have found is Yajñadatta Sarmā, who quotes the whole poem—but discusses only the *vātsalya* aspect—in his *Sūra-sāhitya aura siddhānta* (Delhi, 1955), p. 82.

20. Jagdīś Bhāradvāj, *Kṛṣṇa-kāvya meṃ līlā-varṇana* (New Delhi, 1972), p. 242.

this illusion. The child is anonymous for seven lines of the poem.

But in line 8, the pattern with which we have become so comfortable is rudely interrupted. Repetition has led us to expect a line beginning with *kaba*, "when"; instead it begins with Śyāma—an epithet of Kṛṣṇa. The naming of the god jolts us from drowsy daydream into a fully awake sense of time, place, and person. Abruptly we have Kṛṣṇa placed (in the courtyard), Yaśodā placed (in the house), and both of them occupied ("alone," "at work"); the daydream is over, the stage set for action, all in the space of a line.

The action of line 9 slams into our earlier complacency with the realization that we have been sorely tricked, our contract with the poet violated. We *know* that whirlwind; we know what it portends, and anticipate the consequences of Yaśodā's moment of negligence. Yet the poet has not finished toying with us. Instead of presenting, and resolving, the expected battle, Sūr executes a fade-out at the moment of greatest peril—leaving to the audience the task of completing a tale they know by heart. It is in the process of retelling the story themselves that the audience is led forcibly to remember that the helpless child of lines 1 to 7 is neither helpless, nor an ordinary child.

It should be apparent that I, like Bhāradvāj, find the locus of Sūr's "skill" or "cunning" in the *virodhātmakatā*—the "conflict." But this appears to be a minority position. In study after study, the *pada* is presented as an example of unalloyed *vātsalya*; it also appears, in study after study, in a radically abbreviated form. This abbreviation is certainly not based on considerations of space; the entire poem is ten lines in length, and the usual surgery performed by the critics shortens it by a mere three lines. Nor does the solution lie in a discrepancy between the edition of the *Sūrsāgar* used in this study and that used by other critics. The texts do indeed vary in minor ways, but all editions agree on the number and disposition of the lines in "Yaśodā daydreams." The phenomenon might still be of no more than passing interest were the excised lines of little importance to the poem as a whole, but in fact the converse is true: the three commonly deleted lines completely reverse the sense of the preceding seven. In my terminology, the critics have seen fit to edit out the epiphany.

A typical response is that of K. B. Jindal, who prefaces his remarks on the child-poems with words of high praise for the entire *bālalīlā* corpus:

> (T)he first one-thousand verses of the tenth canto of the Sursagar have no parallel in the literature of the world. Each verse is a complete picture of the child in a particular mood or at a particular stage of his development. All the one thousand deserve to be studied to appreciate fully how deeply Surdas has penetrated into the child mind.[21]

Having thus portrayed Sūr as above all a master of psychological realism, Jindal supports his case with several examples—including "Yaśodā daydreams," which he introduces with another brief comment, quoted here in full:

> In his [Sūr's] verses we can almost see the child playing with the mother. What are the ambitions of a woman when she first rises to the dignity of a mother? She weaves cobwebs of imagination and looks forward to the day when the child in her lap will toddle and lisp.[22]

The version of the *pada* that follows is at least in conformance with Jindal's introduction; it consists of lines 2 through 7 only. Line 1 ("Yaśodā daydreams" in my translation) has presumably been subsumed under Jindal's prefacing remarks, and its deletion need occasion no surprise. What does surprise is the deletion, without comment, of lines 8

21. Jindal, p. 109.

22. Jindal, p. 111. Jindal does not footnote his source; however, the lines he does cite are all identical in form with those of the Venkaṭeśvara Press edition—which contains the missing lines. (See Caturvedī, p. 142, for variant readings.)

through 10. In Jindal's version, there are "waves of emotion" but no *virodhātmakatā*; a reverie but no whirlwind; a child but no god.

When we turn to other critics, we find that the same lines (8, 9, and 10) have been cut by Harbaṃs Lāl Śarmā,[23] Munśīrām Śarmā,[24] Premnārāyaṇ Ṭaṇḍan,[25] and Charles S. J. White.[26] Śaśi Tiwārī gives only lines 3 and 4.[27] Like Jindal, all of the latter critics portray the *pada* as an excellent illustration of Sūr's skill at describing parental fantasies; like Jindal, none of them alludes to the *tṛṇāvarta* episode.

23. *Sūra aura unakā sāhitya* (Aligarh, 1958), p. 320.

24. *Sūradāsa kā kāvya-vaibhava*, p. 151.

25. "Sūr kā vātsalya varṇana, kucha prasaṅga," in Harbaṃslāl Śarmā, ed., *Sūradāsa* (Delhi, 1973), p. 112. Perhaps Ṭaṇḍan's most striking bit of surgery is performed on *Sabhā* 681. The full poem is translated in Part Two. It begins:

"Taking foot in hand, he sticks his toe in his mouth;
The Lord lies alone in his swing,
  playing happily by himself."

The *remainder* of the poem describes the scenes of apocalypse envisioned by all the gods of the universe, who, seeing Kṛṣṇa again in this iconographically suggestive pose, prepare for the seas of *pralaya*. Ṭaṇḍan, however, deletes all but the first two lines and thus is able to comment of the poem: "One day the child Kṛṣṇa was lying on a swing. He grabbed his big toe and put it in his mouth. This scene is extremely realistic; from time immemorial chubby little boys lying in swings have always sucked their big toes" (p. 110).

26. "Kṛṣṇa as Divine Child," p. 173. White does note elsewhere in the article that "The Cosmic Kṛṣṇa unites, in Sūrdās's writing, with the infant" (p. 174). Indeed, Jindal, too, is by no means blind to the presence of the divine in Sūr's verse ("Both Sur and Tulsi wanted to stress the divine element in the incarnation," p. 107). The point here is not that the "censors" fail to see either aspect, but simply that they appear to regard them as separable; they seem not to consider important the interaction of cosmic and commonplace in the same poem. Jindal comes very near a recognition of the potential for irony when he notes that "To intensify the supernatural element [Sūr] makes Krishna perform all the miracles even as a child" (p. 108); but I think he misses the point entirely when he charges that "We lose sight of the divinity of Krishna when we find his ears being boxed, his hands being tied, his acts being censured by his mother, and his comrades taking liberties with him" (p. 138). Not so; as we shall see, Sūr reminds us of Kṛṣṇa's divinity with sufficient frequency to make the sight of God having his ears boxed one of awesome irony.

27. *Sūra ke Kṛṣṇa*, p. 49.

Clearly, six of the seven critics cited are not very interested in the reversal, the epiphany, or whatever we are to call the change that occurs in the second half of the poem; and unless the critics say that they perceive a reversal, it is impossible to prove that they do so. It is quite possible, however, to establish that such deletions are too systematic to be coincidental; that there exists a definable set of poems in which the critics are seeing *something* which they consider at best peripheral to the poem's main theme; and that this "something" is consistently identical with the "something" I have called epiphany. It is, for example, that thing which occurs, most unambiguously, in lines 5 and 6 of *calata dekhi jasumati sukha pāvai*:

1 Yaśodā delights in watching him walk.
2 Clumping along on faltering feet,
 showing off when he sees his mother,
3 He walks as far as the doorstep,
 but returns again and again;
4 Stumbles and falls, but can't quite cross,
 and the gods are made to wonder;
5 *For he makes in a second a million worlds,*
 *and destroys in a second a million more;*
6 *Yet he sits in the lap of Nanda's wife*
 *as she teaches him to play,*
7 And she leads him by the hand
 across that doorstep,
 step by step by step.
8 The sight of the Lord of Sūr
 stuns the minds of gods and men.[28]

Jindal prefaces his discussion of this *pada* with the comment (again quoted in full):

> A toddling child's attempt to cross the doorstep and the insurmountable barrier before him are a common occurrence in every home. But none could have depicted better than Surdas has done this common phenomenon in the life of our children.[29]

28. *Sabhā* 744; Caturvedī p. 215.
29. Jindal pp. 109–110.

Jindal then gives the original Braj for lines 2, 3, 4, and 7. His deletion of line 1, as in "Yáśodā daydreams," presumably reflects nothing more than a sense that the introductory *ṭeka*[30] is made unnecessary by his own prefacing remarks. No such excuse can be made in the case of lines 5, 6, and 8: "For he makes in a second a million worlds" etc. In this instance, there can be absolutely no doubt that Jindal has erased the epiphany. (In this instance, there can also be no doubt concerning Jindal's awareness of the existence of the lines: he has replaced lines 5 and 6 with two proper and explicit rows of ellipsis marks.)[31]

Jindal's treatment of the verse is characteristic of that administered by the critics to all the poems traditionally known as the *pāṃvoṃ-calnā-pada*, the *padas* which describe Kṛṣṇa learning to walk. There are twenty-three of

30. *Ṭeka*: "prop,"' the half-line which usually begins a *pada*, and which is, in most styles of performance, repeated several times during the course of the poem (usually at the end of every couplet). The rhetorical function of the *ṭeka* in the performance of a *pada* has been described by Gaurīśaṅkar Miśra, who in turn cites his debt to Brajeśwar Varmā: "By presenting the central mood of the entire *pada* in a few concise and well-constructed words in the form of a *ṭek*, the poet produces a particular charm in his *pada*" (*Sūra-sāhitya kā chandaḥ-śāstrīya adhyayana* [Allahbad, 1969], p. 16). The repeated effect of this first line should be kept in mind when reading all *padas*; I shall refer to its specific rhetorical functions only when they are other than the obvious one of reinforcement of "contract."

31. Ṭaṇḍan cleanses the poem still more thoroughly of the cosmic. His version of the poem begins with "Yaśodā delights" and ends with "but can't quite cross," allowing him to comment only that: "Kṛṣṇa rapidly learned to crawl; but he still couldn't cross the threshold. When, after several attempts, he fell, the clever child began to turn back as soon as he reached the threshold. Seeing this, his mother is overjoyed" (p. 112). Ṭaṇḍan seems determined to prove at all costs the thesis stated in the first paragraph of his article: "The love of parents for their offspring, and of elders for small, chubby and cheerful children: to describe this is *vātsalya-rasa*. . . . Sūr's poetry contains extensive description of this vātsalya" (p. 107). The thesis itself is indisputable; what is amazing is that, with all the *padas* of "straight" *vātsalya* to choose from, Ṭaṇḍan chose nearly half his examples from the "epiphany" poems, and then went through such editorial gymnastics to make them come out *vātsalya*.

these; eleven are most explicit examples of epiphany.[32] The latter contribute to a particular irony, and to a recurrent and often explicit message. The irony is that of a god who must learn to walk; the message is one we shall soon see again: Kṛṣṇa places himself voluntarily under the control of his true devotee. Yet irony and message alike are ignored by the majority of critics, who describe the *pāṃvoṃ-calnā* poems as examples of realistic description, and limit their examples to the twelve *padas* in which no explicit irony is in evidence. Here Bhāradvāj joins the majority. His description of the *pāṃvoṃ-calnā* poems is limited to a single paragraph which, while aptly summarizing the human actions involved in the narrative, makes no mention whatsoever of epiphany, *virodhātmakatā*, irony, reversal, or even the fact that Kṛṣṇa is God.[33]

While one may speculate on the question of just what it is that prompts such abridgement,[34] what concerns me here is less the reason than the fact. Two poems that I consider as among the best examples of epiphany, are presented by a considerable number of critics as among the best examples of *vātsalya*; yet they perceive in those same poems elements which are incompatible with that sentiment. By their deletions, the critics confirm part of my thesis: that audience

32. I consider "explicit" *Sabhā* numbers 731, 737 and 742–750; as less explicit, numbers 730, 732–736, 738–741, 751–752.

33. Bhāradvāj p. 224.

34. A partial answer is implicit in a most revealing paragraph in Jagdīś Gupta's *Kṛṣṇa Bhakti Kāvya*: "There is another noteworthy peculiarity of the portrayal of Kṛṣṇa's *bāla-līlās* by the poets [Sūrdās, Nandadās, Paramānandadās], and that is the mixture of the supernatural and cosmic form with commonplace human emotions. From the viewpoint of *rasa*, such descriptions appear to be impediments to its full appreciation [*rasāsvādana*]; but at the same time, the introduction of the cosmic produces a sense of mystery which, by creating surprise, wonder, and curiosity, awakens toward the object of emotion [*ālambana*] a strange attraction, thereby compensating for the abovementioned flaw" (p. 162). Gupta's *apologia* is clearly a response to a felt, if seldom expressed, criticism of Sūr's mixing of *laukika* and *alaukika* ("commonplace" and "cosmic") elements—and it is precisely this mixture that results in what I have been calling epiphany.

experience of these poems—not just mine, but theirs also—is complex, is composed of conflicting elements. By their recognition of the *vātsalya* portion of the poems as being particularly well done, they support two more arguments that I should like to make: first, that while the epiphanies may have received little critical acclaim as such, they cannot be dismissed as inferior examples of Sūr's craftsmanship; second, that an effective reversal away from *vātsalya* requires that the *vātsalya* portion itself be persuasive.

Clearly, the "censors" consider the essence of these poems to lie in the *vātsalya* itself, while for me that essence lies more in the reversal. Even assuming this a point of reasonable disagreement, we may still approach the question: what relationship exists between *vātsalya*—a category whose validity I most emphatically affirm—and epiphany?

It would appear that epiphany is possible only after distraction; that is, Sūr must first draw his audience away from the fact of Kṛṣṇa's divinity before he may reveal—return—that divinity to them. One of Sūr's favorite strategies for achieving such distraction is to generate the strongest possible sense of *vātsalya*. This strategy is most certainly not the exclusive property of the *Sūr-līlā*; a similar relationship, between flashes of revelation and the oblivion engendered by love, is evidenced in the very plot of the *Kṛṣṇa-līlā* as it appears in the tenth *skandha* of the *Bhāgavata Purāṇa*, that most definitive of sources for the Gopāla-Kṛṣṇa mythos.[35]

## 3. *Vātsalya-bhāva and the forgetful audience*

> . . . he glanced up at the clock of the Ballast Office and smiled:
> —It has not epiphanized yet, he said.
> —*Stephen Hero*[36]

35. For an exhaustive discussion of the relationship between the *Bhāgavata* narrative and the *Sūrsāgar* see Ved Prakāś Śāstrī, *Śrīmadbhāgavata aura Sūrasāgara kā varṇya viṣaya kā tulanātmaka adhyayana* (Agra, 1969).

36. p. 213.

Early in the tenth *skandha* of the *Bhāgavata*, the child Kṛṣṇa decides to reveal himself to Yaśodā in his full, cosmic form. The mechanics of this revelation are characteristically devious. Kṛṣṇa swallows a handful of mud, and is tattled on by brother Balarāma; when reproached by Yaśodā, he declares his innocence, opens his mouth, and invites her inspection:

> She then saw in his mouth the whole eternal universe, and heaven, and the regions of the sky, and the orb of the earth with its mountains, islands, and oceans; she saw the wind, and lightning, and the moon and stars, and the zodiac; and water and fire and air and space itself; she saw the vacillating senses, the mind, the elements, and the three strands of matter. She saw within the body of her son, in his gaping mouth, the whole universe in all its variety, with all the forms of life and time and nature and actions and hopes, and her own village, and herself. Then she became afraid. . . .[37]

Here is epiphany with a vengeance, and Yaśodā was understandably a bit shaken—but not for long. Five verses later, we are told:

> Once the Gopī had perceived His true self, the Lord spread over her the *māyā* of Viṣṇu, in the form of maternal love;
>
> And the Gopī, losing her memory at once, took her son upon her knees; and her heart filled again with affection for him, as it was before.[38]

This merciful oblivion is required for more than the maintenance of Yaśodā's sanity; it is also essential to the continuation of the narrative itself. At this point the Kṛṣṇa story has hardly begun, and Kṛṣṇa's divine nature must remain unknown, to Yaśodā and everyone else, if subsequent scenes are to achieve the desired effects. In the immediately following episode, for example, a harried Yaśodā takes after a

37. *Bhāgavata* X:viii:37–38. The translation is from Wendy Donniger O'Flaherty, *Hindu Myths* (Baltimore, 1975), p. 220.

38. *Bhāgavata* X:viii:43–44. Eugene Burnouf, ed. and French trans., *Le Bhāgavata Purāṇa* (Paris, 1898).

naughty and recalcitrant Kṛṣṇa with a stick. The episode ultimately arrives at an explicit message regarding the relationship between deity and devotee, but meanwhile the narrative itself is a lighthearted romp, its humor generated by the irony of "woman-with-stick-chases-God." This irony would be quite impossible had Yaśodā not already forgotten her recent brush with the Godhead; it would be another scene entirely, one rather of awe than of amusement, were we to view Yaśodā as a woman who *knowingly* sets out to punish the Lord of the Three Worlds with a willow-switch.

Yet if the present incident requires for its effect that Yaśodā be ignorant of Kṛṣṇa's divinity, it demands from the audience just the opposite. The irony is of the Oedipal variety—"*we* know, but *she* doesn't"—and in the midst of the chase, the audience is given a gentle reminder of who the quarry really is: "the Gopī chased after Him, He who is beyond the reach even of the Yogīs and all their austerities."[39] That nudging relative clause is thus itself a minor epiphany, but with the audience, not Yaśodā, as recipient; it is revelation delivered in a whispered aside, for our ears only.

As the episode continues, it provides another and more explicit example of the same phenomenon. Yaśodā's anger subsides and she abandons the stick. She is still determined to punish Kṛṣṇa, however, and decides to tie him to a heavy mortar. A second narrative aside now reminds the audience both of Kṛṣṇa's true identity, and at the same time of Yaśodā's ignorance regarding that identity:

> Thinking Him her son, Him for whom there is neither inside nor outside, whom nothing precedes nor follows, who Himself precedes and follows, who is without and within the world, who *is* the world,
>
> Unmanifest, Adhokṣāja Himself in human form—Him the Gopī tied to the mortar, like a common child. . . .[40]

There can be no doubt but that this is an "epiphany" in the same sense as that revealed to Yaśodā in the verses quoted

39. *Bhāgavata* X:ix:9.
40. *Bhāgavata* X:ix:13–14.

earlier; if anything, the cosmic spectacle presented here is more awesome than the other. Yet it is equally clear that the audience is the body to be enlightened in this instance; Yaśodā herself continues to regard Kṛṣṇa as "a common child."

Thus there are two sorts of revelation in the *Bhāgavata* narrative: in some episodes Kṛṣṇa's divinity is revealed to the characters, in others to the audience alone. Referring to the former (although in different terms) Archer speaks of the "amnesia" that follows each revelation:

> From time to time the cowherds realize that Krishna is Vishnu and adore him as God. Then amnesia intervenes. They retain no recollection of the vision and see him simply as a youthful cowherd, charming in manner, whose skill in slaying demons arouses their love.[41]

As we have seen, this "amnesia" is a narrative necessity; the characters must forget, if they are to be eligible for subsequent revelations. But why should this be any less true of the audience? The "audience epiphanies" are obviously intentional; that is, we are obviously intended to remember. Does this not require that we first be led to forget?

It does indeed, but the claim requires some clarification. It is axiomatic that the intended audience for the *Bhāgavata*, or for a poem by Sūr, should begin with a full consciousness of Kṛṣṇa's identity; and this consciousness can never be totally lost. But it can be blunted; it is possible for the *childness* of the child to be pushed further to the front of our consciousness than the *identity* of the child. It is possible for the audience, caught up in the events of the narrative, to begin to view those events through the clouded vision of the characters themselves.

There is thus a sense in which it is possible to speak of "amnesia" with regard to the audience as well. But what are the mechanics of this temporary oblivion? Again, a compel-

41. W.G. Archer, *The Loves of Krishna in Indian Painting and Poetry* (New York, 1957), p. 29.

ling parallel exists in the *Bhāgavata* narrative. Returning momentarily to the episode of the "mouth-epiphany," we find the spell induced on that occasion described as the *māyā* of *putrasneha*: "the magic of mother-love" in Raghunathan's translation. It is maternal love that induces Yaśodā to forget the fearsome spectacle of Kṛṣṇa's cosmic form; once she has returned to regarding him affectionately as her son, she is no longer capable of seeing the godhead behind the human child.

This *putrasneha*, "mother-love," obviously has its audience-centered counterpart in the *vātsalya-bhāva* of Rūpa Goswāmin's system; and it is here that we return to my thesis. I suggest that the tale of the child Kṛṣṇa—as related in the *Bhāgavata*, but even more in the Sanskrit *āśiḥ* tradition, and still more in the *Sūrsāgar*—may be viewed as a sequence of alternating revelations and distractions. This is obviously true from the viewpoint of the characters, each of whom (other than Kṛṣṇa himself)[42] repeatedly glimpses, and repeatedly loses sight of, Kṛṣṇa's true nature. I contend that it is equally (if less obviously) true from the viewpoint of the audience.

Each of Sūr's epiphanies, we shall see, is intended to recreate this cycle for the audience, not simply to describe it, but to make the audience experience both phases, distraction and revelation. In many of these poems, *vātsalya-bhāva* serves Sūr as *putrasneha* served Kṛṣṇa: it provides an intentionally misleading sense of protective, parental affection, the "real" purpose of which is to distract the audience for a time from the divinity of Kṛṣṇa. Sūr's epiphanies, I shall demonstrate, are in no way mere narrative conveniences, reminders to a woefully forgetful audience. Sūr intends us to forget, Sūr *guides* us to forget; for only after we have to some extent "forgotten" may we be reminded; only after "amnesia" is epiphany a *poetic* possibility.

42. This marks a significant difference, I think, between the Kṛṣṇa-*līlā* in the *Bhāgavata* and that in the *Sūrsāgar*: Sūr's Kṛṣṇa is often trapped in his own *māyā*, and has to be reminded who he is (usually by Balarāma).

## 4. *The poem as event*

> Mood is what is sought, though the grand successes of Sanskrit I would say go beyond mood to a sort of universal revelation, to what James Joyce, drawing on the vocabulary of religion, called an epiphany.
>
> —Daniel H. H. Ingalls, *Sanskrit Poetry*[43]
>
> How culious an epiphany!
>
> —James Joyce, *Finnegans Wake*[44]

Having speculated on the assumptions that underlie previous studies of Sūr, it is time I stated the assumptions that inform this one. They are by no means original, but I think they bear repeating.

The first assumption is that a poem is a message, from a given poet to a given audience, whose proper transmission depends upon (among other things) poet and audience sharing a common language, and not only language in the ordinary sense, but also the more specialized language of poetic convention. (In the case of *Kṛṣṇa-kāvya*, this common language would of course include the broad outlines of the Kṛṣṇa-mythos.) The second assumption is that a poem, like any verbal message, *is an event occurring in time* and that time therefore plays a major role in the structuring of poetry, time both in the sense of "duration" and in the sense of "sequence."

The latter point may seem too obvious to need repetition, but I suspect that it is often overlooked by *literate* audiences. Northrop Frye has aptly characterized the dilemma of the literate critic:

> When a critic deals with a work of literature, the most natural thing for him to do is to freeze it, to ignore its

43. Daniel H.H. Ingalls, trans., *Sanskrit Poetry from Vidyākara's "Treasury"* (Cambridge, Mass., 1968), pp. 30–31.
44. James Joyce, *Finnegans Wake* (New York, 1939), p. 508.

> movement in time and look at it as a completed pattern of words, with all its parts existing simultaneously. This approach is common to nearly all types of critical techniques: here new and old-fashioned critics are at one. But in the direct experience of literature, which is something distinct from criticism, we are aware of what we may call the persuasion of continuity, the power that keeps us turning the pages of a novel and that holds us in our seats at the theatre.[45]

This is all the more important in the case of poetry composed for oral performance. When poetry is performed orally, the audience will necessarily experience it sequentially, and they will necessarily be conscious of duration. They cannot reread or skip, thereby altering the sequence, nor can they control the rate of their absorption, since the performer (as well as, in the case of most poetry, the meter and therefore the poet himself) determines the pace at which they will receive the lines, and thus determines the interval that will pass between their perception of one line and another. The problem of the overliterate audience underlies at least part of the difference between the approach used here, and that used by the "censors." If we may "freeze" the poem in time, viewing it as a "completed pattern of words," we may also perceive, and isolate, smaller patterns (such as, for example, a pattern developing *vātsalya*) and then chip away the surrounding dross. These static patterns cease to exist if we perceive the poem as an event, a thing in constant motion whose patterns *must* manifest themselves in sequence.

The third assumption is that the short lyric poem constitutes a *unitary* message, using that term in the sense defined by Leonard Nathan: "Unity is an order whose conclusion was implicit in its own premises, in its own beginnings, and whose principle could be abstracted by a careful analysis of its parts *as they develop.*"[46] This last assumption requires somewhat

45. Northrop Frye, *Fables of Identity: Studies in Poetic Mythology* (New York, 1963), p. 21.

46. Leonard Nathan, "Conjectures on a Structural Principle of Vedic Poetry," *Comparative Literature* 28, 2 (Spring, 1976): 124.

more justification than the other two. Nathan raises the question with regard to Vedic poetry: are we not being "parochial," he asks, in assuming that "unity"—axiomatically a desirable quality in Western poetry—should be similarly valued in the poetry of another tradition?[47]

If we were to postulate a set of critics whose expectations of poetry did not include "unity," then there would be nothing the least bit odd about the abridgements of "Yaśodā daydreams." In insisting that the lyric be regarded as a whole, am I then placing unreasonable demands on the poem and its tradition?

I think not. As the Sanskritist will soon discover, the poems here called "epiphanies" are very much in the tradition of the Sanskrit *subhāṣita*; and whatever the assumptions of the modern wielders of Sanskrit critical theory, certainly nothing could be more unitary in structure than the Sanskrit stanza. Sūr's epiphanies, I shall argue, *are* unitary; their conclusions *are* implicit in their premises; and an "abstraction of their principles" will be the concern of Part One of this book.

The three chapters that follow examine progressively smaller units of structure. Chapter II treats *narrative* structure—the tale told by each poem, and its relation to the larger narrative of the Kṛṣṇa mythos. Chapter III deals with individual forms of contrast, comparison, and "revelation," and their relation to the structures of whole poems. Chapter IV deals with the level of prosody and syntax, and the relations between the forms of language and the figures of poetic expression. At each level, my approach has been very much like that proposed by Stanley Fish: to ask at every turn, "what does this word, phrase, sentence, paragraph, chapter, novel, play, poem, *do*?"[48]

47. Nathan, p. 124.

48. Stanley Fish, *Self-Consuming Artifacts: The Experience of Seventeenth-Century Literature* (Berkeley, 1972), p. 387.

## Chapter II

# NARRATIVE STRATEGIES

## 1. *Contract, closure, and the omniscient audience*

> Now a whole is that which has a beginning, a middle, and an end.
>
> —Aristotle, *The Poetics*[1]

> I'll tell you a story
> About Jack a Nory,
> And now my story's begun;
> I'll tell you another
> Of Jack and his brother,
> And now my story is done.
>
> —Nursery rhyme[2]

An intriguingly symmetrical contrast presents itself in two recent studies of poetic structure. Lewis Queary, in his analysis of three Shakespearean plays, pairs *structure* with *contract* as his primary analytical tools.[3] Barbara Herrnstein Smith, in a study of "how poems end," deals with the "close relationship between poetic structure and closure."[4] Queary views the structure of a literary work as the realization of its beginning; Smith views structure as that which leads the work to its conclusion. The two approaches are obviously complementary; the two terms seem made for each other; and it requires little imagination to see that, between them, they provide a useful framework within which to view *structure*. As we shall see, it is a framework

1. Aristotle, "On the Art of Poetry," in T.S. Dorsch, trans., *Classical Literary Criticism* (Baltimore, 1965), p. 41.
2. Raymond Briggs, ed., *The Mother Goose Treasury* (Middlesex, 1973), p. 176.
3. "Structure is the complex realization and fulfillment of contract, while contract is the generator of structure, and a part of it" (Lewis B. Queary, *Contracts and Structure in Macbeth, Antony and Cleopatra, and Coriolanus.* Ph.D. dissertation, University of California, Berkeley, 1973, p. 39).
4. Barbara Herrnstein Smith, *Poetic Closure: A Study of How Poems End* (Chicago, 1968), p. 4.

singularly appropriate to the shape of Indian narrative verse.

A close look at the definitions provided by Queary and Smith seems warranted, for the terms will appear frequently in the following pages. Queary distinguishes two types of contract between playwright and audience, a distinction to which we shall soon return:

> In order to keep the audience in their seats, the playwright must promise some sort of circus. In order to position them in a complex way he must provide them with a frame, a paradigm, a viewpoint from which they can come to care about the play in the way he wants them to. I intend to discuss both processes under the term *contract*, a term which I hope implies the active participation of the audience in the meaningful event that is the play. . . . The opening of any play makes a contract with its audience. The contract may be held to throughout and provide a straightforward guide to the audience . . . or it may be incomplete or misleading in varying degrees.[5]

Smith approaches the definition for her term *closure* by distinguishing between "stopping" and "concluding":

> The ringing of a telephone, the blowing of the wind, the babbling of an infant in its crib: these stop. A poem or a piece of music concludes. We tend to speak of conclusions when a sequence of events has a relatively high degree of structure, when, in other words, we can perceive these events as related to one another by some principle of organization or design that implies the existence of a definite termination point. Under these circumstances, the occurrence of the terminal event is a confirmation of the expectations that have been established by the structure of the sequence, and is usually distinctly gratifying. The sense of stable conclusiveness, finality, or "clinch" which we experience at that point is what is referred to here as *closure*.[6]

She frames the relationship between *structure* and *closure* in terms of the poem in motion:

5. Queary, pp. 3–4.
6. Smith, p. 2.

> The description of a poem's structure, then, becomes the answer to the question, "What keeps it going?" To think of poetic structure in this way, rather than as an organization of, or relationship among, elements, is to emphasize the temporal and dynamic qualities that poetry shares with music. Moreover, it allows the possibility of a corollary question, namely, "What stops it from going?"[7]

The relationship between Queary's *contract* and Smith's *closure* may be stated quite simply: closure entails the fulfilling of at least one contract; strong, "clinching" closure requires the simultaneous fulfillment of several contracts—formal, thematic, syntactic.

Perhaps the stress on beginnings and endings deprives the Aristotelian middle of its due, yet Sūr's narrative poetry operates under certain constraints which together present a strong argument for regarding closure and *initial* contract as preeminent structural units. As Edward Said observes, "a beginning immediately establishes relationships with works already existing, relationships of either continuity or antagonism or some mixture of both";[8] and while much of Said's study of "beginnings" in Western literature necessarily focuses on relationships of antagonism, in the case of Vaiṣṇava poetry the emphasis must be on continuity. It must be remembered that while Sūr's poems are self-contained *formal* units, they are not self-contained *narrative* units. Rather, they are parts of a longer narrative, one already known to the audience, and fixed firmly in outline as a matter of religious dogma—for this is, after all, the biography of a god. Said asks: "Is the beginning of a given work its real beginning, or is there some other, secret point that more authentically starts the work off?"[9] For Sūr's verse, that "point" is to be sought in the audience's detailed knowledge of the mythos. The fact of an omniscient audience who knows the

7. Smith, p. 4.
8. Edward W. Said, *Beginnings: Intention and Method* (New York, 1975), p. 3.
9. *Beginnings*, p. 3.

whole course of our poet's story, and furthermore an audience of true believers who expect that story to stay on course, limits his major narrative choices to two.

We may imagine the situation to be rather like having the whole story on tape, and the tape one that the audience has heard a hundred times before. The man controlling the tape, however, need not play it in its entirety. He still has two interpretive choices: when to turn it on, and when to turn it off. His choices will not affect the narrative, or the audience's knowledge of the narrative; but they will most certainly affect the audience's *reexperience* of the narrative.

The full consequences of audience omniscience may perhaps best be demonstrated by comparing a *Sūr-pada* with a poem from the Western tradition which, while striving for similar effect, operates within the realm Burke calls the "psychology of information."[10] One such is Edwin Arlington Robinson's "How Annandale Went Out":

"They called it Annandale—and I was there
To flourish, to find words, and to attend:
Liar, physician, hypocrite, and friend,
I watched him; and the fight was not so fair
As one or two that I have seen elsewhere:
An apparatus not for me to mend—
A wreck, with hell between him and the end,
Remainded of Annandale; and I was there.

"I knew the ruin as I knew the man;
So put the two together, if you can,
Remembering the worst you know of me.
Now view yourself as I was, on the spot—
With a slight kind of engine. Do you see?
Like this. . . . You wouldn't hang me? I thought not."[11]

The poem is in many ways similar to "Yaśodā daydreams." Both poems build toward an unexpected and terrifying realization, followed by an abrupt closure; both involve the audience as accessories to terror by the perversely indefinite

10. Kenneth Burke, *Counter-Statement* (London, 1953), pp. 29–44.
11. Harry Brown and John Milstead, eds., *Patterns in Poetry: An Introductory Anthology* (Glenview, Ill., 1968), p. 39.

manner in which the instrument of terror is introduced. "With a slight kind of engine. Do you see? / Like this . . ."; and the audience is compelled to imagine for itself a "slight kind of engine," and to envision an act performed "Like this. . . ." The confession is made all the more gruesome by forcing the audience to participate in its unfolding. In "Yaśodā daydreams," the "instrument of terror" is of course Tṛṇāvarta, but the demon is nowhere named; it is rather introduced, with exaggerated vagueness, as "*a* whirlwind." (The indefiniteness is "exaggerated" in that the indefinite article *ika* is displaced from its normal syntactic position—in this case, at the beginning of the sentence—to the very end: "andhavāha uṭhyau *ika.*") The effect is much the same as that in "Annandale"; it is the audience who is forced to say to itself, "But that's not just *a* whirlwind, that's *Tṛṇāvarta*!"

The difference comes in closure. In Robinson's poem, unlike Sūr's, the tale necessarily concludes with the poem. The audience knows no more of the episode, of Annandale, or of the narrator than the poet chooses to tell; we have barely time to glimpse the "crime" before we are told that judgment has been passed, and we are given no basis upon which to dispute that judgment. "You wouldn't hang me? I thought not." Case closed.

Sūr's closure is quite different; instead of end-stopping the narrative, he simply exits into the ongoing tale of Kṛṣṇa, leaving the audience with the task of finishing up. It is not a task that we can escape; the demon has entered, we know that the battle must follow, that Yaśodā must be distraught and Kṛṣṇa ultimately victorious; knowing this, we will inevitably carry the episode through to completion in our minds. This is the epiphany: that the audience cease to be passive listeners to a story-teller's art, and start to remind themselves of what they already know. Once that process of "active remembering" has begun, it carries with it memories of more than simply "Kṛṣṇa-the-demon-killer"; it sparks in the audience a renewed consciousness of Kṛṣṇa's divinity, largely by bringing home to them just how far astray the early part of the poem has led them from that awareness—just how far, that is, they have been the victims of "amnesia."

The strategy employed in "Yaśodā daydreams" is perhaps the most effective in Sūr's narrative repertoire: a progression from the general to the very specific, concluding with a well-known episode, an episode present, but obscured, throughout the earlier lines. The strategy requires a weak initial contract, one providing only the barest of clues as to the poem's position in the broader narrative; given an informed audience, the poet's first task is to misinform.

The technique is seen at its subtle best in Sūr's rendering of yet another "demon" episode. In this instance the demon is Pūtanā, Kaṃsa's henchwoman of the glib tongue and the poisoned nipples, who flatters Yaśodā into letting her suckle the infant Kṛṣṇa. Several of Sūr's poems describe in grisly detail how Kṛṣṇa, immune to the venomous milk, sucks the murderous wet-nurse dry; her shrivelled corpse is finally dragged away and burned by an awed (and puzzled) populace. But one remarkable *pada* restricts itself to the flattery of Yaśodā, the prelude to Pūtanā's treachery:

1 "Just give me Gopāl for a second, my friend!
2 Let me have a good look at his face,
then I'll give him right back, my friend!
3 So soft his flower-like hands and feet,
I just love those lips, those teeth, that
nose, my friend!
4 His dangling locks, the jewels at his throat—
he's the beauty of a million Kāmas, my friend!
5 I think about him night and day;
*I've* never known such fortune, my friend!
6 Treasure of the Vedas, and of the sages all;
you're just so lucky to have him, my friend!
7 He whose form, in the eyes of the world,
shames a million suns and moons, my friend!"
8 Yaśodā, Sūr dotes on your son,
the Gopīs' darling—and Pūtanā's foe.[12]

12. *Sabhā* 673; Caturvedī p. 130. Caturvedī introduces the *pada* as "*Śri Yaśodā ukti sakhī prati*"—"Yaśodā, to a friend"; but such a reading

The whole point of the poem is that our error has been no less than Yaśodā's; we too have surrendered Kṛṣṇa to this beguiling woman, and we too have realized our mistake too late—not, in fact, until the very last word of the poem: *bairī*, "foe." The violence inflicted by that last word is considerably focused by an ingenious prosodic development. It is an untranslatable phenomenon; to understand it requires a word on Sūr's prosody, and a look at part of the poem in the original. The prosodic element that concerns us here is rhyme. An examination of the last two words in each line (with rhyming syllables capitalized) suffices to illustrate the significant pattern:

| | | | | | |
|---|---|---|---|---|---|
| 1 | . . . . . . . . . . . . . dAI | RĪ | 5 | . . . . . . . . . . . . mAI | RĪ |
| 2 | . . . . . . . . . . . . . lAI | RĪ | 6 | . . . . . . . . . . . . . tAI | RĪ |
| 3 | . . . . . . . . . . . sohAI | RĪ | 7 | . . . . . . . . . . . . bhAI | RĪ |
| 4 | . . . . . . . . . . . . . gAI | RĪ | 8 | . . . . . . . . pūtanā | bAIRĪ |

A single end-rhyme sustained throughout is one of the two schemes most favored by Braj poets of Sūr's era, the other being rhymed couplets. For an audience trained to these conventions, the third occurrence of *-airī* is a contract, not merely for a fourth, but for an indefinite sequence of lines ending in the same rhyme. Each subsequent repetition merely strengthens our expectation of the next; the longer the poem,

---

would make lines 5 and 6 total nonsense. I am joined by Usha Jain and Bruce Pray in identifying the *speaker* as the "friend," and the *person addressed* as Yaśodā. The *bhaṇitā* is grammatically ambiguous on one point: it may be read either as I have translated it, or as "Sūrdās (says), Yaśodā dotes on the Gopīs' darling . . ." etc. The latter reading would make no significant difference in this analysis. To those who may be dubious concerning my identification of the speaker as Pūtanā, I should like to point out the very similar lines used by Pūtanā in another of Sūr's *padas*, *Sabhā* 670:

> Deceitfully Pūtanā came to Braj,
> So beautiful, with her poisoned nipples,
> sent by King Kaṃsa.
> She kissed his face and stared at his eyes:
> "You're so lucky, Nandarānī,
> to have the boy Kanhāi. . . ."

the more it accumulates a formal momentum which threatens to carry it forward indefinitely.

Hence the perennial closural problem: a strong rhyme keeps the poem moving, but how does one make it "stop"? The simplest closural solution (what Smith calls "terminal modification"[13]) is obviously to change the rhyme, thereby breaking the chain of expectations; but for Sūr, this is forbidden by convention. In this instance, the formal solution consists of modifying, not rhyme-scheme but word-boundary. Convention dictates that the last two syllables must rhyme, but these may comprise one word or two. In the poem above, each line *but* the last separates the two rhyme-syllables with a word-boundary: *dai-rī, sohai-rī,* etc. In the final rhyme, however, the gap is closed, the syllables form a single word, and a powerful closure is achieved. But there is a further significance to this particular pattern in this particular poem. The key lies in the words *rī* and *bairī. Rī* (along with its masculine equivalent *re*) has traditionally served Hindi poets as a sort of poor man's rhyme, a device that, in the hands of lesser poets, carried about the same semantic weight as the "with a fal-lal, etc." of a Scottish ballad. In conversation, however, *rī* and *re* perform various expletive functions, in all of which they carry at least two bits of semantic content: they indicate familiarity (of affection or disrespect) with the person being addressed, and they are marked for the *gender* of the person addressed. The familiarity, I have translated in this poem with "my friend"; the gender must simply be kept in mind: from the first *rī,* we know that a woman is being addressed, and addressed in a familiar fashion.

Thus the translations "friend" and "foe," while only partially accurate in a literal sense, reflect the crucial structural fact: the rhyme scheme itself, the major *anti*closural force, also contracts for "familiarity," "friendliness," while that word which (we have seen) provides an ingenious solution to a *closural* problem, is *bairī*—"enemy." Terminal modification

13. Smith, p. 53.

on the formal level violates an anticipated word-boundary; terminal modification on the thematic level violates a trust.

It is a trust we have placed in a woman (a Gopī, we have assumed), a friend of ours, because she was a friend of Yaśodā's (she *spoke* as a friend), and a friend of Kṛṣṇa's (she praised him, didn't she?). What appeared a simple, near-nonsense rhyme has subtly shaped our sympathy from line to line. Even as the *bhaṇitā* prepares us for closure, the change seems merely to be a shift from praise by a nameless Gopī, to a rather formulaic praise by the poet. It is only at the last word, that word for which the entire prosodic structure of the poem has prepared us, that we recognize Pūtanā, and realize that she has duped us precisely as she duped Yaśodā. The poem is over, the deed is done; formal closure coincides precisely with the most dramatic imaginable reversal in audience position: from a sense of sympathy and closeness, to a sense of the deepest loathing. Just as in "Yaśodā daydreams," here too the poet lulls and lures us to the battle-field's edge, then withdraws and leaves the field to us. Once again he swathes us in the commonplace, only to open, briefly, a peephole into the cosmic. Closure violates all but the fine print: You read the contract wrong, the poet seems to taunt; I never told you she *wasn't* Pūtanā.

## 2. *The Eighth Coming*

The darkness drops again; but now I know
That twenty centuries of stony sleep
Were vexed to nightmare by a rocking cradle,
And what rough beast, its hour come round at last,
Slouches towards Bethlehem to be born?
—W. B. Yeats, "The Second Coming"[14]

The tale of Kṛṣṇa, complex as it is, by no means exhausts the Kṛṣṇaite poet's narrative resources. Kṛṣṇa's status as an *avatāra* of Viṣṇu, while challenged by the theologians of Kṛṣṇa-bhakti, was accepted by the poets as a narrative

14. M.L. Rosenthal, ed., *Selected Poems and Two Plays of William Butler Yeats* (New York, 1962), p. 91.

reality; and since Kṛṣṇa is the eighth such *avatāra*, the lives of the seven who preceded him are, in a very real sense, a part of Kṛṣṇa's biography as well.

The very sequence of the ten incarnations itself became the structural principle for a genre, the *daśāvatāra stotra*, which proceeds through the sequence from first to last, from Matsya the fish to Kalki, the horseman of apocalypse. The most famous example is that which prefaces Jayadeva's Sanskrit poem, the *Gītagovinda*. Sūr also employs the genre, although his "*daśāvatāra*" *stotras* never actually get beyond incarnation number eight: his point of perspective is that of the *Kṛṣṇāvatāra*, and the *avatāras* who are to follow, Buddha and Kalki, are of little interest to the poet. The seven *preceding* incarnations, however, are often called upon to establish for the child a heroic past—and, as in the poem below, to strike an ironic contrast between past heroism and present child-form:

1 "Don't go far to play now, Love,
    a bogey-man's come to the woods!"
2 Kṛṣṇa laughed and asked:
    "Who *sent* the bogey-man?"
3 "Such a little thing you let scare you now!"
    laughed brother Balarāma;
4 "You slept on the serpent Śeṣa in the seven nether worlds—
    have you forgotten all that now?
5 When Śaṅkhāsura took the four Vedas,
    and hid them in the sea,
6 In the form of a fish you slew him—
    where was your bogey-man then?
7 You bore mount Mandara beneath the ocean,
    churned the sea for the gods and demons;
8 In the tortoise-form you bore the earth—
    you didn't see the bogey-man there!
9 When Hiraṇyākṣa wanted war,
    and the pride rose in his heart,
10 You took the form of the boar, and slew him,
    and raised the earth upon your tusks!
11 When you took upon yourself that terrible form,
    and rescued Prahlāda,
12 Rending Hiraṇyakaśipu with your claws—
    you didn't see the bogey-man there!

13 You tricked Bali when you came as a dwarf,
and crossed the earth in just three steps;
14 He placed your sweat in the sacred vessel,
and touched your sacred feet!
15 When they slew the sinless sage
and took away Kāmadhenu,
16 Twenty-one times you swept the Kṣatriyas from the earth—
you didn't see the bogey-man there!
17 In the form of Rāma when you slew Rāvaṇa
he of ten heads and twenty arms,
18 When you burned all Laṅkā to a crisp—
you didn't see the bogey-man there!
19 For the sake of your *bhakta* you came to earth
and purged it of all its demons;
20 The Vedas forever sang *'Neti!'*
of this *līlā* of the Lord of Sūrdās!"[15]

But the *daśāvatāra stotra* is not the only, or even the most frequent, strategy by which Sūr plays upon the links between the Kṛṣṇa-story and those of the earlier incarnations; more frequently, those others are summoned individually, their lives and Kṛṣṇa's made to intersect in plausible, but startling fashion. In the poem below, the link forged is between *Kṛṣṇāvatāra* and *Rāmāvatāra*:

1 "Listen, son, and I'll tell you a lovely story."
2 The lotus-eyed was overjoyed;
the clever gem made sleepy sounds.
3 "Daśaratha was a king, of the line of Raghu,
and he had four sons.
4 The greatest, named Rāma,
wed the daughter of Janaka.
5 On his father's oath he left the kingdom,
went into the forest with brother and bride.

15. *Sabhā* 839; Caturvedī p. 365. In the Caturvedī version, lines 3 and 4 are reversed, and "Such a little thing" should read "Mother's tales." Lines 3 and 4 refer to the cosmic form of Viṣṇu, who reclines on the serpent Śeṣa during periods of *pralaya*; lines 5 and 6, to the Matsya ("Fish") incarnation; lines 7 and 8, to Kūrma, the Tortoise; lines 9 and 10 to Varāha, the Boar; lines 11 and 12 to Narasiṃha, the Man-lion; lines 13 and 14 to Vāmana, the Dwarf; lines 15 and 16 to Paraśurāma, Rāma-of-the-Axe; and lines 17 and 18 to Rāma. For outlines of the stories of the *avatāras*, see under Matsya, Kūrma etc. in the Glossary.

6 Then as he, the noble one, lotus-eyed,
ran after the golden deer
7 Rāvaṇa stole Sītā away"—
Nanda's son heard, and awoke, and arose:
8 "My bow, my bow!" shouted Sūr's Lord,
"Lakṣmaṇ!
Give me my bow!"—and his mother drew
back in awe.[16]

At first glance, the poem seems to employ a simple, albeit ingenious, strategy. The mother (Yaśodā) tells her son (Kṛṣṇa) a bedtime story—a perfectly commonplace human activity, and therefore one that focuses our attention on the human aspect of Kṛṣṇa's dual nature. The bedtime story itself is one that any Indian mother might well tell her son: the tale of Rāma and Sītā, of their exile along with Lakąmaṇa in the forest, and of Sītā's abduction by Rāvaṇa. In the last line, however, this seemingly domestic activity of story-telling takes an unexpected twist. Kṛṣṇa, who has fallen asleep, awakes in alarm at the mention of Sītā's peril—and his summons to action in her defense is a jarring reminder that this particular "bedtime story" is one which Kṛṣṇa already knows, and more than knows: he has lived the story himself, since he, like Rāma before him, is an *avatāra* of Viṣṇu.

We, the audience, have ourselves been lulled by the lullaby, lulled for a time into accepting the human, and forgetting the divine, aspect of the *avatāra.* The last line reverses that focus, foregrounding the divine aspect, with the impact of the poem resting on the abruptness of that reversal. Like Yaśodā, we draw back in wonder; but the quality of our awe is different from hers. Her reaction is "My God, what have I spawned?" —but we already know the answer to that question. Our own awe might derive from a different sort of question: how could we have been so foolish as to forget Kṛṣṇa's real identity?

16. *Sabhā* 816; Caturvedī p. 317. Cf. the Sanskrit verse from the *Kṛṣṇakarṇāmṛta* beginning "*rāmo nāma babhūva huṃ* . . ."; Frances Wilson, ed., *The Love of Krishna: The Kṛṣṇakarṇāmṛta of Līlāśuka Bilvamañgala* (Philadelphia, 1975), pp. 166–167.

This distraction, of course, stems from the fact that the poem tells not one story but two: the Rāma-story, framed by the Kṛṣṇa-story. Each provides its own "circus"; to some extent, each operates independently of the other; and closure (along with epiphany) is achieved only by their final confluence.

Lines 1 and 2 establish the contracts for the Kṛṣṇa portion: it will be a childhood-poem, and will provide a story-within-a-story. These lines also establish a contract of some complexity: somehow, we are told, the child is *catura,* "clever," in voicing assent to the telling of the story. This necessarily raises the question: wherein lies the cleverness?

The word "Daśaratha" at the beginning of line 3 (the first name used in the poem, it should be noted) serves a double function. First, it establishes a new contract: the story we are to hear is the *Rāmāyaṇa.* Second, it appears to solve the mystery of Kṛṣṇa's "cleverness"; Kṛṣṇa will allow Yaśodā to proceed unwittingly with the story of his own previous incarnation.

It is at this point, I suspect, that most audiences "have it all figured out." We have received an epiphany of sorts, by the reminder of Kṛṣṇa's participation in the chain of *avatāras.* We have foreseen the irony of Kṛṣṇa smugly listening to a recounting of his own heroic exploits. We have solved the "cleverness" mystery. The contracts of the opening lines seem set aside, the problems solved. The Rāma-story takes over at this point; it is almost as if we have completed one poem, and begun another.

And this second poem employs a most sophisticated strategy for drawing the audience into an involvement with the *Rāma-kathā,* and therefore away from a concern for the *Kṛṣṇa-līlā.* This strategy of distraction (the "amnesia" portion of the poem) is to be sought in the manner by which characters are introduced. Each of the three principals in the *Rāma-kathā*—Rāma, Sītā, Lakṣmaṇa—is introduced first by kinship, and only later by name. The resulting pattern is not unlike a *terza rima,* a rhyme-scheme of ABA-BCB-CDC-etc., with a new contract always established just before the last can be fulfilled, the pattern leapfrogging us forward to the final couplet, in which only the absence of the middle member permits the poem to come to rest. Here the pattern begins with line 3: "and he had four sons." The omniscient audience immediately and inevitably run through the four names in their minds: "Rāma, Lakṣmaṇa, Bharata, Śatrughna. . . ." Hardly has this process begun when the next line confirms our list: "the greatest, named Rāma." But we are not allowed to congratulate ourselves on "solving" the first identity-puzzle before we are, in the same line, given another: "the daughter of Janaka." The poem has now contracted for Sītā's name, as it had for Rāma's; and it is with Sītā's name on our tongues that we enter line 5.

Here we are momentarily frustrated: Sītā is there, but not in name. She is *gharani,* "the wife"; and even before she appears in that guise, another identity-contract is added to the list: *anuja,* the younger brother. We thus enter line 6 with two names, Sītā and Lakṣmaṇa, at the upper level of our consciousness. Line 6 gives us neither, but in removing Rāma from the scene it increases our expectation of both—for we know that, with Rāma off chasing the deer, only the unnamed "wife and brother" remain on the stage.

The Sītā-contract is finally fulfilled in line 7. The pattern of kinship-contract/name-fulfillment is now further reinforced; and at the moment, there is only one contract still to be fulfilled: Lakṣmaṇa.

The second half of line 7 is a pre-closural cue, an alliterative flourish of drums: SU-NI NA-NDA NA-NDA-NA NĪ-NDA NI-*vārī*. At this point we are jerked out of the Rāma-story and back into the Kṛṣṇa-story in a number of ways. First, the line says that we have returned to Kṛṣṇa: "Nanda's son (i.e., Kṛṣṇa) heard, and awoke, and arose." Second, there is the effect of the alliteration itself, in a poem previously rather free of it (the longest sequence heretofore having been SU-*ni* SU*ta,* *i*KA KA*thā* KA*hauṁ,* 1. 1). Third, the reference to "awaking" is a reminder that we too have been "sleeping" through this bedtime story. Finally, the first word of the sequence—*suni*—is the same as the first word of the poem. We have returned full circle.

We are awake, and we have left the Rāma-story; but we left it with one bit of unfinished business: Lakṣmaṇa's name. The name is delayed until just after the *bhaṇitā* (*Sūra prabhu*), so that even the formal contracts have been fulfilled. The entire poem hangs now on a final contract; and the startling manner of its fulfillment—with our "clever" Kṛṣṇa, undone by sleep, revealing himself as a god—provides simultaneously a most striking epiphany and a most powerful closure.

Poems like the "bedtime story," while among the most popular (and at the same time the most *classical*) in Sūr's repertoire, are perhaps the most foreign to the modern Western audience. We are unaccustomed to, and thus unprepared for, a mythology so rich; neither the Graeco-Roman nor the Judaeo-Christian mythos can approach the Indian in terms of the narrative resources available to the poet. The difference is particularly notable in the realm of devotional verse. Consider, for example, Donne's "Temple," fourth of the oft-maligned *La Corona* sonnets:

> With his kinde mother who partakes thy woe,
> Joseph turne backe; see where your child doth sit,
> Blowing, yea blowing out those sparks of wit,
> Which himselfe on those Doctors did bestow;
> The Word but lately could not speake, and loe
> It sodenly speakes wonders, whence comes it,
> That all which was, and all which should be writ,
> A shallow-seeming child, should deeply know?
> His Godhead was not soule to his manhood,
> Nor had time mellowed him to this ripenesse,
> But as for one which hath a long taske, 'tis good,
> With the Sunne to beginne his businesse,
> He in his ages morning thus began
> By miracles exceeding power of man.[17]

As the title indicates, the poem is based on the biblical episode of the child Jesus debating points of Jewish law with the scholars ("Doctors") at the Temple in Jerusalem. The

17. John Donne, *The Divine Poems*, ed. Helen Gardner (Oxford, 1952), p. 3.

octave introduces the situation in a carefully controlled dramatic mode: the narrating voice bids Joseph "turne backe," and we, like Joseph, are held at arm's length while the first four lines dramatize the paradox itself. The next four lines restate that paradox in explicit terms, but still in an ostensibly dramatic form, still ostensibly addressing the question to Joseph. A change of tense in the sestet, however, extends the perspective from a spatial arm's length to the temporal distance of centuries, while shifting the object of address from Joseph to the audience. The technique of an abrupt tense shift is one we shall soon see again: all is now in the past (". . . *was* not soule . . . ," ". . . nor *had* time *mellowed* . . . ," ". . . he . . . *began* . . ."); we now draw back from the stance of spectator to that of speculator, and rather than watching and wondering along with Joseph, we intellectualize our wonder along with the narrator.

It should be clear by now that the use of lines 5 to 8 as a "paraphrase" for Sūr's poem does not abuse the context of the lines: the two poems are strikingly similar in their overall strategy. Both emphasize the paradox of the child-god; both do so by opening with a child and concluding with a god. The first line of each contracts for a poem of *vātsalya* by focusing on a human relationship between parent and child ("Listen, son, and I'll tell you a story"; "With his kinde mother who partakes thy woe"). In each, the child drawn so close at first is distanced beyond approach by the end, for the human relationships with which the audience can identify, and through which they feel a sense of personal involvement with the godhead, have themselves grown distant. We witness Joseph "turne backe," so far so that his presence is no longer felt in the sestet; we are left instead with a god, "By miracles exceeding power of man." Yaśodā too draws back, confused and terrified, from one she had thought her son; and the audience draw back with her. Epiphany—as always, a process of *reminding*—has turned tenderness to awe.[18]

The poems, then, are similar in theme, and to a certain

18. Also see the sonnet "Annunciation," Gardner, p. 2.

extent, in intention. A.B. Chambers, for example, applies to Donne's "Temple" the words of the fifteenth-century *Glossa*: "thus . . . was the double nature of Christ shown";[19] he goes on to claim that the sonnet "looks back to the human frailty of the birth of Jesus . . . and forecasts the end for which he came."[20] It is, of course, just such a "double nature" that concerns us, in the "bedtime story" as indeed throughout this study; and our child foreshadows the hero that will be, as surely as does his the martyr that is to come. But however great their similarities, there is a very apparent difference in the *effects* of the two poems: the Hindi poet delivers revelation in a flash infinitely more blinding than the slow, reasoned realization of "Temple." We applaud Donne's wit, but his is not a miracle in which we have participated; we have been "told," not "shown," in the terms of the now-classic dictum.[21]

I suggest that the difference stems not merely from an ill-matched comparison, but rather from a fundamental difference in the resources available to poets from the two traditions. It is precisely that difference recognized long ago by Antiphanes, who laments:

> Your tragedian is altogether the most fortunate of poets. First his plot is familiar to the audience before a line is uttered—he need only give a reminder. If I just say "Oedipus," they know all the rest: his father was Laius, his mother, Jocasta, the names of his sons and daughter, what he has done and what will happen to him. . . . We comic playwrights have no such resources.[22]

19. A.B. Chambers, "The Meaning of the 'Temple' in Donne's *La Corona*," *Journal of English and German Philology* 59 (1960): 214.
20. Chambers, p. 217.
21. It is perhaps this overly cerebral quality that accounts for the rather lukewarm reception that the *La Corona* sonnets have received from most critics. Leishman, for example, dismisses them as "essentially religious exercises" (J.B. Leishman, *The Monarch of Wit: An Analytical and Comparative Study of the Poetry of John Donne* [London, 1965], p. 259). But cf. Gardner, p. xxii: "perhaps no more than a religious exercise, but it is an accomplished one."
22. Antiphanes, *Poiēsis*; quoted in W.K. Wimsatt and Cleanth Brooks, *Literary Criticism: A Short History* (New York, 1957), p. 30.

"Tradition," says J.V. Cunningham, "is all the ways a particular poem could have been written."[23] Donne's tradition would not permit him a poem like Sūr's; he might look forward to a second coming, but he could not look *back* to one. Sūr, on the other hand, could—and did—look forward to two, and back to seven "comings." The concept of multiple *avatāras* affords the Vaiṣṇavite poet a mythological apparatus of marvellous scope: an intricate maze of narrative strands linking this child at this moment to thousands of characters, episodes, plots, and subplots, spanning all time and all creation. It is a universe far richer in narrative possibilities than that inhabited by Donne—or Herbert, or Crashaw, or for that matter Eliot. Only a Milton or a Dante might construct, at epic length and by recourse to Graeco-Roman as well as Judaeo-Christian sources, a mythic structure of the scope that Sūr found ready-made, and that, given a knowing audience, he might summon up in a single lyric.

## 3. *Bowman and Butterthief*

> Mythology is never the biography of the gods. . . . The deeds of the child Apollo remain Apollonian, and the pranks of the child Hermes are not so much childish as Hermetic.
>
> —C. Kerényi, "The Primordial Child in Primordial Times"[24]

The strategy of "Pūtanā," "Yásodā daydreams," and the "bedtime story"—the strategy, that is, of the rediscovered episode—has long been a part of the repertoire of Indian verse. It is, as we have seen, a tool available only to the poet whose tale is already known to his audience—but then there are few Indian poets, of Sūr's time or before, whose work

23. James Vincent Cunningham, *Tradition and Poetic Structure* (Denver, 1960), p. 18.

24. C.G. Jung and C. Kerényi, *Essays on a Science of Mythology: The Myth of the Divine Child and the Mysteries of Eleusis* (Princeton, 1963), p. 25.

does not presuppose such "omniscience." Only in recent decades has any substantial segment of Indian literature begun to exalt the "new" tale over the "old"; the test of a poet's originality has traditionally been not his ingenuity in creating new material, but his dexterity in demonstrating new relationships between the elements of a well-worn theme. The "rediscovery" strategy achieves this end by garbing the traditional theme in an unfamiliar, and thus temporarily concealing, context.

Yet there is a sense in which Sūr's application of this common strategy is uniquely appropriate to his theme. His impish toying with our sympathies mirrors Kṛṣṇa's own mythic mischief; deception is intrinsically more suited to praise of Kṛṣṇa than to hymning soberer gods. Put rather simplistically, it is difficult to imagine a breach of contract by *maryādā puruṣottama Rāma*, the paragon of social responsibility; such a breach is not the least difficult to imagine, however, in the case of Kṛṣṇa the *mākhan-cor*, the "butterthief" and arch-deceiver of Gokul. Of course, we are now talking about contracts of two quite different sorts, and there is no *a priori* reason why such a difference between the characters of the deities should have its precise counterpart in the structure of their devotees' poetry; yet to a great extent it does. The same basic strategy produced very different results in the hands of Tulsī, Sūr's Rāmaite contemporary.

While best known for his epic *Rāmcaritmānas*, Tulsī was a master of shorter verse-forms as well. His *Kavitāvalī* is a work comparable in design, if not in volume, to the *Sūrsāgar*; it consists of short poems, each expanding on some pivotal episode from the life of Rāma. Among the episodes singled out for such expansion was the *Sītā-svayaṃvara*, the great contest in which Rāma won Sītā's hand by breaking the bow of Śiva, a bow renowned for its role in yet another myth-cycle, the destruction of the Triple City. The most dramatic of Tulsī's verses on the *svayaṃvara* is a *chappai*, a six-line verse divided into quatrain-and-couplet:

1 Shaking,
the ponderous earth, the mountains and seas and the lakes,
the Serpent deafened in that instant:
2 The still and the moving,
the Keepers of the Quarters disturbed,
3 The earth-bearing elephants staggering,
ten-headed Rāvaṇa falling on his face
4 And the chariots of the Gods colliding
with the sun and the chill moon.

5 Amazed
were the Gods, Śiva and Brahmā,
the Boar, the Tortoise and the Snake were shaken;
6 That awesome sound shattered the shell of the universe—
when Rām broke Śiva's bow.[25]

Straightforward in effect, the poem is nonetheless enormously subtle in execution; it demands a close reading. The narrative strategy, of course, is the very one we have been examining, the "rediscovered episode," but with one striking difference. In "Yaśodā daydreams" and the "Pūtanā" poem, we were led first to believe that nothing exceptional was occurring, or would occur, within the frame of the poem. In Tulsī's *chappai,* the opposite is true: we are plunged immediately into what we know to be an event of the greatest consequence, if only we knew *what.* Our ignorance serves to keep us distanced from the "real" events of the poem, from those acts of gods and great men which we sense must lie behind these images of apocalypse; yet at the same time we are drawn into the very midst of the cataclysm itself. The net result—distance from the cause, entanglement in the effect—brings the audience to a position of helpless, insignificant, and uninformed observers of the end of the world.

The tool of our entanglement is syntax. Tulsī skillfully avoids all grammatical indicators of tense through the four lines of the quatrain. This pattern begins with the first word

25. Tulsīdās, *Kavitāvalī,* ed. Satīś Kumār (Delhi, 1971), Bālakāṇḍa 11 (p. 93).

of the poem, *ḍigati*—"shaking." The verb serves as a paradigm for the first four lines: of six predicates in the quatrain, four are *tenseless* participles ("shaking," "staggering," "falling," "colliding"); the remaining two are adjectives, also conspicuously lacking in tense markers: "deafened," "disturbed." The result is a temporal disorientation: there is no time-perspective, no "then" or "now" to hold on to, no sense of "it has happened," or "it is happening at this moment and will pass"; in those four lines there is only a consciousness of "happening," on a scale so immense that time is suspended, transcended, nonessential. We are engulfed because the cosmos, time itself, is engulfed.

Line 5 brings a formal change, in rhyme and meter, required by the conventions of the *chappai*; Tulsī exploits this conventional break most effectively. We are suddenly pulled back to a world which, if still coming to an end, does so in a fashion more orderly than the chaos of the quatrain.

Tulsī began the quatrain with a verbal participle, thereby setting a tenseless paradigm sustained through all four lines; he similarly begins the couplet with a verb, this time in the past tense, and proving equally paradigmatic. There are in the couplet four sentences, and four finite verbs, all in the simple past: *cauṃke* ("were amazed"); *kamalamalyau* ("were shaken"); *khaṇḍa kiyo* ("shattered"); *dalyau* ("broke"). The effect of the tense change is a sudden acquisition of temporal perspective. The cataclysm is no less violent than it was in the quatrain, but we view it now from a distance, through an ordered syntax. The urgency is gone; the event has become history, and we may begin to seek the cause of the eruption through which we have just passed.

The search actually began much earlier, with the *tehi kāla* in line 2. Even in the English translation—"in *that* instant"—the impression conveyed is of a beginning *in medias res*; we feel that we must "catch up," something happened that we missed, and the question "*Why* all this?" is strengthened considerably by the assignation of a definite, but unknown, event in time preceding this atemporal melee. All of this is conveyed in the Hindi as well, but in a fashion that makes the question syntactically compelling: *tehi* is a correlative, not a demonstrative, "that"; it must be followed, eventually, with a relative clause. "Then" must grammatically have its "when."

We thus enter the last line propelled by three powerful anticlosural forces. The first is simply that of conventional form: unlike the *pada* (but like the sonnet), the *chappai* has a necessary and predictable stopping point. The second is the unresolved syntax: we must have a "when" clause. The third is the unresolved thematic question: "What's happening?"

The poet has actively frustrated our efforts at solving this latter question, through a minor diversion in line 3. If we were to view the poem as a static, written, rereadable whole, then "Rāvaṇa falling on his face" would reasonably be interpreted as prophetic: since the scene of the poem is the contest for Sītā, long before the battle with Rāvaṇa, the latter's participation in the universal upheaval might only be a promise of things to come, when Rāma would truly send the demon-king "falling on his face." But if we read/hear/perceive the poem sequentially, at line 3 we do not yet know that the scene is that of the *Sītā-svayaṃvara.* We know only that a cataclysmic event is in progress; we must then assume that the fall of Rāvaṇa is not merely prophesied, but an accomplished fact. In other words, we must assume that the episode being described is the final battle in Laṅkā.

Thus we think we have a solution to the thematic problem. Even when the poem begins to calm and sort itself out in the couplet, we assume the thematic contract fulfilled; and as of the middle of line 6, we know we are only half a line from fulfillment of the formal contract as well. Only the syntactic contract (we think) is still in doubt.

The syntactic contract fulfills itself when "that instant" is finally revealed in the long-awaited "when" clause: "When Rām broke Śiva's bow." The episode is not "Laṅkā" after all. Yet while the thematic solution is not that expected, it is still a contract fulfilled; the episode is in every way compatible with everything in the preceding lines. We began with a description of mighty events, and we sought a mighty cause. That we found it in the *svayaṃvara* episode is surprising only in that we were diverted by the mention of Rāvaṇa; the final episode is equally heroic, and our quest is satisfyingly completed. Closure is achieved by a simultaneous fulfillment of formal, thematic, and syntactic contracts, a fugue returned at last to the tonic.

A closure this tight leaves no room for advancing "beyond the poem"; while we may theoretically tell ourselves the sequel—how the gods rained down flowers, and Paraśurāma was angry, and Rāma and Sītā were married—there is no encouragement to do so; there are no loose ends, nothing to tease us forward. Our omniscience, that internal tape-recorder, has been stimulated into motion, but only to the extent that we have been called on to remember what Śiva's bow was, and why Rāma broke it. This allows us to understand the thematic appropriateness of that final relative clause, to appreciate the event as sufficient cause for a moment of universal chaos. But the moment passes with the poem; the syntax rights itself, time flows again in verbs of reassuring tense. The deed is behind us, and we still breathe; the poem and the cosmos conclude in order and stability. "God's in his heaven, all's right with the world": if one were to search for an equivalent idiom in Hindi, the most likely candidate would be *Rām-rājya*: "the rule of Rāma."

As we have seen, the same episodal strategy leads to quite different results when employed by Sūr. Tulsī used the rediscovery of a known episode to reinforce and clarify the terms of the original narrative contract; in Sūr's hands, the rediscovery leads not to reinforcement but to reversal. In general, Sūr's epiphanies set white against black; Tulsī's merely work for whiter whites. The following *pada*, while texturally far less brilliant than Tulsī's *chappai*, leads the audience to a position of much greater complexity:

1 He tore himself free in anger
2 As his friends all stood and watched,
 and he ran to climb the *Kadamba*-tree.
3 The gang clapped their hands and laughed:
 "Śyām, you ran away! He's got you scared!"
4 Śrīdāmā ran home, crying
 "I'm going to tell Yaśodā!"
5 "Friend, friend!" Śyām called him back.
 "Here, come and get your ball!"
6 Sūr's Śyām tucked the yellow cloth between his knees
 and plunged into the deep.[26]

Again we begin *in medias res*: the contract in line 1 is extremely weak, promising only a conflict. Lines 2 and 3 identify the characters, and clarify the contract: it is now clearly a scene involving Kṛṣṇa and his friends, Kṛṣṇa is apparently the one who fled in anger, and we must assume that the conflict promised is a quarrel among children. The cause of the fight is yet to be determined, however, and an explanation of the issues at stake becomes the main thematic contract of the poem.

In line 4, the adversary is at least identified: we may now safely infer that Kṛṣṇa had a fight with his childhood friend Śrīdāmā; furthermore, we know that Śrīdāmā has what he considers a legitimate grievance to bring before Kṛṣṇa's mother. The thematic problem, one step nearer solution, now narrows to the question: what did Kṛṣṇa do to Śrīdāmā? Line 5 answers that question, as well as confirming our suspicion that Śrīdāmā's cause was just. Kṛṣṇa, *acting out of what we must assume to be the fear of being tattled on*, has called his friend back and promised to return his ball—the ball, we now realize, having been the reason for the fight in the first place.

The poem appears to have fulfilled its old contracts and set no new ones. In line 1 it contracted for the answer to a specific question: who's fighting whom, and why? Lines 2 and 3 provided the "who"; line 4, the "whom"; and line 5,

26. *Sabhā* 1157.

the "why." The appearance of Sūr's *bhaṇitā* as the first word of line 6 confirms our closural suspicions. Convention dictates that a *pada* have an even number of lines, and that the *bhaṇitā* appear no sooner than the penultimate line; therefore, line 6 is necessarily the last. With the thematic problem solved, and formal closure scant syllables away, our guard is down. The poem, we have every reason to believe, holds no more surprises.

But there was one question that we never thought to ask: where was the ball? Had the question been raised at all, we would have given the obvious answer: in Kṛṣṇa's hands. Now we learn differently, as a last and unexpected detail is added to the *vignette*: the ball must have fallen in the water, because it is there that Kṛṣṇa goes to retrieve it.

Of course, it is not just any "water." The word I have translated as "deep" is *dah*. While the word may mean any deep pool in a river, the Yamunā holds only one *dah* for the Kṛṣṇa tale: the *dah* where the serpent Kāliya dwells, poisoning the land of Braj; the *Kālīdaha* in which Kṛṣṇa will fight, in a matter of seconds now, the greatest of his childhood battles.[27] We are left at the final rhyme (*bhaharāi*, "splashing") with a picture positively iconographic. The childish quarrel over a ball fades into insignificance, we are carried beyond the poem and into the battle, and the child has become a god.

And yet we *were* warned: there is the matter of the *kadamba*-tree (line 2). We know that tree; in fact, many in the audience may well have anticipated the *kāliyadaman* episode at the very mention of Kṛṣṇa climbing into its branches.[28] It is the task of the remainder of the poem—of the laughing, hand-clapping, weeping, quarreling, tattling, taunting children—to divert and distract. When the final plunge is taken,

27. It was certainly the greatest in Sūr's estimation, judging from the fact that he devoted 69 *padas* to it (*Sabhā* 1139–1207), making it by far the longest of the demon-slaying episodes.

28. Actually the *Kadamba* tree plays a part in one other well-known episode: the "*cīra-haraṇa*" or "clothes-stealing" episode. See Part Two.

the *kadamba* is remembered; it was the fine print in the contract, and is no less binding simply because we failed to heed it.

Like Tulsī's *chappai*, Sūr's *pada* began by plunging us into frantic activity of unspecified origin; Sūr's poem, like Tulsī's, concludes with a famous and heroic act. But whereas Tulsī end-stops his poem by answering all questions, Sūr urges his audience on beyond closure by violating the powerful, implicit contract for a poem of *sakhyabhāva*.[29] The two poets' approaches to the "rediscovery" strategy differ in more than the mere technicalities of contract: each, in "rediscovering" the episode, has also to some extent reinterpreted it. Tulsī's poem on the *Sītā-swayaṃvara*, for example, ignores Sītā entirely; pride of place is given to the cosmic consequences of the act, and the purpose of the bow-breaking seems less the winning of Sītā than the establishment of Rāma's supremacy in the universal order, a supremacy proved beyond doubt by his ability to *disturb* that order. By a great stroke of good fortune, Sūr himself has provided us with an example of how differently the episode may be treated. In one of his rare poems on the Rāma-incarnation, the Kṛṣṇaite poet delivers a radically different interpretation of the bow-breaking:

1 She gazes at Rāma's body.
2 "Keep him safe, for me,"
she prays to Brahmā;
3 "My father's so terribly strict
about this thing with Śiva's bow;
but Rāma's just a boy!
4 Why should *he* bear the burden of that bow,
sisters,
I ask you: Why?"
5 Knowing Sītā's doubt, Sūr's Lord
took the bow upon his fingertips. . . .
6 At its breaking, the great kings there assembled all
scattered and hid,
as the stars flee the rising sun.[30]

29. *Sakhyabhāva*: see Chapter I.
30. *Sabhā* 467.

Sītā's Rādhā-like concern for Rāma dominates the Sūr poem entirely. The bow-breaking is subordinated to the love affair; it is a strutting Rāma Sūr gives us, flexing his muscles for his lady-love and only incidentally destroying in the process the bow that once downed the Triple Cities. But perhaps the most telling line of all is that in which Sūr emphasizes Sītā's "doubt." With few exceptions, "doubts" concerning the omnipotence of Rāma play little part in Tulsī's verse: indeed, as others have noted, Tulsī often goes out of his way to launder those very episodes which might, in more classical renderings, permit us a moment's anxiety. Macfie observes:

> Tulsidas is unwilling to face the consequences of a real incarnation. When Rama acts like a man, he does so in sport. When he is weary, when he swoons, when he finds it difficult to defeat Ravan, when he asks questions as if he did not know, some explanation must be found. It is said that it was Rama's pleasure that it should seem so. And to that extent his incarnation is not real. . . .[31]

With Sūr, precisely the opposite is true: Sūr's narrative interpolations often seem intended to imbue the character of Kṛṣṇa with a far greater degree of pathos than appears in more classical versions of the tale. As we have seen, the *kāliyadaman* episode is a case in point, and I think we may profitably examine yet another *pada* on the episode (again, a *pada* that illustrates the "rediscovery" strategy):

1 Then the child Kṛṣṇa jumped out of bed:
2 "Mother, where are you?
 Why did you leave me alone?"
3 Nanda awoke and Yaśodā awoke,
 and they called him to their side.

31. J.M. Macfie, *The Ramayan of Tulsidas; or, The Bible of Northern India* (Edinburgh, 1930), p. 149. Cf. K.B. Jindal: "Both Sūr and Tulsi wanted to stress the divine element in the incarnation. Tulsi achieved this purpose by repeatedly reminding his readers that whatever commonplace Ram does is just to gratify his devotees. Otherwise, '. . . his state is kingly. Thousands at his bidding speed and post on Land and Ocean without rest.' Sūr regarded it as puerile to describe in so many words the divinity of Krishna" (*A History of Hindi Literature* [Allahabad, 1955], pp. 107–108).

4 "You were asleep, what woke you up?"
  they asked as they lit the lamp.
5 "In my dream, somebody pushed me
  and I plunged into the *Yamunā-dah*!"
6 Yaśodā said to Sūr's Śyām:
  "Don't be afraid, my love."[32]

The appeal of the poem lies in the very real fear shown by a child who must on the morrow do a god's job of work. Sūr gives us no reason to assume that the fear is feigned. Indeed, in Sūr's version of the episode, Kṛṣṇa often acts in a fashion most *un*godlike. The ultimate act, the battle with Kāliya, not only saves the land of Braj, but is in fact paradigmatic for Kṛṣṇa, arriving in time of great need. But the course of that arrival is here made devious; it may lead to heroism, but the heroic act is initially motivated by a most unheroic sequence. Kṛṣṇa is first frightened by, and then appears to ignore, a prophetic nightmare. The stage is set for heroism only when he becomes angry at a friend. He runs away; he takes the plunge only when prompted by the threat of parental punishment and the taunts of his playmates. God saves the world—but on a dare, motivated by fear and pride. Sūr's Kṛṣṇa, here and elsewhere, is a complex (that is to say, human) character, even when performing his most godlike deeds.

While the point may be debated for many of Sūr's poems,[33] these *padas* would suggest that Sūr's Kṛṣṇa himself sometimes forgot, or at least doubted, the extent of his own powers. The

32. *Sabhā* 1135.

33. There are certainly *padas* in which the child Kṛṣṇa shows himself to be aware of his own divinity; in *Sabhā* 886, for example, Kṛṣṇa himself says:

"I've taken birth in Gokul for the fun of it;
  I'll eat everyone's butter!
Yaśodā thinks I'm a child;
  I'm going to have a time with the Gopīs!"
Sūr's Lord says affectionately,
  "These are my own Braj-folk."

Yet there are other poems which are equally explicit in portraying Kṛṣṇa as *un*aware. See for example *Sabhā* 839, translated in Part Two, section II, poem 9.

fact of his doubt (however temporary) is important: if Kṛṣṇa never doubted, then we would have no cause to do so, and therefore it is impossible that we should feel protective toward the child. This protectiveness is Yaśodā's trademark and a paradigm for *vātsalya-bhāva*; more important for our purposes, it is a necessary precondition for epiphany. We must to some extent share the Brajvāsī's fear at Tṛṇāvarta's entrance, Yaśodā's terror at the unveiling of Pūtanā, and Kṛṣṇa's prophetic dread of the battle with Kāliya. Paradoxically, each poem cited leads us to a realization of Kṛṣṇa's omnipotence by first giving us cause to doubt it. Each drops us on the threshold of a battle, and closes with that battle still in doubt. We must hurry forward and reassure *ourselves* of the outcome, thereby reminding ourselves that Kṛṣṇa, doubts and all, is God as well as child.

## Chapter III

# THE VERBAL ICON

### 1. *Signs and tokens*

> She came up close and washed her lord,
> and at once she recognized that scar,
> which once the boar with his white tusk
> had inflicted on him, when he went to
> Parnassos, to Autolykos and his children.
> —*The Odyssey of Homer*[1]

Something happens—or is about to happen—in the poems so far examined. Anonymous friend turns notorious fiend; a swirl of dust takes on familiar form; a child's dream, and a lost ball, lead us to the bottom of a well-known pool; a sleeping child shouts for a hero's bow. In each instance it is an act, witnessed or imminent, which reminds us how deceptive is Kṛṣṇa's child-form: he does, and knows, things impossibly beyond his years. In this and the following chapter, we shall examine a very different sort of poem, one that focuses not on the child's occasional godlike acts, but rather on the deeds (and misdeeds) of a very ordinary child, viewed against the background of his extraordinary potential for action. In this second class of poems, nothing remarkable happens—but much, we are told, is possible:

1 When Mohan grasped the churn
2 At the touch of hand to curds, clay jar and churning-cord,
  the Sea, the Mountain, and the Serpent knew fear.
3 Sometimes he measures the world in three steps;
  sometimes he can't cross the doorstep.
4 Sometimes the very gods cannot reach him;
  sometimes he plays with Nanda's wife.
5 Sometimes he's not content with the whole Sea of Milk;
  sometimes he delights in simple butter and curds.

1. *The Odyssey of Homer*, trans. Richmond Lattimore (New York, 1968), p. 292.

6 Not even Śeṣa can tell the tale
of the *līlā* of the Lord of Sūrdās.[2]

Kṛṣṇa, the young butterthief, lays a fond hand on his mother's butterchurn, and the universe trembles with recognition: for when last the Lord applied himself to a churning, the consequences were far-reaching. On that occasion the object of his labors was the primal *Kṣīrasāgara*, the Sea of Milk; the churning-cord was the world-serpent Vāsuki, pulled at one end by the assembled gods and at the other by the host of demons; and the churn was Mount Mandara, upturned and resting on the patient, unyielding back of the Tortoise—the second incarnation of Viṣṇu, and thus an earlier manifestation of Kṛṣṇa himself.

In the course of that enterprise, the gods and demons successfully churned from the sea (and subsequently fought over) nine great treasures of antiquity, among them the Moon and *amṛta*, the nectar of immortality. But the focus of this poem is the process, not the product. Standing with his hand on the churn, the child becomes for a moment an icon, a reminder both of his deeds in an earlier life and of the enormous power latent in his tiny limbs. Indeed the whole scene is iconographic, a reduction in scale of the great Churning. The first two lines of the verse establish a correspondence between the paraphernalia of the earthly churning and those of the cosmic: Serpent, Sea, and Mountain see in their tiny counterparts the threat of a replay of their ordeal. But the domain of that suggested threat goes beyond the participants in the ancient Churning; here, as in many of Sūr's poems, the audience is reminded that the very stability of the created universe is subject now to an infant's whim.

2. *Sabhā* 762; Caturvedī p. 253. There is one significant difference between the *Sabhā* and Caturvedī readings: in line 4, Caturvedī reads *tāhi*, "him," in place of the second occurrence of *kabahuṃ*, "sometimes." It is difficult to justify this reading, since as Caturvedī himself notes, the Agra, Navalkishore, and Venkateshvara Press readings all agree with the *Sabhā* reading of *kabahuṃ*.

The icon is neatly framed; the poem develops an ordered contrast between cosmic and commonplace, child and god, by confining the halves of Kṛṣṇa's identity within distinct prosodic units. In line 1, we are presented simply with a boy and a butterchurn; in line 2, beginning precisely at the mid-line caesura, we perceive the earthly churning as synecdoche for the cosmic. Lines 3, 4, and 5 present variations on the theme, each illustration occupying precisely one line, and each line carefully confining child and god to opposite sides of the midline break: first half, god; second half, child. The structural separation is still further emphasized by the device of beginning each half-line with the same word, *kabahuṃ*, "sometimes," and by concluding each half-line with a rhyme-word; that is, by pairing the conventional end-rhyme in each line with an unconventional, and contrasting, midline rhyme:

| | | | |
|---|---|---|---|
| 1 | . . . . . . . . . . . . . . -āni | | |
| 2 | . . . . . . . . . . . . . . | / | . . . . . . . . . . . . . . -āni |
| 3 | SOMETIMES . . (god) . (m)ā(p)ata | / | SOMETIMES . . (child) . . . .-āni |
| 4 | SOMETIMES . . (god) . (p)āvata | / | SOMETIMES . . (child) . . . -āni |
| 5 | SOMETIMES . . (god) . (bh)āvata[3] | / | SOMETIMES . . (child) . . . -āni |
| 6 | . . . . . . . . . . . . . . | / | . . . . . . . . . . . . . . -āni |

Within this frame, the poem digresses from the "churn" theme for two lines (3 and 4), then restores it in line 5; once again the *Kṣīrasāgara* and the butterpot are placed in opposition. All the time this cosmic reflection and trepidation have been going on, we are reminded, the child Kṛṣṇa has been idly twirling his mother's butterchurn. The frame closes; the icon is restored to life.

A similar strategy informs a large number of Sūr's poems. *Laukika* and *alaukika*, the commonplace and the cosmic, are

3. In the internal rhyme patterns of lines 3, 4, and 5, note that, since *m, p, v,* and *bh* are all labials, the regularity is actually greater still: i.e., if we allow *B* to represent any labial consonant, then all three words—*māpata, pāvata,* and *bhāvata*—may be represented as: *BāBata.* It is interesting to note that such homorganic alliteration has been "rediscovered" in the West by Kenneth Burke, who devotes several pages to the subject. He begins with the phrase from Coleridge, "bathed by the mist," of which he claims: " 'b— b— the m—' is a *concealed* alliteration" (*The Philosophy of Literary Form* [New York, 1957], p. 296).

isolated within the confines of some structural frame; correspondences are fixed between elements of the child's temporal world and the atemporal universe of Viṣṇu. We are led repeatedly to glimpse a shadowed icon[4] standing just behind the boy of flesh-and-blood. The possible forms such a contrast may take are nearly inexhaustible, but there are a few that Sūr favored above others, and we may profitably examine a sampling of these. In the present chapter, we shall confine ourselves to phenomena that survive translation reasonably intact; finally, Chapter IV will treat two frames—one syntactic, the other prosodic—that require a closer look at the forms of Sūr's language.

## 2. *Figures of deceit*

If mountains shiver in the cold
with what
will they wrap them?

If space goes naked
with what
shall they clothe it?

If the lord's men become worldlings
where will I find the metaphor,

O Lord of Caves
—Allama Prabhu
(trans. A. K. Ramanujan)[5]

The sky is as vast
as the sky; the sea's only simile
Is the sea. The battle of Rāma and Rāvaṇa
was like the battle of Rāma and Rāvaṇa.
—Vālmīki, *Rāmāyaṇa*[6]

4. While I am of course indebted to W.K. Wimsatt and Monroe C. Beardsley's *The Verbal Icon: Studies in the Meaning of Poetry* (Lexington, Ky., 1954) for the title of this chapter, the term *icon* is used here in a sense very different from (and far more literal than) that employed by Wimsatt and Beardsley.

5. A.K. Ramanujan, trans., *Speaking of Śiva* (Baltimore, 1973), p. 151.

6. Cited in Vāmana, *Kāvyālaṅkāra sūtravṛtti*, 4:3:14.

The simile (or, more precisely, the *upamā*) is the most conspicuous rhetorical figure in Sūr's repertoire; it is also the single most important figure in Sanskrit rhetoric and poetics;[7] and latter-day practitioners of the classical *alaṅkāraśāstra* express some rather definite views as to what are, and are not, appropriate uses of the figure. There are some who have suggested, most delicately, that Sūr's passion for the simile occasionally overstepped the bounds of decorum. Manmohan Gautam, discussing the *alaṅkāras* in Sūr's *bhramargīt*, has a short section entitled *upamā kī vikṛti*—"defects of simile." He prefaces the section by suggesting that "mental bitterness" occasionally gives rise to "unbecoming" similes. He seems particularly disturbed when a Gopī tells Uddhava that changing a person's nature is like "trying to straighten a dog's tail, or drag a crow from his carrion-feast."[8] Gautam gives no further explanation of his judgment, leaving the similes to speak for themselves. Pundit Rāmcandra Śukla, perhaps the most brilliant and certainly the most biting pen in Hindi, articulates his distaste at greater length:

> In his description of physical beauty and dress, ornaments, etc., Sūr becomes possessed by a madness for similes, and he goes on piling simile upon simile, conceit (*utprekṣā*) on conceit. In this madness he sometimes loses all Sense of Proportion.[9]

The capitalization, Sense of Proportion, is Śukla's; he turns from Hindi to English for this concept. Śukla's prime example consists of two lines:

> The buttered bread gleams in Hari's hand
> As when the Hog raised the earth with all its
> mountains
> upon the very tips of his tusks.

"What a distance," exclaims Śukla, "lies between a bit of

7. Edwin Gerow, *A Glossary of Indian Figures of Speech* (The Hague, 1971), p. 140.
8. Manmohan Gautam, *Bhramaragīta kā kāvya-vaibhava* (Delhi, 1967), pp. 90–91.
9. Rāmcandra Śukla, *Sūradāsa* (Varanasi, 1948), p. 181.

buttered bread, and the globe of the earth!"[10] But the distance may not actually be as great as it appears; for while there is undeniably an incongruity in the simile, it is a most functional and systematic incongruity.

We are faced with a minor textual problem: all available editions of the Sūrsāgar interpose two lines between the two given by Śukla. However, it seems unlikely that the Pundit would have withdrawn his objections if presented with the poem in its *Sabhā* form:

1 The buttered bread gleams in Hari's hand
2 As if a petaled lotus, knowing the moon its foe,
    clutched the nectar cupped in its heart.
3 He stuffs it into his lotus-mouth—
    and bears a simile so stout:
4 As when the Hog raised the earth with all its
    mountains
      upon the very tips of his tusks.
5 Naked, smiling, he grasps his topknot
    and dances 'round his father.
6 Let Sūr eat the leavings of his Lord,
    so beautifully smeared with spit.[11]

The contract in line 1 is for a poem of very straight *vātsalya*; the simile in line 2 is strikingly beautiful, and classical in its decorum. Playing on the conventional enmity between moon and day-blooming lotus, it gives detail and motive to the sparse picture in the first line: butter becomes as precious as nectar, and shines as if reflecting moonlight; the hand takes on fingers, soft as petals—but clenched, possessive. The *mākhan-cor,* theft accomplished, clutches his booty and glances furtively about for his moon-faced Gopī victim.

The first half of line 3 retains most of the decorum, and part of the figure: lotus-hand fills lotus-mouth. But the second half of that line takes us entirely by surprise: the poet

10. Śukla, p. 181.

11. *Sabhā* 782; Caturvedī p. 273. The sole translatable difference between the two readings is that in Caturvedi's version Kṛṣṇa dances around his mother (*māta*) rather than his father (*tāta*). I have used the *Sabhā* reading here simply because it is better known; the variant reading makes no difference in the present analysis.

positively leaps into his poem, *and tells us explicitly what he intends to do*. The words could well be Śukla's: "a simile so stout." The audience has no choice but to give its full attention to a simile so announced. When it proves hyperbolic—unduly hyperbolic, Śukla felt—we are still forced to remind ourselves: yes, but the poet warned us it would be odd; and if he was aware, if he knew what he was doing, the hyperbole must be there for a reason.

The reason, I suggest, is that what masquerades as a simile is actually something else entirely. A simile is an explicit statement of similarity, but it is at the same time an implicit statement of non-identity. Gerow, in discussing the notion of *upamā* in Sanskrit poetics, defines it as "the comparison of one thing with a substantially different thing," and adds: "All comparisons involve an element of non-identity."[12] Yet in line 4 of the poem above, the form of a simile, implying non-identity, merely serves to mask complete identity: Kṛṣṇa is not "like" Varāha the Hog, he *is* Varāha the Hog, *avatāra* number three, just as he is Rāma and all the other *avatāras*. The butterball now poised on Kṛṣṇa's teeth is no less precious than was the earth poised on his tusks a scant few births ago—or, more precisely, the earth is no more precious than the butter, for the creation of both is merely Kṛṣṇa's *līlā*, with the child "Himself the Play, Himself the Player, Himself the Playground."[13] With this revelation, the poem loses its initial decorum: there are to be no more moonbeams, no more lotuses. A naked child, limbs greased with butter, dances a dance at once comic and awesome: for we have seen this drooling child bear the earth like a juggler's ball in another age; and the Śiva-like dance reminds us that he will one day tire of the game, and drop his butterball earth back into the seas of *pralaya*.

12. Gerow, p. 140.

13. Aurobindo, defining *līlā* in *A Glossary of Sanskrit Terms in the Life Divine*; quoted in Jagdīś Bhāradvāj, *Kṛṣṇa-kāvya meṃ līlā-varṇana* (New Delhi, 1972), p. 7n.

Sūr's work abounds in similes like that of the Hog, figures that tease us with their near-truth, forcing *us* to make the final leap of identification, to brush aside the "seems" and proclaim "is." What are we to call such figures? There may indeed be no handy label, but we do have an intriguing parallel from the English tradition: Sūr's "similes" bear an uncanny similarity to those Miltonic figures of which Isabel MacCaffrey says:

> (Milton) is not so much joining different objects as observing the same thing on a smaller or larger scale. . . . (T)he same forces operate in all parts of a self-consistent, mutually dependent universe.[14]

Stanley Fish dubs the figure "pseudo-simile":

> By "pseudo-simile" I refer to the characteristic manoeuvre by which what is offered as an analogy is perceived finally as an identity. That is, the simile ostensibly compares *A* with *B* (Satan with Leviathan, Satan's host with Pharoah's legions), but ends by discovering that *B* is a manifestation, in another form, of *A* or, alternatively, that both are embodiments of a complex entity *C*.[15]

But it is MacCaffrey who most elegantly captures the spirit of that Miltonic "manoeuvre": "Milton's epic similes are loopholes into history: they allow us to see the archetypes surrounded by their ectypes."[16] The description is as apt for Sūr as for Milton; and while Pundit Śukla may read Sūr's "loopholes into history" as lacking all "Sense of Proportion," I suggest that they are better read as attempts to convey the *cosmic* proportions of the poet's theme.

In the poem above, we had the poet's own word that the simile was peculiar; in that below, the deceptive nature of the figure is made equally explicit, but only after we have

14. Isabel MacCaffrey, *Paradise Lost as "Myth"* (Cambridge, 1959), p. 142.
15. Stanley Fish, *Surprised by Sin: The Reader in Paradise Lost* (Berkeley, 1971), p. 310.
16. MacCaffrey, p. 133.

been led to experience it ourselves. In this *pada*, perhaps the *tour de force* example of Sūr's "pseudo-simile," we progress from statements of physical similarity between Kṛṣṇa and Śiva, to an explicit acknowledgement of the joint godhead:

1 "Sisters, take a look at Nanda's son!
2 With his dusty, matted locks
Hari's made himself look like Hara![17]
3 That necklace of blue silk and gems—
for a minute I thought it a snake!
4 Rattle in hand, Hari laughs;
Hara beats his drum and dances.
5 Gopāl wears a garland of lotus—
how shall I describe it?
6 It's like the elephant's trunk resting at
Hara's throat—
*that's* the look it has!
7 That string of pearls
gleams on Śyām's black body, like—
8 Like Gaṅgā, fearing Gaurī
and clinging to Hara's neck!"
9 Seeing the lion-claw pendant at his breast,
the women wonder anew:
10 It was like the young moon, slipped from the brow
to the breast of Tripurāri.
11 The Limbless saw the limbs and paused,
taking Nanda's son for Hara;
12 May you live forever in the heart of Sūr,
O image of Śyāma-Śiva![18]

Fish argues that within the Christian tradition "the informed reader would recognize Christ in Moses, or even in Hercules, without having to see them isolated together in the artificial confines of a rhetorical figure."[19] A similar, perhaps stronger,

17. Throughout the poem, correspondences are made between features associated with the iconography of Kṛṣṇa (Hari) and that of Śiva (Hara); for the most part the references to Śiva are those that emphasize his destructive role, and thus contrast most sharply with the apparent harmless benevolence of the child. For those unfamiliar with the iconography of Śiva, see Śiva, Tripurāri, and Kāma in the Glossary.
18. *Sabhā* 788; Caturvedī p. 245.
19. Fish, *Surprised by Sin*, p. 311.

argument may be applied here; the informed Indian audience will have no difficulty recognizing one form of the godhead in another. Thus we may perceive the link as soon as the first foot of line 2.[20] "Dusty, matted locks" leads us by an immediate metonymic association to Śiva; the explicit statement of the second foot merely serves to confirm this recognition. Like the Gopī, we too discovered the "Śiva-ness" of Kṛṣṇa by recognizing the iconographic feature itself.

Hence revelation occurs in line 2. The Gopī, thinking Kṛṣṇa mortal, sees the similarity to Śiva as accidental; we perceive it as inevitable. What, then, does the *rest* of the poem do? Does it simply play variations on a theme, prolonging our enjoyment of dramatic irony ("*we* know, but *she* doesn't"), while providing the poet an opportunity to demonstrate his ingenuity in constructing figures? I will admit this as one possible response, but there is another; and it is again structure that gives us a clue to the poet's intention.

The first structural element may be quantified. In lines 1 to 4, Śiva enters the poem gradually, expanding his territory line by line. He is totally absent in line 1; in line 2, he appears only in the last two words, *hara-bheṣu*; in line 3, he has nudged Kṛṣṇa aside and appropriated the entire second foot; and in line 4, he crowds his way two syllables into the first foot as well, thus occupying momentarily more space than Kṛṣṇa:

1 . . . . . . . . . . . .
2 . . . . . . . . . . . . / . . . . . . . . hara-bheṣu
3 . . . . . . . . . . . . / phaniga dhokhaiṃ jāi
4 . . . . . . . hara / nacata ḍamaru bajāi

Now the pattern of expansion changes to one of alternation. For the next six lines, the deities will occupy alternate lines,

20. I shall use the term *foot* to describe the prosodic unit on either side of the midline *caesura*, or *yati*: that is, each line consists of two *feet*, divided by a caesura. The use of the English term here is necessary because of a certain inconsistency in Hindi prosody in defining terms like *carana* and *pāda*.

lines 5, 7, and 9 being devoted to descriptions of Kṛṣṇa, and lines 6, 8, and 10 providing comparisons with Śiva. In the final couplet, lines 11 to 12, the two are inseparable structurally as well as metaphysically.

Line 4 is clearly a major structural pivot. It was here that Śiva "gained the most ground," after which the unit of comparison shifted from the line to the couplet; it is also here that the poet begins to show himself behind the scenes. For the first three lines, the poet's craft is kept as unobtrusive as possible, while we watch the Gopī's "naive" discovery. Before line 4, no explicit word of simile occurs; the comparisons are made, rather, in a casual, conversational syntax. In line 2, Kṛṣṇa has made himself in Śiva's form (*hara-bheṣu kiye*); in line 3, the blue necklace "deceives" the Gopī into thinking it a snake (another metonym for Śiva). But on the other side of line 4, when the pattern of alternation begins, we perceive the poet behind the Gopī, for she switches to a mode of discourse readily identifiable as "poetic": conventional similes using *manau*, "like/as." The poet's intrusion continues in the last couplet: the Gopī disappears entirely, and he speaks in his own voice and his own name, directly addressing the joint divinity.

But the voice of line 4 is unidentifiable, and it contains no simile, however disguised. Rather, it delivers a startlingly direct statement of identity only slightly less explicit than that of line 12, and it does so with powerful prosodic and syntactic support. The prosodic support is simple and direct: a conspicuous (and appropriately kinaesthetic) sequence of sixteen short syllables, double the length of any other in the verse:[21]

21. In the Caturvedī reading, the sequence is somewhat shorter (eleven syllables) but is still by far the longest in the verse. The metrical scheme given above is that of the *Sabhā* text, with parentheses indicating points at which the Caturvedī reading differs. The Caturvedī readings for the portions in parentheses are as follows: Line 4, (–); 5, (– ∪ ∪); 6, (∪ ∪ – ), (∪ – –); 7, (–); 8, (– ∪ – – – ∪ – ∪ ∪ – ∪ ∪ ∪ ∪ – – ∪); 12, (–).

1 ∪∪––∪–∪∪–∪
2 –∪–∪∪∪–∪∪–∪∪∪–∪∪–∪
3 –∪–∪∪–∪∪∪∪∪∪∪∪–––∪
4 ∪∪∪–∪∪∪∪∪∪∪∪∪∪∪(∪∪)∪∪∪–∪
5 ∪∪∪–∪∪–∪(∪∪–)∪–∪–∪–∪
6 –∪––∪(–∪∪)∪∪(––∪)––∪
7 –∪∪∪––∪–∪∪–∪∪∪(∪∪)–∪
8 (∪––––∪∪∪∪∪∪––∪∪–∪)
9 –∪–∪∪∪∪∪∪∪–∪––∪∪–∪
10 –∪∪∪∪∪–∪––∪∪∪–∪∪–∪
11 –∪–∪∪–∪∪∪––∪∪∪∪∪–∪
12 –∪–∪∪–∪–(∪∪)–∪∪∪––∪[22]

Prosody calls our attention to the line; syntax now makes the equation. The equational form of the line loses its impact in translation, for it rests upon a precise syntactic and semantic *chiasmus*:

| | | | | | | | |
|---|---|---|---|---|---|---|---|
| khunakhunā | kara, | haṃsata | hari, | hara | nacata | ḍamaru | bajāi |
| rattle | hand | laughing | Kṛṣṇa, | Śiva | dancing | drum | beating |
| rhythmic accompaniment | | action | subject, | subject | action | rhythmic accompaniment | |

No matter how quickly we "recognized" Śiva in line 2, nothing has prepared us for this; we enter the line with a laughing, clapping child, and leave it with the *tāṇḍava*, Śiva's frenzied dance of universal destruction.

The remainder of the poem, I suggest, is a game of sorts. We have "seen"—that is, we have been led to remember—the oneness of Kṛṣṇa and Śiva. Now we are dared to keep this vision firmly in sight, as the poet attempts to lead us away. Each simile denies the oneness as strongly as it proclaims the similarity; furthermore, each serves as a temporal buffer between one deity and the other: the two-syllable *manau* is in

22. A detailed explanation of the rules of Braj prosody appears in Chapter IV.

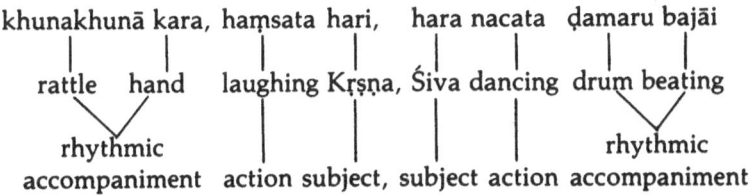

each case extended by auxiliary phrases of comparison—"How shall I describe it?" . . . "*That's* the look it has." The similes become almost blatantly coy; they compartmentalize the deities, and we must actively resist their logic to maintain the vision of line 4: Kṛṣṇa is not *like* Śiva; Kṛṣṇa *is* Śiva. The final couplet comes as a reward, a chance for self-congratulation, as first Kāma and finally the poet himself confirm the identity. Kāma still does so in a figure of similarity (seeing the body [like] Śiva's, he fears another roasting), but the explicit barrier of the simile is gone. The *bhaṇitā* removes the last shred of doubt: Sūr admits that his similes meant more than they said.

This same extravagance, this penchant for stretching the terms of a simile across eons of mythic time, marks Sūr's use of even the most conventional figures. We may take as examples several variations on the stock comparison of "face" and "moon," an association in which the qualities of roundness and cool brilliance are customarily emphasized. In its simplest and most common form, the comparison contains no hint of the mythic, as in this anonymous stanza from the *Subhāṣitaratnakoṣa*:

> Behold the risen face-moon of my darling
> wherein the only blemish is
> that I've compared it to the blemished moon.[23]

But the moon also plays a role in a great many tales from the lives of gods and demons. Lunar eclipses, for example, occur when the moon disappears into the maw of the demon Rāhu, a conceit that enables the Maithili poet Vidyāpati to say of Rādhā:

> The tresses stray across her face, hiding its beauty;
> Rāhu lusts for the circle of the moon.[24]

23. Ingalls, p. 130.

24. Vidyāpati, *Vidyāpati-gīta-saṃgraha*, ed. Subhadra Jha (Varanasi, 1954), p. 83. The translation is mine.

Vidyāpati's figure dips lightly into the mythic, demanding of its audience only that they remember Rāhu's eclipsing function. But when Sūr, in a description of the young brothers Kṛṣṇa and Balarāma, plays on the same association, he makes it a major excursion into mythology: Rāhu is introduced, most obliquely, through his demon-mother:

> Tresses stray across a face, doubling its beauty
> As when the crescent moon is embraced
> by the son of Siṃhikā.[25]

We must remember who Siṃhikā was, before we may identify her son and thus "solve" the simile. But Siṃhikā's name immediately brings to mind her single claim to fame, her battle with Hanumān—and hence her association with the tale of Rāma, Viṣṇu's previous incarnation.[26] Rāhu thus becomes more than a mere figure of comparison, and Siṃhikā more than an irrelevant digression: Rāhu's mother was Rāma's foe; he who was Rāma is now Kṛṣṇa; Kṛṣṇa's face, eclipsed by a lock of hair, is "as if" devoured by Rāhu. Once again, the parts of a cosmological unity have been drawn together by the net of a seeming simile.

Less tenuous than Viṣṇu-Kṛṣṇa's link with the moon's eclipser is his association with the moon herself. At the churning of the Milky Ocean (in which, it will be remembered, the Tortoise-incarnation played a major role) the moon was the first object recovered from the sea. Sūr alludes to this episode in another moon-face simile: when Yaśodā awakens the child Kṛṣṇa by pulling the cover from his face, we are told that his face is:

> like the full moon, appearing through the parted froth
> when the gods churned the milky sea.[27]

There is a chill, haunting irony in the double vision that the line provides us: in one world a child's sleepy face emerges

25. *Sabhā* 802; Caturvedī p. 301.
26. See Rāhu; Siṃhikā; Rāma, in the Glossary.
27. *Sabhā* 822; Caturvedī p. 326.

from a rough blanket; in another, the moon surfaces slowly from the depths of a prehistoric sea, the world's first moonrise watched by a solemn host of gods and demons as they labor at the great churn—which in turn rests on the back of this same sleepy child, then in the form of a monstrous Tortoise.

Of course, these last two similes are as obscure as they are rich; indeed, they are rich precisely because of their obscurity, precisely because they demand so much of their audience. It may be argued that they demand too much, that a poem in motion leaves no time for such associations. Ultimately the question rests on how sophisticated we assume the poet's intended audience to have been in matters mythological; and this we may not know. In any case, Sūr frequently prepares his reader for such rich (and opaque) figures by prefacing them with others more straightforward. The manoeuvre is much like that described by Winifred Nowottny, in reference to English poetry:

> Probably one reason why, in our poetry, there are so many cases where the poet begins with a simile and goes on to a metaphor, is that he must first introduce his comparison explicitly, otherwise nobody would recognize it.[28]

Nowottny cites, as one example of this move, Cleopatra's description of Antony:

> his delights
> were dolphin-like; they showed his back above the elements
> they lived in.[29]

Similarly, Sūr prepares us, in yet another *pada*, for the complex association of child-face, moon, and primal Churning:

> 1 With a clatter Hari put on the necklace
> 2 And it was like a pair of moons, both poised
> above a new-formed, rain-dark cloud.

28. Winifred Nowottny, *The Language Poets Use* (New York, 1962), p. 68.

29. Nowottny, p. 51.

3 Once he bore the Mountain and the Tortoise,
the gods and the demons and the Snake,
with never a moment's fear;
4 Now the Gopīs must help him bear the weight
of the gold he wears so proudly on his arms.
5 Sūr's Śyām peers into the jar of curds
and face will not part from reflected face;
6 As if two moons emerged from the churning,
as if illumined by the light of his laugh.[30]

The poem develops in three distinct movements, each bound within a couplet, and each couplet in turn isolating the terms of contrast or comparison within separate lines. As in so much of Sūr's verse, prosodic units are employed to order the steps of an argument; the line-by-line progression provides a frame as tight as the numbered headings of an outline.

One line of each couplet describes an action performed by the child Kṛṣṇa, the other expands upon the description through explicit figures of comparison or contrast—in the first and last couplets, by explicit simile; in the second, by explicit reference to the child's mythic past. The portrait that emerges in the three descriptive lines is one that has become a cliché of Indian calendar art: the child Kṛṣṇa, donning heavy (presumably gold) necklace and armbands, and peering hungrily into a jar of butter or curds. But it is in the remaining lines, those ostensibly providing a figurative background for the child's actions, that the important "events" of the poem actually occur.

The first simile, while the more opaque for a Western audience, is actually the more conventional of the two. To decipher it requires only one item of rather specialized information: we must know the sort of necklace that Sūr and his audience envisioned Kṛṣṇa as wearing. Frequent mention is

30. *Sabhā* 759; Caturvedī p. 237. The first line presents problems of translation and interpretation. The *Sabhā* version (*kalabala kaiṃ hari āri pare*) seems to bear little relationship to the simile of line 2, and yet line 2 is clearly intended to expand on line 1. The Caturvedī reading, *kalabala te hari hāra pare*, makes sense if interpreted as *hāra pahire*, "put on the necklace," rather than *hāra paḍe*, "fell/was defeated."

made throughout the *Sūrsāgar* (and by other poets as well) of Kṛṣṇa's *keharīnakha* or *baghanakha*, a pair of claws from a tiger, framed in gold or silver, and worn as a pendant—as described here in another *pada*:

> The string of pearls gleams on Śyām's breast,
> and the *baghanakha* glitters from its midst,
> like two moons surrounded by the stars.[31]

Thus in the present verse, the "two moons" of line 2 are the crescent tiger-claws of the necklace, shining against the "raincloud" of his body.[32] The latter association, between Kṛṣṇa's dusky skin and a dark cloud, had been a literary cliché for centuries before Sūr's time; an Indian reader would no more pause at the mention of Kṛṣṇa's "cloud-dark" body or "moon-bright" face than would an English reader at "ruby lips" or "eyes like limpid pools."

The moons, of course, are to reappear in the final couplet; but by that time their significance will have undergone a substantial change, a change for which the intervening lines, 3 and 4, prepare us. This middle couplet establishes a most straightforward contrast between clumsy child and awesome past; and while studiously avoiding any mention of "moons," it sets us up for the final couplet by introducing, in unambiguous terms, the role played by Viṣṇu-Kṛṣṇa in the churning. When the "two moons" now return in line 5, this time as the face and its reflection, we can no longer ignore the association between "moon" and Kṛṣṇa; the episode having been mentioned, we are prepared to make the connections in line 5—and to have them confirmed in line 6: "As if two

31. *Sabhā* 757. The couplet does not appear in Caturvedī's reading (Caturvedī pp. 233–234). For an illustrated description of the twin-clawed *baghanakha* (*vāganakha*) necklace, see Mahādevśāstrī Jośī, ed., *Bhāratīya saṃskṛtikośa* (Poona, 1974), vol. 8, p. 552.

32. This is actually one of two possible readings; the other is that the "two moons" are (1) Kṛṣṇa's necklace and (2) his face itself. The second reading is in fact more in keeping with the final simile in line 6, and while, to the Western audience, it may seem farfetched indeed, it was the *sole* reading that occurred to one knowledgeable informant, Tej Bhatia.

moons emerged from the Churning. . . ." Only at the end do we realize that, throughout the seemingly diverse figures of the poem, there have been in reality only two terms of comparison, two spheres of association: Nanda's courtyard, and the Sea of Milk. Village idyl and cosmic enterprise are revealed as being—in MacCaffrey's phrase—"parts of a self-consistent, mutually dependent universe." The jar of curd is the Sea of Milk by synecdoche, not—as stated—by analogy; Kṛṣṇa the child stumbles under the weight of his tiny bracelets, even as Kṛṣṇa/Viṣṇu/Kūrma the Tortoise supports the Churning-mountain, and Kṛṣṇa *parabrahma* supports in turn the Tortoise; a god's face is reflected in a primal sea, a sea contained in a child's clay jar, while the moon rises, and rises again.[33]

It is a satisfying occurrence when the forms of rhetoric themselves mirror the substance of belief; there is a sense, I think, in which Sūr's "pseudo-simile" constitutes such a case. It is a central point of doctrine for the *Vallabha-sampradāya*, the sect which claims Sūr as a follower, that the icon of Kṛṣṇa must not be regarded (as icons are regarded in many sects) as a mere symbol of the godhead; rather, the icon is to be treated as the *svarūpa*, the "true form," of God himself. For the Vallabhite, the relationship between icon and godhead is essentially one of scale, a substitution of microcosm for macrocosm. The latter relationship is, in the terms of Western *rhetoric*, that of synecdoche—or more broadly, the relationship of metonymy, using the term in the sense employed by Wellek and Warren:

> Recently some bolder conceptions of metonymy as a literary mode have been suggested, even the notion that metonymy and metaphor may be the characterizing structures of two poetic types—poetry of association by

33. There is of course another association evoked by Kṛṣṇa's reflection in the jar of curds: the age-old Indian metaphor of the changeable "world of name and form" as a mere (and multiple) reflection of an absolute reality.

> contiguity, of movement within a single world of discourse, and poetry of association by comparison, joining a plurality of worlds. . . .[34]

The strategy of pseudo-simile appears to exploit the tension between these two modes of discourse, between what Roman Jakobson calls the "metaphoric and metonymic poles."[35] "Other poets' similes join two universes of discourse in such a way as to imply and *confirm* their more usual separation," argues Fish[36]—in contradistinction, of course, to the pseudo-similes of Milton. We might paraphrase for Sūr: other poets (and sects) establish, between the terms of a simile as between the icon and the godhead, relationships that are essentially metaphoric; Sūr, however, garbs metonymic relationships in metaphoric guise, presenting us with ambiguous figures that permit a double vision, seeing at once the "plurality of worlds" within Kṛṣṇa's *līlā*, and—through a window of metonymy—the unity beyond.

### 3. *Frames for the icon: paratactic, sequential*

> I saw a peacock with a fiery tail
> I saw a blazing comet drop down hail
>   I saw a cloud with ivy curled around
>   I saw a sturdy oak creep on the ground
> I saw an ant swallow up a whale
> I saw a raging sea brim full of ale . . .[37]

> Solomon Grundy,
> Born on a Monday,
> Christened on Tuesday,
> Married on Wednesday,
> Took ill on Thursday,
> Worse on Friday,
> Died on Saturday,

34. Rene Wellek and Austin Warren, *Theory of Literature* (New York, 1949), p. 200.
35. Roman Jakobson and Morris Halle, *Fundamentals of Language* (The Hague, 1956), p. 90.
36. Fish, *Surprised by Sin*, p. 311.
37. Raymond Briggs, ed., *The Mother Goose Treasury* (Middlesex, 1973), p. 195.

Buried on Sunday.
This is the end
Of Solomon Grundy.[38]
—Nursery rhymes

The unity described in similar figures by Sūr and Milton is perhaps most clearly visible to the blind: the two poets shared a darkness as well as a rhetoric. But whatever their points of agreement, the *bhakta* and the Puritan were poles apart in their attitudes toward the proper *forms* of poetry. Milton damned all rhyme, and couplet-rhyme above all, as "the jingling sound of like endings."[39] But for Sūr and his tradition the rhymed couplet was the basic unit of structure, just as a rather loosely ordered string of such couplets was the dominant structural mode. In the present section we shall briefly examine the significance of this generalization, before turning to some equally significant exceptions.

The phenomenon is well illustrated in the very similes discussed above. The similes of Milton's epic are themselves most often epic in proportion, having neither couplet nor stanza to confine them. Sūr, on the other hand, invariably trims each simile (as we have seen) to fit precisely within the frame of a single rhymed couplet. This perfect congruence of couplet and figure appears to be the legacy of an oral tradition, one in which composition was a modular process. Framed by a couplet, a simile (or any figure) becomes a self-contained, and hence portable unit. For the medieval poets, a well-made couplet was public property. It might reappear, with minor tailoring, in the works of several poets; it might be shifted from poem to poem, or from point to

38. *The Mother Goose Treasury*, p. 140.

39. "Not without cause therefore some both *Italian* and *Spanish* Poets of prime note have rejected Rime both in longer and shorter Works, as have also long since our best *English* Tragedies, as a thing of itself, to all judicious ears, trivial and of no true musical delight; which consists only in apt Numbers, fit quantity of Syllables, and the sense variously drawn out from one Verse into another, not in the jingling sound of like endings, a fault avoided by the learned Ancients both in Poetry and all good Oratory" (from Milton's preface to the second edition of *Paradise Lost*. Merrit Y. Hughes, ed., *Paradise Lost* [New York, 1962], p. 4).

point within a single poem, to suit the needs of an individual performance; or it might be matched with others of its kind, strung together like beads of uniform shape, to construct a poem like "Śiva-Śyāma," in which each simile-couplet presents another variation on the central theme.

The "variations on a theme" pattern is extremely common, not only in Sūr's verse but in that of most of his contemporaries as well. In most cases a string of such "variation" couplets is framed by two couplets explicitly introductory and closural in function. In the following *pada*, for example, each couplet but the first and last is built around a simile:

A
1 The two boys frolic as one.
2 Footsteps stumbling,
    swinging their dust-drawn limbs,

B
3 They toddle along the road, anklebells tinkling,
    shrieking each to each,
4 *Like* a pair of tender goslings
    enraptured with their own new speech.

C
5 At a tiny waist, a gold-belled belt
    gleams a slivered gleam,
6 *As* gold upon a touchstone
    leaves a thin and gleaming slash.

D
7 Earrings glitter in lovely ears;
    a lotus-pair, swaying, swaying,
8 *As* when Bāsava sent the sacrifice
    at the Life-poet's command.

E
9 Locks of hair stray across a face,
    doubling its beauty,
10 *As* when the crescent moon was embraced
    by the son of Siṃhikā.

F
11 Now they dash to the door,
    now to father Nanda's side;
12 Their Gopī-mother takes the hand of Sūr's own Lord
    and kisses him.[40]

Such poems present in effect a three-part "argument": thesis; examples; summation. The structure is seen most clearly in

40. *Sabhā* 802; Caturvedī p. 301. The simile in lines 7 and 8 is most obscure. I have given one possible reading in a footnote in Part Two.

those poems that are explicitly polemical. Kabīr's *Bījak* provides some of the finest examples:

1 There is no-one, no-one, no-one like Rāma!
A 2 How can a fool understand?
But you, O wise man, ponder:
3 Many the Rāmacandras so austere
B who preserved the world;
4 Many the flute-bearing Kṛṣṇas—
but none reached the Whole.
5 They took the forms of fish and tortoise and boar,
C they took the name of Dwarf;
6 Many were the Buddhas, the stainless—
but none reached the Whole.
7 Many the *siddhas*, the *sādhakas* and *saṃnyāsīs*
D who wandered in the forest;
8 Many the *munis* who bore the name Gorakha—
but none reached the Whole.
9 Even Brahmā knows Him not,
E nor Śiva, Sanaka nor the rest;
10 Kabīr calls to you, asking: Man,
how may *you* then know Him?[41]

The pattern is precisely that which Barbara Smith has termed *paratactic*, as opposed to *sequential* or *associative*; and it is interesting to note that Smith, discussing parataxis in English poetry, also relates this structural mode to an oral tradition, and to poetry "intended for musical rendition":[42]

> Paratactic structure appears frequently in nursery rhymes, traditional lullabies, and in those folk songs which seem to contain, between their fixed opening and close, an almost infinitely expandable and contractable number of verses. . . . Although the opening and closing verses have thematic characteristics appropriate to their positions in the sequence, the central verses may be

41. Kabīr, *Kabīra-bījaka*, Śukdev Sinha, ed. (Allahabad, 1972), p. 117. The translation is mine. I have translated the word *anta* (literally "end") as "Whole," since a more literal translation, "none reached the *end*," would not convey clearly the sense: that is, none have reached the *end* of his qualities; none have exhausted him.

42. *Poetic Closure: A Study of How Poems End* (Chicago, 1968), p. 98.

> omitted or rearranged without affecting the thematic coherence of the whole song, and verses which provide additional variations on the common theme may be interpolated almost indefinitely.[43]

Merely substitute "couplet" for "verse" and Smith's description could be applied as well to the *bhajans* of Mīrābāī, the *śabdas* of Kabīr, the *padas* of Tulsī's *Vinaya Patrikā*, or the *abhaṅgas* of Tukārām. It would seem no great exaggeration to claim parataxis as the structural principle most characteristic of the North Indian *bhakti* lyric.

But however useful the generalization, we must not fail to note the exceptions; for there is another, more judgmental issue linked to that of structure. There can be little doubt that the predominantly paratactic structure of *bhakti* poetry, along with reflecting a particular style of composition and performance, also lends the verse much of its celebrated "folk" simplicity. Significantly, Smith observes that parataxis is particularly characteristic of "primitive and naive styles",[44] and while I have yet to see *bhakti* poetry described as "primitive," yet words like "naive" (or "rough, rugged, free, spontaneous") are commonplace in discussions of *bhakti* literature. These are not, of course, unsympathetic portrayals; on the contrary, they mirror the prevailing, and undeniably appealing image of the *bhakti* poet as a rebel bard, scornful of social as well as literary convention, bursting into spontaneous—and by implication, unstructured—song. There is undoubtedly much truth in this stereotype; it would be hard to disagree with van Buitenen when he says of *bhakti* poetry that its "basic character is more vital than polished, more vivid than refined."[45] Yet we must not allow our admiration for this vitality and apparent simplicity to blind us to the possibility that there is, after all, an underlying "polish" and "refinement." "Spontaneity," A. K. Ramanujan cautions, "has its

43. *Poetic Closure*, p. 99.
44. *Poetic Closure*, p. 98.
45. In Edward C. Dimock et al., eds., *The Literatures of India: An Introduction* (Chicago, 1974), p. 21.

own rhetorical structure."[46] And Smith, speaking again of the English tradition, goes even farther: "The quality of naïveté suggested by this [paratactic] structure has in fact been exploited by poets when certain effects are wanted, such as forthrightness, honesty, or simplicity."[47]

Whether or not we suspect Sūr of having been disingenuous in his choice of form, it is certainly the case that a general tendency toward repetitive, paratactic structure contributes an undeniable "folk" texture to his verse. And yet there is also ample evidence of a far more subtle sense of structure, one that comprehends the *pada* as a thoroughly unified whole rather than a mere string of couplets. This is particularly evident in the two poems we shall examine next: poems that exploit, through a single, extraordinarily sophisticated strategy, the audience's knowledge of a given sequence: in the one case an anatomical sequence, in the other a mythological sequence. Whereas the poems of the preceding section framed child and god in alternate lines of a repeated figure, those now to be examined effect a progressive transformation, from line to line, of child into god and back again.

The first example belongs to a genre traditionally associated with a still young, but sexually precocious Kṛṣṇa: the *murlī-gīt* or "flute-songs." These poems characteristically describe both the seductive powers of the archseducer's flute, irresistibly drawing the Gopīs to Kṛṣṇa, and at the same time the Gopīs' jealousy of that hollow bamboo reed which dares to spend more time at Kṛṣṇa's lips than they do:

1 Gopāl does love that flute,
2 Sisters! Though she makes our Nanda's-son
  dance so many dances;
3 Makes him stand upon one foot,
  and orders him about,
4 Bends his tender body to her will,
  crooks his waist at her command—

46. Ramanujan, *Speaking of Śiva*, p. 38.
47. Smith, *Poetic Closure*, p. 102.

5 He's a slave now, our wise man; a cripple!
She bows the neck of Him who bore the Mountain!
6 Lying couched upon his lip,
she compels his fingers to caress;
7 Furrowed brow, wide-eyed and nostrils flared,
she turns his wrath on us—
8 And thinking him happy
even for a second, Sūr,
she shakes him head to toe.[48]

In traditional taxonomies the flute-songs are customarily assigned to the *śṛṅgāra*, or erotic, *rasa*; this particular verse might further be classified as an example of *vipralambha* or "love in separation," and within *vipralambha* as an example of the subtype *māna*—that mixture of love and pique experienced by a woman whose man has done her wrong. The terms are wholly appropriate to a description of the *Gopīs'* mood: filtered through their jaundiced eyes, a catalogue of the dancing Kṛṣṇa's charms becomes a clinical description of a Kṛṣṇa possessed and in pain, controlled by the Gopīs' cruel rival, the flute. Yet as the bizarre portrait unfolds, it reveals a form increasingly familiar; we are gradually reminded that it is a god's anatomy before us, as the jealous litany is transformed into an iconographic blueprint.

I think it useful at this point to quote briefly from Gopinath Rao, who enumerates, in his *Elements of Hindu Iconography*, the attributes required in a statue of Veṇugopāla, or "Kṛṣṇa-with-flute":

> (T)he rapture of music has to be clearly depicted on his face. . . . This image of Kṛṣṇa is made to stand erect, with the left leg resting on the floor, and the right leg thrown across behind or in front of the left. . . . The flute is held in both the hands and the end of it is applied to the mouth. . . . There should be three bends in the body.[49]

48. *Sabhā* 1273.

49. T.A. Gopinatha Rao, *Elements of Hindu Iconography* (New York, 1968), p. 208.

The last requirement, the "three bends," refers to the pose known as *tribhaṅga*, in which the bent knee of the dancer's raised leg forms the first bend, with the second and third formed by graceful tilts at waist and neck.

The presence of the *tribhaṅga* in this verse has of course been noted by other critics. Indeed, as the poem is read by Munśīrām Śarmā, the pose is the whole *point* of the poem; and it is interesting to note that Śarmā, in espousing this view, feels compelled to counter the conventional expectation—namely, that the "point" of the poem would be its *rasa*. I quote here from Śarmā's study entitled *Sūradāsa kā kāvya-vaibhava*:

> The suggestion of *śṛṅgāra* in this verse—was that really Sūr's goal? No; think a bit, consider a moment. What is Sūr really writing, wrapped within these *bhāva*-s? Something quite ordinary. Sūr wants to portray the *tribhaṅga* pose, which Śrīkṛṣṇa adopts as he plays the flute. The picture is completed, but the reader only manages to understand it after reflecting for a moment.[50]

I agree with everything in Śarmā's analysis except for his concluding statement. The reader, I suggest, does not have to "reflect for a moment," not, at least, after the picture is completed. Rather, the reader has been led to recognize the iconographic form through a process of progressive revelation, guided by a clever variation on a classical poetic device: the so-called *nakha-śikha*, the head-to-toe (or more precisely "toenail-to-topknot") description of the beloved's charms.

The *nakha-śikha* appears first in line 3, from which point it is developed in a thoroughly systematic fashion: each line carries us precisely one step upward in this anatomical sequence. In line 3, Kṛṣṇa is made to "stand upon one *foot*"—thus lifting the other to create the first bend of *tribhaṅga*. In line 4, the flute "crooks his waist"—and gives us bend number two. Line 5 completes the *tribhaṅga* with a flourish, while

50. Munśīrām Śarmā, *Sūradāsa kā kāvya vaibhava* (Kanpur, 1965), p. 216.

continuing the upward progression of *nakha-śikha*: the *neck* is bent—as the third bend of the stylized pose, from our viewpoint; from the Gopīs', as a neck bowed meekly in submission; but also, in a brief narrative allusion to Kṛṣṇa's divinity, as that neck which once bore the weight of Mount Govardhana.

Yet even as the icon emerges before our eyes, the Gopīs continue to vent their spleen, all unknowing, on a god. Their increasingly grotesque misconception of the pose serves as ironic foil to our steadily clearing vision; behind the explicit description, unseen by the Gopīs but visible to the audience, there materializes limb by limb the static, eternal Veṇugopāla, poised as if in a bronze *tribhaṅga*—bronze flute on bronze lips, bronze limbs thrice-bent on a temple altar. The bronzing of the man is neatly framed by the *nakha-śikha*. In line 2, Kṛṣṇa "danced"; but in lines 3 through 7 he is moved, puppet-like, one joint at a time; the statue is fashioned bend by bend, all motion localized. The essential *tribhaṅga* is of course complete with the third bend at line 5, but the anatomical contract for completion of the *nakha-śikha* propels us upward, from "neck" in line 5 to "lip" in line 6. Line 7 closes the series with an ingenious variation, one which, I shall argue in a moment, is essential to the poet's strategy. We jump from "lips" in line 6 to "brow" in line 7, and at this point we fully expect to move higher still; but then we are led, unexpectedly, to retreat: from brow to eyes, from eyes to nose—stopping just short of the "lips" of the preceding line.

This crucial seventh line also fills in the details of the icon, while demonstrating again how distorted is the Gopīs' vision. Iconographer Rao says of the pose, "The rapture of music has to be clearly depicted on his face"; but "furrowed brow, wide-eyed and nostrils flared/he turns his wrath on us," say the Gopīs. The sequence completed, line 8 concludes with a summary of that sequence: Kṛṣṇa is shaken "head to toe"—or literally, "earth to head." The finished puppet is set in motion again; bronze melts to flesh; God dances again as a cowherd in the forest of Brindāban.

Before proceeding to a discussion of the second poem, let us summarize those aspects of the first that will prove crucial to the comparison. The poet established a contract with his audience for a sequence of predictable direction and duration; the regularity of that progression, and hence its predictability, was emphasized by limiting its advance to precisely one step per line, but in the penultimate line the poet's contract was violated in two ways. First, the sequence took three steps in a single line; second, the sequence changed its direction, descending when a continued ascent was expected. The *significance* of this pattern, and of the deviation in the penultimate line, will become clearer when we examine the same strategy in a very different context.

The second poem is a *daśāvatāra stotra*, and is thematically very similar to the other example of that genre examined in Chapter II: in both, the irony of the child-god is developed in the form of a bold taunt, addressed to the child who is so comically unaware of his own divinity:

1 What happened to that strength of yours, God?
2 The strength by which you plunged as the Fish into the sea,
 took back the Vedas, and slew the ancient demon;
3 The strength by which you took the mountain on your
 Tortoise-back,
 and thus contrived to churn the sea;[51]
4 The strength by which you took upon your Boar's tusks
 the Earth, as if it were a flower;
5 The strength by which you split Hiraṇyakaśipu's breast,
 and bestowed a wealth of kindness on your devotee;
6 The strength by which you once trapped Bali,
 and measured the Earth in just three steps;
7 The strength by which you took form
 to place upon the Brahmin the *tilak* of your protection;[52]

51. Variant readings exist for the last part of line 3. The *Sabhā* edition gives *kiyau vimāna*; the Agra edition (as listed by Caturvedī) *kiyau paramāna*; I find most plausible the Navalkishore Press reading (also as listed by Caturvedī): *kiyau vidhāna*.

52. Line 7 appears to refer not to any specific episode, but rather to Paraśurāma's general role as defender of Brahmins and foe of Kṣatriyas.

8 The strength by which you cut off Rāvaṇa's heads,
  and made Vibhīṣaṇa king at last;
9 The strength by which you broke the pride of Jāmbavat;
  the strength by which you heard the plea of Earth.
10 Sūrdās says: Now you can't even cross the threshold of
  your house!
  You just stand there; Lord, you don't *know*![53]

Line 2 begins the *daśāvatāra* sequence with incarnation number one, the Fish; lines 3 through 9 advance through the list in traditional order, introducing (and this is most crucial to the strategy) precisely one *avatāra* per line: the Tortoise in line 3, the Boar in line 4, the Man-lion in 5, the Dwarf in 6, Paraśurāma in 7, Rāma in 8, and in line 9 Kṛṣṇa, the eighth incarnation. Here the sequence stops, two *avatāra*-s short of completion.

Of course, it serves the poet's purpose to stop it precisely when he does. The *daśāvatāra* sequence is employed as a flashback, albeit of cosmic scale—plunging us back to the very beginnings of the Vaiṣṇavite mythos, then bringing us forward, step by step, to the "present" of the Kṛṣṇa-incarnation. For the poem to *complete* the sequence, by going *beyond* Kṛṣṇa to the two incarnations that are to follow, Buddha and Kalki, would be to destroy the effect of the flashback. And yet I suggest that this truncated series, necessary as it is, presents the poet with a structural problem, for which he has devised a structurally ingenious solution.

The problem is simply that once the poet has embarked upon this well-known progression, he has in a sense established a contract with the audience to follow it through to the end. By line 3 or 4 of such a poem, I suspect that most audiences who already know the sequence will have recognized it here, and will have begun actively to anticipate each new incarnation. Each subsequent line merely confirms this contract, and thus heightens our anticipation of the next *avatāra*; the poem is propelled with ever-increasing momentum toward the very clear target of incarnation number ten.

53. *Sabhā* 745; Caturvedī p. 216.

The task facing the poet is thus to terminate the sequence at number eight, and yet to do so in an aesthetically persuasive manner; that is, to achieve closure, a satisfying (rather than frustrating) sense of the poem having come properly to rest.

Let us defer for a moment discussion of how the closural problem is resolved, and turn to a brief examination of the formal skeleton of the poem, those patterns of sound and syntax that serve to make the initial sequence even more compelling. Some of these patterns of regularity are those imposed by the conventions of the *pada* genre. By convention, all lines but the first are of equal metrical length, and are divided by a pause into two roughly equal segments; all employ end-rhyme, each line in this case ending in the syllables *-āna*. The first, metrically shorter line, known as the *ṭek* or 'prop,' functions much like a refrain. Finally, the last line contains the poet's *bhaṇitā*, or signature: Sūrdās.

But of greater interest for the purposes of this study are those additional elements of regularity that the poet himself has superimposed onto the conventional framework. By far the most compelling of these is the repetition, at the beginning of each line but the last, of the phrase *jihiṃ bala*, "The strength by which," with each repetition syntactically linked to the correlative phrase at the beginning of line 1: *so bala*, "that strength." These first nine lines thus constitute a single sentence (a fact somewhat obscured in translation): a main clause in line 1, followed by eight relative clauses in apposition. The entire sentence is a single elaborate question, for which the final line provides, if not an answer, then at least a context: the question has been occasioned by the sight of the child Kṛṣṇa—who once in an earlier incarnation traversed the universe in a mere three steps—thwarted now at the raised doorstep of a village house.

The positioning of those relative and correlative articles, *so* and *jihiṃ*, at the *beginning* of each line is crucial: the first nine lines are thus bound "fore and aft," their structural discreteness emphasized by the repetition both of initial pronoun and of final rhyme, with the pattern broken only by the abrupt appearance of the name Sūrdās at the beginning of line 10. The cumulative effect of this repetition may most succinctly be conveyed by repeating the first and last words of each line:

so bala . . . bhagavāna
jihiṃ bala . . . purāna
jihim bala . . . vidhāna
jihiṃ bala . . . samāna
jihiṃ bala . . . nidhāna

—and so forth. A repetition so prolonged is itself a powerful contract for continuation; each repetition strengthens our expectation of the next, and the poem threatens to go on forever. Now it must be made to stop, and it is the penultimate line, here as in the previous poem, that provides the stopping power. It does so by the simultaneous employment of two devices—one thematic, the other formal, and both devices that we have already seen.

At the formal level, line 9 alters (without actually violating) the contract for repetition of the phrase *jihiṃ bala.* The phrase does indeed appear as expected at the beginning of the line, but it also *re*appears, most unexpectedly, immediately following the midline break. As in the preceding poem, here also the unit of repetition abruptly shortens, in this instance from line to half-line. The same device, I might note in passing, serves as a preclosural cue in a large number of Sūr's poems. Its effect is to blunt the forward momentum of a pattern of repetition, and thus to prepare us for the pattern's total disappearance in the final line.

Returning from form to theme, we find the penultimate line to be the thematic pivot as well. This is the line, remember, in which we have long anticipated the appearance of the Kṛṣṇa incarnation; yet we are halfway through the line before we realize that Kṛṣṇa has indeed arrived on schedule. The first half of the line—"The strength by which you broke the pride of Jāmbavat"—appears at first to be wholly anomalous. Since Jāmbavat's fame rests primarily on his role as ally of Hanumān and Rāma, the mention of Jāmbavat leads us to assume ourselves still in the *Rāma* incarnation—which, if the poet is true to his contract, we should have left behind us in the preceding line. But line 9 becomes still more surprising as the first clause completes itself: for while, as we have just reminded ourselves, Jāmbavat was the *ally* of Rāma, yet now "that strength" is being used to "break his pride."

We may justifiably feel a moment's disorientation; and by the time the light dawns, I suspect that most of us will have fallen into the intended trap. The poet has not broken his contract after all, but he has most certainly tampered with the fine print. While Jāmbavat's greatest fame may indeed derive from his part in the story of Rāma, he plays a role in the story of Kṛṣṇa as well; but it is in an episode from the adulthood of Kṛṣṇa, long after Kṛṣṇa has left the land of Braj (and thus, for all practical purposes, left the purview of *bhakti* poetry) that Kṛṣṇa encounters Jāmbavat, and engages in a quarrel over a famous jewel. The details of the quarrel are unimportant here; what is important is that the issue of the gem is resolved *only when Jāmbavat recognizes in Kṛṣṇa his erstwhile ally,* Rāma—whereupon his posture changes from one of enmity to one of devotion renewed, and his pride is broken indeed.[54]

There are two possibilities. Either we do not remember this reasonably obscure encounter—in which case line 9 will make no sense at all—or else we remember the manner in which Jāmbavat was humbled, and thus remember that *he* remembered. The ambiguity of Jāmbavat's role, linking as it does the Rāma and Kṛṣṇa incarnations, serves to blunt the forward thrust of the *avatāra*-sequence. It starts us "back up the line," reminding us of that fact which the appositional relative clauses have been syntactically affirming all along: Kṛṣṇa, as Jāmbavat remembered, *was* Rāma, and Paraśurāma, and Vāmana, and all the rest.

54. *Bhāgavata* X:1:vi. For a translation of the episode, see N. Raghunathan, trans., *Srimad Bhāgavatam* (Madras, 1976), vol. II, pp. 370–373.

But there is one final anomaly in the penultimate line: the second half of the line does in *fact* carry us a small step backward—not to an earlier *avatāra*, but to the origins of this one: Kṛṣṇa, we are reminded, came to Braj at the request of Earth.[55] The line thus brackets the child-Kṛṣṇa—first overshooting, all the way to the adult Kṛṣṇa reigning in Dwārakā; then swinging back to a time before the child's birth; and finally, like a pendulum coming to rest, dropping us into the "slot" for which the whole poem has served as background: a moment taken from the childhood of Kṛṣṇa, a moment of apparent weakness bracketed by long ages of greatness.

I think it beyond debate that the two poems above, and a great many like them throughout the *Sūrsāgar*, demonstrate a sense of structure that comprehends the poem as a unity, with its parts tightly ordered, their relationships fixed; but then it is equally beyond debate that a somewhat greater number of Sūr's poems exhibit a structure basically paratactic, and that yet a greater number fall somewhere between these two structural poles. The claim here is not that Sūr abandoned that paratactic design which characterizes *bhakti* verse as a whole; the claim is simply that his verse evidences an awareness of, and a control over, both modes. Indeed, if we assume an audience accustomed to the less tightly ordered verse of earlier *bhaktas*, for Sūr to employ a structure too self-consciously "sophisticated" might well have been simply bad rhetoric, sounding more of the *paṇḍit* than of the god-drunk devotee. In this regard, it is interesting to note that even within such closely sequential verses as the flute-song and *daśāvatāra* poems, the *illusion* of parataxis is to a considerable extent retained. Both poems observe the familiar tripartite division: introductory line (or couplet); a string of parallel examples, each occupying the same prosodic space; a concluding line (or couplet). In the case of the *daśāvatāra pada*, the epanaphoric repetition of *jihiṃ bala* bears all the *formal* earmarks of a loosely cumulative structure; in the

55. See Introduction.

flute-song, an inattentive reader (or listener) might well perceive the Gopī's description as a spontaneous, and unordered, catalogue of grievances. In both cases, the central portion of the verse is indeed in the time-honored mold of variations-on-a-theme, but with one enormous difference: the variations are subtly but irresistibly directed toward a predetermined goal; the poems' beginnings lead, by routes almost insidiously direct, to their conclusions.

"An obvious characteristic of the medieval literary lyric is 'enumerative' structure"—so says Leonard Nathan of quite a different tradition.[56] Nathan observes that the catalogue, of lover's charms or sinner's ills, marked the medieval English lyric, but that the sixteenth century (Sūr's own, I cannot resist noting) saw the introduction of a structure which, while still superficially employing the catalogue, had moved to a tighter order, producing such transitional works as Gascoigne's "Lullabie." Coincidence of time aside, it is tempting to suggest that some such transition is a nearly inevitable development; perhaps in each tradition of any antiquity there must be a Gascoigne or a Sūr, conscious at once of the rhetorical force of the compelling sequence, and of the limitations imposed by an audience suspicious of rhetoric.

## 4. *The irony of it All*

> OEDIPUS: Could I have told that you'd talk nonsense, that
> You'd come here to make a fool of yourself, and of me?
> TEIRESIAS: A fool? Your parents thought me sane enough.
> OEDIPUS: My parents again!—Wait: who were my parents?
>
> —Sophocles[57]

56. Leonard Nathan, "Gascoigne's 'Lullabie' and Structures in the Tudor Lyric," in *The Rhetoric of Renaissance Poetry*, ed. Thomas O. Sloan and Raymond B. Waddington (Berkeley, 1974), p. 59.

57. Sophocles, "Oedipus Rex," *The Oedipus Cycle*, Dudley Fitts and Robert Fitzgerald, trans. (New York, 1939), p. 22.

BALARĀMA (to Kṛṣṇa): White is Nanda,
and Yaśodā white;
How come *you're* so black?
—Sūrdās[58]

Human anatomy supplied the major principle of structure in the "flute-song," as did a repeated (and deceptive) comparison in "Śiva-Śyāma." Yet by their two quite different routes—the one sequential, the other paratactic—both poems led us to glimpse the form of an icon lurking behind a body of flesh and blood; and in neither poem would we have seen the icon half so clearly were it not so grossly misrepresented by the Gopīs. The harder the Gopīs try to push God from his pedestal, the more we are called upon to push him back again.

The stratagem is ubiquitous; it is employed, in one form or another, in almost every *pada* we have examined. And were Sūr a Western poet, we would unhesitatingly label the device "dramatic irony." But then, as we are constantly reminded, Indian conceptions of "dramatic" are very different from those held in the West. It is a cliché of Indological studies, for example, that tragedy is foreign to the Indian theatre. The "cruelties of Choice and Chance" bring Oedipus to irresistible, and irreversible, ruin; but to Duṣyanta they must give no more than a moment's pause—a fascinating complication in the plot, but one over which the original (and proper) order must ultimately triumph. Yet while *Oedipus* must have a tragic, and *Śakuntalā* a happy, ending, there is at least one respect in which these two archetypal plays end very much alike: both conclude with the discovery by the characters of that which the audience knew all along. Sophocles' audience possesses from the beginning the fatal knowledge that the poet denies to Oedipus himself: who fathered, and who mothered him; who it was he slew, and whom he bedded. Kālidāsa's Duṣyanta, spell-struck, may forget the fact of his marriage to Śakuntalā, and fail to recognize his own son; the audience makes no such errors. In both plays, and in much of the literature of both traditions, a great deal

58. *Sabhā* 833.

of what we perceive as "drama" springs from what has been called "dramatic irony": the audience's acute sense of being privileged spectators, of knowing more about the characters and their fate than do the characters themselves.

In the case of Sūr's verse, the most common victims are the Gopīs, but they are by no means the only characters so treated. Almost everyone associated with Kṛṣṇa plays the fool's role at some point or another, from Yaśodā, cautioning her supposed son against the bogey-man, to the sundry demonic assassins who vow (with premature bravado) to dispose of the "infant." The only character who consistently escapes the role—the only character, indeed, who appears never to lose sight of Kṛṣṇa's true identity—is his "brother" and co-*avatāra*, Balarāma. Balarāma often serves the poet as an all-knowing narrator, whose frequent asides direct the audience to ironies concealed from the other characters—as when Yaśodā has "punished" Kṛṣṇa by tying him to the mortar:

> Haladhara saw Śyāma, and smiled:
> "Who can bind this one,
> and who can set him free?"[59]

But it is Kṛṣṇa himself to whom Balarāma most often addresses his "reminders," always in the process accentuating what is undoubtedly the sharpest irony of all: that Kṛṣṇa should fall victim to the ruse of his own *līlā*. We have seen one such example: the first *daśāvatāra* poem, in which Balarāma teases a timid Kṛṣṇa while recalling for him (and for us) his heroic past. There are other examples in which Balarāma's knowing taunts become more outrageous still:

> 1 "Mother, Brother's always teasing me!
> 2 He says, 'Yaśodā bought you,
> who says she gave you birth?'
> 3 What can I do? I'm so mad
> I can't go out and play.
> 4 Again and again he asks:
> 'Who's your mother,
> who's your father?

59. *Sabhā* 998.

5 White is Nanda, and Yaśodā white;
how come *you're* so black?'
6 The other boys all snap their fingers
and laugh to see me dance.
7 You sure know how to beat *me*,
but you never get mad at Brother!"
8 Yaśodā heard Mohan's angry words
and was amused.
9 "Listen, Kānha: your brother's a liar,
he's a scoundrel from birth!
10 I swear by the cows we live by:
I *am* mother,
you *are* son."[60]

There is nothing subtle about the irony in this *pada*; revelation here is less a matter of a single, startling jolt of recognition, than a series of hammer-blows—in the form of Balarāma's taunts—each driving deeper the wedge between Kṛṣṇa the sulking tattle-tale and Kṛṣṇa *parabrahma*. Balarāma, of course, is at least half right; Kṛṣṇa is not the son of Nanda and Yaśodā, and Yaśodā's naive reassurance is all the more ironic for being, in the original, technically correct: *hauṃ mātā, tū pūta*—"I am mother, you are son." Mother and son they are indeed, but not (as each believes) each other's.

But the fictive relationship accounts for only part of the irony: for when Balarāma "deduces" that the dark-skinned Kṛṣṇa could not be the son of fair Nanda and Yaśodā, the implications go farther than a question of paternity. "Kṛṣṇa"; "Śyāma"; both mean "black," and the color is a major feature of Kṛṣṇa-iconography. Purāṇic accounts, as we have seen, trace the origins of Kṛṣṇa's blackness to the black hair of Viṣṇu from which he was conceived (in the womb, it must be remembered, not of Yaśodā but of the noblewoman De-

60. *Sabhā* 833; Caturvedī p. 371. For the Caturvedī reading, line 6 would translate: "The other boys all snap their fingers and laugh/and Balabīra teaches them (i.e., eggs them on)." Line 8 in the Caturvedī reading would translate: "Yaśodā saw Mohan's angry face/and was amused." The variations are minor, and certainly make no difference to this analysis.

vakī); and a great many later poets (not excluding Sūr) depict Rādhā swooning with love at the sight of her own black hair; or compare Kṛṣṇa with a black and life-giving raincloud; or otherwise exalt his blackness. Sūr, however, seems determined to bring myth to terms with reality, and the reality of North Indian society is that black is *not* beautiful. The assumption underlying Balarāma's taunt is not merely that somewhere Kṛṣṇa must have another set of parents, but also that those parents must themselves be black, *and therefore low caste.* Kṛṣṇa, Balarāma jeers, is both low-born and a changeling; and the stinging half-truth prompts the audience to recall how high was his birth in fact.

This almost perverse demythification of the sacred might be construed as an attempt at social commentary—in this case, as a parody of contemporary attitudes toward race and caste. Certainly such satire would be in the great tradition of *bhakti* poetry. But Sūr is no Kabīr; his barbs, if barbs they are, are gentle and good-humored. I suspect that the basic intention of such poems is less to satirize that which is objectionable, than to give new life to that which is sacred but clichéd; to set the icon in motion again by the sheer novelty of viewing it through the distorting glass of social prejudice. Much the same strategy is applied, in another poem, to the sacred dual name Rādhā-Kṛṣṇa. For the worshipper this name has a mantric quality, evoking the mystery of the *yugala,* the union of the Lord and his *śakti*; but here it is spoken in tones of disdain and mockery by Rādhā's protective (and class-conscious) mother:

"Why do you keep going to *their* house?"
At home her mother scolds her,
  but she's not a bit afraid.
"Rādhā-Kṛṣṇa, Kṛṣṇa-Rādhā!
It's all over Braj,
  it's so shameful!
*You're* the daughter of the great Vṛṣabhānu;
  but *that* one has no caste, no rank.
Stay away from Gokul!

Haven't you had your fill of shame?"
The mother lectures the daughter,
but the daughter wavers not;
she only smiles. . . .[61]

Rādhā appears no more aware than is her mother of her lover's true identity, unless we read some such awareness into that nicely ambiguous smile. But the audience knows, and shares at least that part of Rādhā's smile which is addressed to her mother's folly: for the audience hears at once the *mantra* and the taunt, the sacred name and its absurdly distorted echo.

The irony is not always so heavy-handed, however; in particular, it softens noticeably when the target is Yaśodā, rather than the Gopīs, Rādhā, or Kṛṣṇa himself. Most poems that make Yaśodā the target of dramatic irony evoke a sense more of awe than of mirth. Yaśodā, it must be remembered, is the paradigm of the *vātsalya* mode of *bhakti*, just as Rādhā is the model for the *madhura*; great stress is placed on Kṛṣṇa's willing submission to a devotee whose love for him is untempered by fear, or awe, or expectation of reward. Those poems that focus on Yaśodā's naive, but loving, assertion of authority over the source of *all* authority, exemplify better than any others the strategy here called "iconographic": they play the temporal against the timeless, revealing a source of limitless power restrained by a mortal hand:

The arm that saved Prahlāda
and tore open Hiraṇyakaśipu's breast—
Yaśodā grabs that very same arm
and says: "Hold still now, love!"[62]

The following poem, for example, returns to the theme of the fictive relationship, but this time with a feather-light touch, confined to a single disturbing phrase in the second half of line 6:

61. *Sabhā* 2326.
62. *Sabhā* 746.

1 In the jewel studded courtyard of Nanda
the two Brothers are at play.
2 The White and the Black, such a pair they make!—
Balarāma and Kanhaiyā.
3 Lovely locks dangling,
yellow *bindu* on their brows,
4 The lion-claw necklace agleam on their breasts,
lifting the sorrow of the saints.
5 And Yaśodā and Rohiṇī together,
devoted mothers both,
6 Snapping their fingers to make them dance,
*thinking the children their sons.*
7 The blue and yellow silks
are pleasing to the eye;
8 Suraja sings the praises
of the joy of children at play.[63]

The early lines of the poem lead us away from any conscious awareness of the pretense underlying Kṛṣṇa's presence in the house of Nanda. Even when the poet refers to Yaśodā and Rohiṇī as the "mothers," nothing tempts us to contradict him; we accept the relationship as not only right and proper, but indeed as sacred. Nor do the first five lines encourage us to dwell upon the divinity of the "brothers." True, several attributes metonymic for the divine pair are named: their colors (black and white—line 2); the traditional colors of their clothing (yellow for Kṛṣṇa, blue for Balarāma—line 7); the *Hari-nakha,* or lion-claw pendant of Hari (line 4). Yet while we know at each step that we are in the presence of Kṛṣṇa and Balarāma, they are not portrayed as a particularly *alaukika* pair; the only explicit move into the *alaukika* comes when the *Hari-nakha* lifts the "sorrow of the saints" (line 4), and even this reference to their divinity is so formulaic as to lose any revelatory impact.

63. *Sabhā* 734; Caturvedī p. 201. The fourth edition of the *Sabhā* text reads "*Kanhaiyā*" ("Kṛṣṇa") instead of "*nanhaiyā*" ("children") in line 6; however, the third edition reads "*nanhaiyā,*" as does Caturvedī. I think we are safe in assuming the "*Kanhaiyā*" reading to be a misprint.

In short, the child-gods and their "mothers" are described with a stylized decorum; they live in an in-between world (Sūr's "little world of sweet dreams," Dwivedi called it[64]) filled neither by the dung-smoke of an *ahīr* village nor by the battle cries of gods and demons. We are reminded that these are exceptional children, children of legend, for the iconographic elements are present; but these elements are not ordered, contrasted, isolated. There is nothing to force a separation of *laukika* and *alaukika*—nothing, that is, until line 6.

In the second half of that line, the level "semi-*laukika*" tone of earlier lines is disturbed by the reminder—"*thinking*" them their sons—that the children are not their sons at all. The phrase may strike us first as a total non sequitur; certainly it is incompatible with all that has gone before. But as recognition dawns, the tranquil scene takes on an awesome new dimension: the "mothers," unaware that the children before them jointly comprise the lord of all creation, dare through ignorance to snap their fingers and put God through his paces. The stylized scene has lost all cohesion; Yaśodā and Rohiṇī descend to the human, Kṛṣṇa and Balarāma rise to the cosmic. Then the poem moves past the moment of revelation. Sūr drops the curtain again, and returns us to the "world of sweet dreams," with a final couplet that proceeds as if nothing had happened. Indeed, from the viewpoint of the characters, nothing has; only the audience has seen the gulf between what appears, and what is. For them, the deceit of the mother-son relationships has become yet another synecdoche for the much larger deceit of the entire Braj-*līlā*: nothing about Kṛṣṇa is ever quite what it seems.

64. Ram Avadh Dwivedi, *A Critical Survey of Hindi Literature* (Benares, 1966), p. 69.

Chapter IV

# STRATEGY AND THE FORMS OF LANGUAGE

## 1. *The hand that ropes the wind: figures of contiguity*

Those who sharpen the tooth of the dog, meaning
Death
Those who glitter with the glory of the hummingbird, meaning
Death
Those who sit in the stye of contentment, meaning
Death
Those who suffer the ecstasy of the animals, meaning
Death

Are become insubstantial, reduced by a wind,
A breath of pine, and the woodsong fog
By this grace dissolved in place

—T.S. Eliot, "Marina"[1]

Throughout the preceding chapters, an effort has been made to confine discussion to more or less translatable phenomena. This has proved a less formidable constraint than one might imagine. The ways in which the world's poetries resemble one another are often more striking than the ways in which they differ; and since in any case an "exhaustive" study of Sūr, or any other poet, lies beyond the scope of this or any other volume, it has been possible to pick and choose: to examine those phenomena which, like the simile, have precise English analogs and to ignore others, such as prosody, which wholly fail to survive outside the medium of their original language.

But in every poem discussed, these untranslatable forces have, of course, been at work. Sometimes, as in the case of alliteration, they have served a largely ornamental function; more often, they have participated in the very structures we have been examining. Where that participation seemed especially crucial—as in the rhyme-scheme of the Pūtanā poem

1. T.S. Eliot, *The Complete Poems and Plays, 1909–1950* (New York, 1952), p. 72.

or the metrical focus in the fourth line of "Śiva-Śyāma"—it has been noted; elsewhere the reader has simply been left to imagine (as readers must do with all translated literature) that much has been lost in translation.

The present chapter is intended in part to give the reader some idea of what it is that translation loses. The phenomena to be discussed here are language-bound, and the discussion will of necessity be more technical than in preceding chapters. It will also, mercifully, be shorter. I have selected for discussion two aspects of Sūr's use of language: the first a syntactic device, the second a metrical device. The particular selection reflects a second intention of the chapter: for while the two phenomena to be discussed are ubiquitous, not only in the works of Sūr but in those of other *bhakti* poets as well, they appear nonetheless to have escaped previous critical attention. I think it a most unfortunate oversight, for the phenomena that concern us here provide some of the most convincing evidence of Sūr's fine sense of poetic structure.

"The syntactical forms used in poetry," argues Donald Davie, "may or may not be identical with those of prose; but . . . where they are identical, this identity of form masks an entirely different function."[2] Some forms, we might add, have been more successful than others in masking their poetic function. A case in point is that of the simile versus the relative clause. While the former has long been the acknowledged property of poets and rhetoricians, the latter has been ceded, with scarcely a shot fired in protest, to the grammarian. And yet both are "syntactical forms"; both serve to relate one thing to another; and both have functions that are "poetic" as well as functions that are "prosaic." "She's like a day in Spring" we immediately identify as a "simile"; "She's like my aunt in Pittsburgh" we perceive as "literal statement."[3] But

2. Donald Davie, *Articulate Energy* (London, 1955), p. 23. I am greatly indebted to Davie's discussion of the role of the relative clause in Sackville's "Henrie Duke of Buckingham."

3. The debate over what constitutes "figurative" language is, of course, perennial. In this regard, I am attracted to Stephen Ullmann's observation: "It is an essential feature of a metaphor that there must be a

so conditioned are we by traditional taxonomies that when we encounter a figurative application of the relative clause (and it is the thesis of this section that such encounters are frequent) we are unlikely even to notice the phenomenon, and less likely still to have a name for it.

Indian taxonomies are no more helpful than those of the West in giving us a name for the figure; and yet it would be difficult to read the *Sūrsāgar* without concluding that here, at least, the relative clause is performing a very specialized rhetorical function. A slightly closer examination reveals that this particular application of the relative clause appears in much the same contexts, and serves many of the same functions, as those of the simile. Consider, for example, two couplets from different *padas*, both of which we have already examined elsewhere:

1 Seeing the lion-claw pendant at his breast,
  the women wondered anew:
It was LIKE the young moon, slipped from the brow
  to the breast of Tripurāri.[4]

2 The arm WHICH saved Prahlāda
  and tore open Hiraṇyakaśipu's breast—
Yaśodā grabs THAT very same arm
  and says: "Hold still now, love!"[5]

---

certain distance between tenor and vehicle. Their similarity must be accompanied by a feeling of disparity; they must belong to different spheres of thought. If they are too close, they cannot produce the perspective of 'double vision' peculiar to metaphor" (*Style in the French Novel* [Cambridge, 1957], p. 214). Certainly the terms of Sūr's similes—as well as, we shall see, his relative clauses—"belong to different spheres of thought." Nowottny, commenting on Ullman, observes further that "This curious situation, where there has to be a similarity between two things sufficient to hold them together and a disparity between them sufficient to make their encounter exciting, raises considerable difficulties of terminology" (Winifred Nowottny, *The Language Poets Use* [New York, 1962], p. 53). I intend to stay clear of that terminological battlefield; I am content to endorse the Ullman/Nowottny view of what characterizes metaphoric, as opposed to routine, speech, and to note that it is a distinction particularly applicable to the present discussion.

4. *Sabhā* 788; Caturvedī p. 245.

5. *Sabhā* 746. For mythological references, see Glossary under Narasiṃha.

The simile *compares* Kṛṣṇa's pendant with Śiva's moon; the relative clause *equates* the arm of Kṛṣṇa, the eighth *avatāra*, with that of the fourth, Narasiṃha. But in both cases, and in scores of similar examples throughout the *Sūrsāgar*, a correspondence is established that proclaims, obliquely or directly, Kṛṣṇa's participation in an all-encompassing godhead.

Similes that suggest, and relative clauses that declare, that divine unity are probably the most conspicuous figures in Sūr's rhetorical arsenal; and while not every relative clause in the *Sūrsāgar* makes an explicit statement of Kṛṣṇa's dual nature, the overwhelming majority do precisely that—an extraordinary statistic when one considers the literally infinite number of possible (and prosaic) applications of the construction. Equally extraordinary is the almost formulaic regularity with which the contrasting clauses are ordered: relative clause, god; correlative clause, child:

| | |
|---|---|
| JĀKĪ *citavani kāla ḍarāi* / | HE WHOSE glances frighten Time itself / |
| TĀHI *mahari kara-lakūṭa dikhāi.* | HIM his mother threatens with a stick. (*Sabhā* 747) |
| JIHIṂ *ḍara bhramata pavana, ravi-sasi, jala,* / | HE, the fear of WHOM drives wind and water, sun and moon, / |
| SO *karai ṭahala lakuṭiyā sauṃ ḍari.* | HE moves at the threat of a little stick. (*Sabhā* 1010) |
| JO MŪRATI *jala-thala maiṃ vyāpaka, /nigama na khojata pāi,* / | WHICH FORM pervades earth and sea,/ yet is not to be found in the Vedas,/ |
| SO MŪRATI *taiṃ apanaiṃ āṅgana/ cuṭakī dai ju nacāi.* | THAT FORM you cause to dance at a snap of your fingers, here in your very own yard. (*Sabhā* 981) |
| JE *giri kamaṭha surāsura sarpahiṃ / dharata na* | HE WHO bore the Mountain and the Tortoise, the |

| | |
|---|---|
| *mana maiṃ naiṃku ḍare, /* | gods and the demons and the Snake, with never a moment's fear, |
| TE *bhuja-bhūṣana-bhāra parata, kara / gopini ke ādhāra dhare.* | HE falls from the weight of his bracelets, stands only with the Gopīs' helping hands. (*Sabhā* 759) |

As the examples illustrate, the semantic function of the relative clause construction is the same in Hindi as in English: it relates two propositions through a single, shared, coreferential term. The *form* of the construction is significantly different in the two languages, however, and there are at least two aspects of this difference that have poetic consequences. The first concerns the positioning of relative and "main" clauses; the second concerns the positioning of the relative pronoun.

The English relative clause, in normal usage, clings solidly to the phrase that it modifies—as in this example, to which we shall soon return:

> The force *that through the green fuse drives the flower*
> drives my green age. . . .[6]

In Hindi the two clauses have a far greater degree of independence; as the examples show, relative and correlative clauses in Hindi stand as complete and separate sentences, either of which may precede the other. For our purposes, the significance of this clausal separation is that it permits a congruence between the parts of a sentence and the parts of a poem. In each of the examples given, and in almost every instance throughout the Sūrsāgar, the clausal separation of child and god is reinforced by a prosodic separation as well. In two of the examples, relative and correlative clauses are divided by the midline caesura; in the other examples, each

6. Dylan Thomas, "The force that through the green fuse drives the flower," *The Collected Poems of Dylan Thomas* (New York, 1957), p. 10. The emphasis is mine.

clause constitutes one line of a couplet. The latter pattern is the more common, and is one that should be familiar by now. It is of course precisely that which we have already observed in the case of the simile: a comparison packaged in a couplet, and thus a ready-made unit for inclusion in a paratactic string. It is not surprising, then, to find *padas* consisting almost entirely of relative-correlative couplets, just as we found *padas* constructed around a string of simile-couplets:

1 Look, see the state of the Stateless One!
What a form he's taken for himself!
2 He whose home is the Three Worlds,
what a dump he's landed in!
3 Whose umbilicus bore Brahmā,
fulfilling all his yogic vows,
4 His umbilicus the Braj-girl seized
and sliced, and tied with twine!
5 The face which Śiva gazed upon in meditation,
making it the object of his veneration,
6 Is kissed by the woman Yaśodā,
embracing her nursing child!
7 Those ears which hear the cries of mankind,
and speed Him from Garuḍa's back to their relief—
8 Yaśodā leans near those very same ears
and coos and sings and whispers.
9 The nourisher of the cosmos, the lifestaff of all,
frets about a little butter.
10 With a million vast worlds in his every hair
he lies in a narrow cradle.
11 The arm that saved Prahlāda
and tore open Hiraṇyakaśipu's breast—
12 Yaśodā grabs that very same arm
and says: "Hold still now, love!"
13 He whose vision gods and sages sought in vain,
and Śambhu fixed ever in his mind,
14 *He*, O Sūr, is right here in Braj,
a playful cowherd in Gokul![7]

7. *Sabhā* 746; Caturvedī p. 217. For the Caturvedī reading, line 10 would translate as: "That Mountain-Lifter, heavier than Govardhana, lies in a cradle." Line 3 refers to the Vaiṣṇavite concept of Brahmā as born from a lotus in Viṣṇu-Kṛṣṇa's navel; lines 11 and 12 refer to the deeds of the fourth *avatāra* of Viṣṇu, Narasiṃha, the Man-lion. See Brahmā, Garuḍa, Narasiṃha in the Glossary.

Five of the poem's seven couplets follow a single pattern. The first line of each presents an *alaukika* proposition, the second a *laukika*. Yet in each case the two are spanned by an entity which, syntax commands, must be contained in both universes: an umbilicus; a face; a pair of ears; an arm. Paradoxically, it is this shared term, this grammatical spike bonding child to god, which makes the relative clause so natural a vehicle for extravagant contrast; like Donne's famous "soules," the lines of each such couplet are made to "endure not yet / A breach, but an expansion."[8]

But there is a second aspect of the Hindi relative clause that helps to explain the poet's singular infatuation with the construction; and this concerns the relative pronoun, that word which signals the intention of the clause. Whereas in English the "which" or "who" or "that" of the relative clause lies buried in its sentence, the Hindi counterpart, in the most common pattern, begins its clause; in fact both clauses, correlative as well as relative, are customarily headed by pronominal indicators of their function. In a poem like that above, in which line- and clause-units coincide, the result is a pronominal *epanaphora*, a pattern of repetition as conspicuous at the beginning of each line as is that of rhyme at the end. When, as here, rhyme and epanaphora work in concert, the result is a couplet bound fore-and-aft, a marvellously tight prosodic unit.

We have already seen this combination, of course, in the second *daśāvatāra* poem, where the relative pronouns combined with a single, sustained rhyme to bind the *line* as a unit:[9]

*Which* strength . . . . . . . (rhyme *A*),
*Which* strength . . . . . . . (rhyme *A*),
*Which* strength . . . . . . . (rhyme *A*),
*Which* strength . . . . . . . (rhyme *A*). . . .

8. John Donne, "A valediction: forbidding mourning," *The Major Metaphysical Poets of the Seventeenth Century*, ed. Edwin Honig and Oscar Williams (New York, 1969), p. 71.

9. See Chapter III.

But in the present example, with *couplet*-rhyme and *alternating* relative and correlative pronouns, it is the couplet rather than the line that becomes a unit of prosodic focus—as well as, of course, the rhetorical unit of contrast:

*Which* umbilicus . . . . . (rhyme A),
*That* umbilicus . . . . . . (rhyme A)!

*Which* face . . . . . . . . . . (rhyme B),
*That* face . . . . . . . . . . . . (rhyme B)!

*Which* ears . . . . . . . . . . (rhyme C),
*Those* ears . . . . . . . . . . . (rhyme C)!

As we have seen many times before, the rhetorical force of a pattern so regular becomes most apparent when the pattern is interrupted. In the earlier, *daśāvatāra* poem, deviation consisted of an increase in the tempo of repetition; here, the significant deviation occurs when, for the space of a couplet, the pronominal skeleton disappears altogether. The effect is a dramatic reduction in the distance between *laukika* and *alaukika*. The clausal pattern, it must be remembered, served to keep child and god syntactically separate even as they were metaphysically identified; in each couplet the child was the "base term" (the foreground) and the god the "figurative term" (the background). We do not realize how much we have come to rely on this separation until it disappears in lines 9 and 10, resulting in a moment of prosodic, syntactic, and metaphysical vertigo:

The nourisher of the cosmos, the lifestaff of all
  frets about a little butter.
With a million vast worlds in his every hair
  he lies in a narrow cradle.

Prosodically, we lose epanaphora; "rhythmically," which is not quite the same thing, we experience diminution: the unit of contrast shortens from couplet to line, the temporal distance between our perceiving the child and perceiving the god is cut in half. But most important, we lose the perspective given by that comforting relative clause, which showed us a god while pushing him firmly, syntactically into the background. Suddenly the barrier dissolves; god moves forward to join child in a most disturbing couplet.

There is a word or two yet to be said on this "anomalous" couplet; but what has already been said may be clarified somewhat by turning briefly to another, similar poem, in this case one from the English tradition. There is a second purpose to be served by this particular comparison. I suggested earlier that the relative clause has not received its due from the rhetorician; that its form often conceals its poetic function; and that while that form is less concealing in Hindi than in English, its rhetorical role in both languages is more pervasive than is commonly recognized. Consider, then, the poem that made Dylan Thomas famous:

*The force that* through the green fuse drives the flower
Drives my green age; *that* blasts the roots of trees
Is my destroyer.
And I am dumb to tell the crooked rose
My youth is bent by the *same* wintry fever.

*The force that* drives the water through the rocks
Drives my red blood; *that* dries the mouthing streams
Turns mine to wax.
And I am dumb to mouth unto my veins
How at the mountain spring the *same* mouth sucks.

*The hand that* whirls the water in the pool
Stirs the quicksand; *that* ropes the blowing wind
Hauls my shroud sail.
And I am dumb to tell the hanging man
How of my clay is made the hangman's lime.

The lips of time leech to the fountain head;
Love drips and gathers, but the fallen blood
Shall calm her sores.
And I am dumb to tell a weather's wind
How time has ticked a heaven round the stars.

And I am dumb to tell the lover's tomb
How at my sheet goes the *same* crooked worm.[10]

Considering the volume of critical comment engendered by

10. *Collected Poems*, p. 10. The emphasis is mine.

this poem, it is astounding that there has been, apparently, no discussion of the relative clause as its syntactic framework.[11] Yet for those schooled in the conventions of *Sūr's* poetry, the pronominal skeleton of Thomas's poem positively shouts from the page; and no less conspicuous is the moment of vertigo in the fourth stanza when, as in Sūr's fifth couplet, that comforting framework dissolves:

| | |
|---|---|
| Stanza 1,2,3: | The force THAT .................. |
| | ..................; THAT ........... |
| | ................. . |
| | .................................... |
| | ..............(same).............. |
| Stanza 4: | ....................................; |
| | .................................... |
| | ................. . |
| | .................................... |
| | .................................... |
| Coda: | .................................... |
| | ..............(same).............. |

11. Not even by those critics who do comment on syntactic repetition in the poem. William Tindall, for example, notes the epanaphora: "Our sense of regular process is aided, as in 'The Boys of Summer,' by verbal repetition. First lines, except for that of the coda, begin with 'The.' Fourth lines begin with 'And.' Last lines, except for that of the first stanza, begin with 'How' " (*A Reader's Guide to Dylan Thomas* [New York, 1962], p. 39). Tindall's myopic approach supports arguments made above concerning the importance of the fronting of relative pronouns in Hindi. Tindall recognizes the *prosodic* importance of the first-word position, but apparently looks no farther; he totally fails to see the relational component of syntactic repetition. William Moynihan makes the opposite error; he perceives recurring "meaning," but misses the all-important pronouns: "Thomas employs this device [syntactical repetition] in numerous ways throughout his poetry . . . 'The Force that through the Green Fuse' being the best example. In each of the poem's four stanzas, the first line makes a declarative statement, the second develops the statement in terms of the narrator, the third concludes the statement, the fourth contains the refrain "And I am dumb to . . . ," and the fifth line deals with what the poet is dumb to tell. This repetitive syntax conditions the mind in a more effective way than the reader realizes . . ." (*The Craft and Art of Dylan Thomas* [Ithaca, N.Y., 1966], p. 149). That it does; far more effective, in fact, than Moynihan realizes.

But the similarities go beyond syntax. Elder Olson echoes the standard, and obvious, interpretation when he claims that the Thomas poem serves to "mediate the relation between man and his universe as one of microcosm and macrocosm."[12] The terms will serve Sūr's poem nearly as well as *laukika* and *alaukika*, and so we might render the paradigm for each poem as follows:

| | |
|---|---|
| SŪR:<br>(lines 3–8, 11–14) | RELATIVE macrocosm,<br>CORRELATIVE microcosm. |
| THOMAS:<br>(stanzas 1–3) | RELATIVE macrocosm<br>CORRELATIVE microcosm; RELATIVE macrocosm<br>CORRELATIVE microcosm. |
| | macrocosm<br>SAME AS microcosm. |

In the Thomas poem as in Sūr's, the pronominal frame is both a link and a barrier between microcosm and macrocosm; when the frame disappears, so does much of the sense. Significantly, that fourth stanza has inspired a dazzling variety of exegetical gymnastics by the critics.[13] I shall join the fray by suggesting that it is the *function* of the stanza to be obscure. It makes us work; it makes us strain to see through the poet's eyes, and it does so precisely by knocking from under us the props of ordered syntactic figuration. Before, the unity of man and nature was proclaimed within the framework of a repeated relative clause; now, that unity is illustrated in lines whose syntax permits no clausal separation of the two. The stanza begins "The lips . . . ," and we automatically prepare for "The lips *that* . . ."—but find instead,

12. Elder Olson, *The Poetry of Dylan Thomas* (Chicago, 1954), p. 46.

13. "(L)ove is blood, blood collected in a pool, as in a black eye, the pressure of which is eased by the suction of Time. This blood is, of course, at the 'fountain head,' which must be the heart" (Clark Emery, *The World of Dylan Thomas* [Miami, 1968], p. 271). " 'Fallen blood' is that of birth and death. When the latter, it will calm mother's sores" (William Tindall, *A Reader's Guide to Dylan Thomas*, p. 41). "Time is a leech, which sucks at the fountain head of Love, making a sore wound. But the loss of blood, in keeping with archaic lore, is beneficial" (Ralph Maud, *Entrances to Dylan Thomas' Poetry* [Pittsburgh, 1963], p. 70).

"The lips of time." Human and cosmic have merged syntactically into one, no longer separable by the "turn on a pronoun."

Finally, closural strategies in both poems exploit the *return* to order. In fact, viewing the fourth stanza of the Thomas poem as the loosening of a figured structure serves to explain "why" the poem must have its final truncated stanza: it is these two lines that return us to our stable world, presenting once again an equation with its terms neatly separated, and explicitly labelled as "same." Similarly, lines 11 and 12 of the Sūr poem again return child and god to alternate lines; pronouns return to frame the separation while guaranteeing the identity. The relief we feel at the resolution of a prosodic deviation is matched by the far greater relief of a god who stays in his place:

> The arm that saved Prahlāda
> and tore open Hiraṇyakaśipu's breast—
> Yaśodā grabs that very same arm
> and says: "Hold still now, love!"

## 2. *The union of sound and sense*

> *Śabdārthau sahitau kāvyam*
> —Bhāmaha[14]

When we think of prosody, we tend to think first in terms of rules and types; that is, we think in terms of a system that is largely prescriptive and taxonomic. Yet in most poetries, those aspects of prosody that are left to the poet's discretion are as numerous as those that are regulated by convention; and it is often in the areas least governed by the rules that the choices made by a poet are most revealing of his skill. A competent versifier complies with the structure imposed by convention. A poet imposes upon that convention a structure of his own.

This is particularly so in the case of a poet like Sūrdās, whose genre, the *pada*, is governed by very few and simple rules indeed. The latter claim may at first seem inconsistent

14. Bhāmaha, *Kāvyālaṅkāra*, 1:16.

with the existence of a massive body of literature on the subject of Hindi prosody. Kellogg does not exaggerate when he suggests that "In no modern language, probably, has prosody been so elaborately developed as in Hindi";[15] and Gaurīśaṅkar Miśra, in his *Sūra-sāhitya kā chandaḥ-śāstrīya adhyayana,* devotes 640 pages to a classification of the seventy-odd meters employed by Sūr alone.[16] But the apparent complexity of the system attests more to the subtlety of the taxonomists than to any real complexity in individual meters: of those employed in the *Sūrsāgar,* all but a handful are governed by a few quite simple rules.

As we have noted, the *pada* customarily contains an even number of lines—most often six to ten, but occasionally as few as four or as many as a hundred—of which all lines but the first, the *ṭeka,* are of equal length. Two common rhyme-schemes are employed: couplet-rhyme, and a single rhyme sustained throughout the *pada.* The metrical basis is quantitative; the unit of quantity is the *mātrā* (mora), with a short syllable counting as one *mātrā* and a long syllable as two. The rules for syllable-length are somewhat involved, but in general a long syllable is one that either contains a long vowel, or ends in a consonant.

The quantitative prosody of Hindi is clearly similar to that of Greek and Latin, but with one crucial difference: in the meters of the *pada,* the *sequence* of long and short syllables is unregulated. There are, in fact, only three defining variables for the several meters: (1) the length of a line—that is, the total number of *mātrā* in each line; (2) the position of a caesura (*yati*), usually occurring at or near the midpoint of the line; (3) the pattern of long and short syllables occupying the final three or four *mātrā* of each line. For example, Miśra defines the *sāra* (by far the most common *pada* meter) as consisting of a line of twenty-eight *mātrā,* divided by a caesura into two segments (here termed "feet") of sixteen

15. S.H. Kellogg, *A Grammar of the Hindi Language,* 3rd edition (London, 1938), p. 546.

16. Gaurīśaṅkar Miśra, *Sūra-sāhitya kā chandaḥ-śāstrīya adhyayana* (Allahabad, 1969).

and twelve, and usually ending in two long syllables.[17] Thus the last two lines of *Sabhā* 782, the "Boar" poem, would be scanned as follows, with (/) indicating midline caesura and (//) indicating line-end:

∪ ∪ ∪ – ∪ ∪ ∪ – ∪ – ∪ ∪ ∪
5. *na- ga- na gā- ta mu- su- kā- ta tā- ta ḍhi-ga/*
– ∪ ∪ ∪ ∪ ∪ ∪ – –
*nṛt-ya ka- ra- ta ga- hi co-ṭī//*
– ∪ ∪ ∪ ∪ – ∪ – ∪ – ∪ ∪
6. *sū- ra- ja pra-bhu kī la- hai ju jū- ṭha-ni/*
– ∪ ∪ ∪ ∪ ∪ ∪ – –
*lā- ra- ni la- li- ta la- po- ṭī//*

The count would then be:

*Line 5, first foot*: 3 longs equals 6 *mātrā*, plus 10 shorts equals *16 mātrā/*
*second foot*: 3 longs equals 6 *mātrā*, plus 6 shorts equals *12 mātrā//*
*Line 6, first foot*: 4 longs equals 8 *mātrā*, plus 8 shorts equals *16 mātrā/*
*second foot*: 3 longs equals 6 *mātrā*, plus 6 shorts equals *12 mātrā//*

The two lines rhyme (as, in this case, do all lines in the *pada*) in *-oṭī*, an ending that satisfies the *sāra* requirement for two long syllables. The remaining four lines of the *pada* are equally consistent with the rules of *sāra-chanda*; and the traditional prosodist, having classified the meter and pronounced the verse free of defects, would, in all probability, leave the matter there. At most, he might go on to comment upon the internal rhyme in line 5 (*gāta musukāta tāta*), or the alliteration in line 6 (*lārani lalita lapoṭī*).

He would be most unlikely, however, to comment upon the phenomenon of interest here: that the second feet of lines 5 and 6 are metrically parallel, each following the pattern: (– ∪ ∪ ∪ ∪ ∪ ∪ – –). Such parallelism is not covered by the rules; it is not a constant feature of any of the meters; indeed, there is no ready term available to describe the phenomenon. It is not, in short, a matter of concern for the taxonomist.

17. Miśra also includes under the *sāra* heading those lines ending (∪ ∪) or (– ∪).

Its structural significance, however, is considerable. In this instance the effect is to strengthen closure, an effect that becomes apparent when we examine the parallel feet in the metrical context of the poem as a whole: in a poem (and a tradition) for which metrical *irregularity* is the norm, the final and unexpected regularity is most conspicuous:

| | *First foot* | *Second foot* |
|---|---|---|
| *Line 1* (*ṭeka*) | ∪∪∪∪–∪∪–∪∪––/[18] | |
| Line 2 | ∪∪–∪∪∪∪–∪–∪∪∪/ | ∪–∪–∪∪––// |
| *Line 3* | ––∪∪∪∪–∪∪–∪∪ | /∪∪–∪∪–––// |
| *Line 4* | ∪∪∪–∪–∪∪∪∪∪∪–/ | ∪–∪∪∪–––// |
| *Line 5* | ∪∪∪–∪∪∪–∪–∪∪∪/ | –∪∪∪∪∪∪––// |
| *Line 6* | –∪∪∪∪–∪–∪–∪∪ | /–∪∪∪∪∪∪––// |

While the pattern in a sense "begins" in line 5, we do not of course *perceive* any regularity until line 6; that is, nothing about the pattern of line 5 leads us to anticipate its repetition in line 6. It is only the final foot of the final line that establishes the sense of an unusual degree of order.

Such metrically parallel sets of feet are ubiquitous, not only in the works of Sūr, but in those of Tulsī and Kabīr as well; and while a great deal more work on the subject is necessary—including the laborious scansion of thousands of lines of verse—it would not be surprising to find that metrical parallelism played a major role in all North Indian *bhakti* verse. That the phenomenon has heretofore received little or no critical attention may in part be explained by the prosodic unit involved: parallels rarely involve the line as a unit, but rather link either the segments preceding, or (more commonly) the segments following, the caesura; and while "line" and "caesura" are recognized prosodic units, the two segments on either side of the caesura (here referred to as "feet") are not standard units of analysis in Hindi poetics.

18. The *ṭeka* is not a full line; there seem to be no clear rules regarding its prosody.

The predominance of specifically second-foot parallelism is hardly surprising; like rhyme, such parallelism serves to tighten the *end* of a line-unit, and thus serves to strengthen line-level closure. There is classical precedent as well: the *anuṣṭubh*, that most common of Sanskrit meters, also tightens at the end of each prosodic unit (in this case the *pāda*, or quarter): whereas the first four sylllables in *anuṣṭubh* are a matter of free choice for the poet, three of the last four are regulated. In the quarters of a *śloka*, as in the lines of a verse by Sūr, opening halves are metrically "loose," closing halves metrically "tight."

Closure is only one of several rhetorical functions served by metrical parallelism, but it is certainly the simplest to illustrate and explain. Of the poems discussed in this and preceding chapters, four exhibit second-foot parallels in the final two lines. In addition to the "Boar" poem described above, they are the "two mothers," "See the state," and "two moons." The final two lines of each are scanned below; note the added reinforcement of alliteration in "see the state" as well as in "Boar":

(a) "See the state" (meter: *sāra*, 16–12), lines 13, 14:
jā- kau dhyā-na na pā- yau su- ra mu- ni/
*saṃ-bhu sa- mā- dhi na ṭā- rī//*
so- ī sū- ra pra-ga- ṭa yā bra-ja maiṃ/
*go- ku- la go- pa bi- hā- rī//*

(b) "two mothers" (meter: *upamāna*, 13–10), lines 7,8:
nī- la pī- ta pa- ṭa o- ṛha-nī/
*de- kha-ta ji- ya bhā-vai//*
bā- la bi- no- da a- nan-da sauṃ/
*sū- ra- ja ja- na gā- vai//*

(c) "two moons" (meter: *tāṭaṅka*, 16–14), lines 5,6:
sū- ra syā-ma da- dhi bhā-ja- na bhī-ta- ra/
*ni- ra- kha-ta mu- kha mu- kha taiṃ na ṭa- re//*

bĭ- bĭ cān-dră-mā mă- naū mă- thĭ kā- ṛhē/
*bĭ- hẵ- să- nĭ mă- nă- hŭ̃ pră-kā- să kă- rē//*

Of those parallel sets that occur in *non*-final positions, a great many signal thematically crucial junctures. Consider, for example, the metrical scheme of *Sabhā* 744, "Yaśodā delights"; the relevant pattern is underlined in lines 4,5, and 8:

(Meter: *sāra*, 16–12)

| | | |
|---|---|---|
| Line 1: | ∪∪∪–∪∪∪∪∪∪∪––// | |
| Line 2: | ∪∪∪∪∪∪∪∪∪∪––∪∪ | /∪∪––∪∪––// |
| Line 3: | –∪∪–∪∪–∪∪∪∪∪∪ | /∪∪∪∪––––// |
| Line 4: | ∪∪∪∪∪∪∪∪∪∪∪∪–∪∪ | /∪∪∪∪–∪∪––// |
| Line 5: | –∪∪–∪∪∪∪∪∪–∪∪ | /∪∪∪∪–∪∪––// |
| Line 6: | ––∪––∪––– | /–––∪∪––// |
| Line 7: | ∪∪∪∪∪∪∪∪–∪–∪– | /∪∪∪∪∪∪∪∪––// |
| Line 8: | –∪–∪∪∪–∪–∪∪∪ | /∪∪∪∪–∪∪––// |

The first appearance of metrical patterning in the poem serves to link lines 4 and 5. As we saw in Chapter I, it is these lines that intrude Kṛṣṇa *parabrahma* into an otherwise tranquil and domestic scene, an intrusion that some Hindi critics appear to have found unwarranted:[19]

4 He stumbles and falls, but can't quite cross,
*and the gods are made to wonder;*
5 For he makes in a second a million worlds,
*and destroys in a second a million more.*

But the "focusing" function of the pattern in lines 4 and 5 is further extended by a third occurrence of the same pattern, in the final line. The latter repetition is doubly interesting. First, the final line returns to more than a metrical pattern; it returns to the *alaukika* Kṛṣṇa of lines 4 and 5 as well, and in fact parallels line 4 in phrasing as well as meter:

Line 4, second foot: *sŭră mŭnĭ sōcă kărāvāi*
"(It) causes gods and sages to think"

19. See Chapter I.

Line 8, second foot: *nără mŭnĭ būddhĭ bhŭlāvai̅*
"(It) makes men and sages forget their minds (i.e. lose their senses)"

But aside from the linking function served in this poem by a last-line return to an earlier pattern, the poem illustrates a phenomenon of wider, possibly even universal, significance: the closural effect of what Barbara Smith calls "return to the norm after a deviation." It is a strategy learned by every English-speaker as a child, in the rhyme- and meter-scheme of every limerick:

There was a young lady from Niger
Who smiled as she rode on a tiger
They returned from the ride
With the lady inside
And the smile on the face of the tiger.

In the last line of the limerick, as in the last line of the Sūr poem, the return of an interrupted pattern brings an almost physical sense of satisfaction, of renewed order and stability, and hence of closure. It is a strategy illustrated more clearly still in the metrical scheme of another *pada*, *Sabhā* 972 (translated below, Part Two):

| | | | |
|---|---|---|---|
| Line 1: | ∪ – – – ∪ ∪ – – ∪ ∪ – / | | |
| Line 2: | – – ∪ ∪ – – ∪ ∪ – – | / ∪ ∪ ∪ ∪ – ∪ ∪ ∪ ∪ – // | (A) |
| Line 3: | ∪ ∪ ∪ ∪ ∪ ∪ – – ∪ – ∪ – | / ∪ ∪ ∪ ∪ – ∪ ∪ ∪ ∪ – // | (A) |
| Line 4: | – ∪ ∪ ∪ ∪ ∪ ∪ – ∪ – ∪ – | / – ∪ ∪ – ∪ ∪ ∪ ∪ – // | (B) |
| Line 5: | – ∪ ∪ – ∪ ∪ – ∪ ∪ – – | / – ∪ ∪ – ∪ ∪ ∪ ∪ – // | (B) |
| Line 6: | – ∪ – ∪ – ∪ ∪ ∪ ∪ ∪ ∪ ∪ ∪ | / ∪ ∪ ∪ ∪ – ∪ ∪ ∪ ∪ – // | (A) |

Here we are faced with not merely one, but two patterns of second-foot regularity (labelled *A* and *B*). If we ignore for the moment the always-anomalous *ṭeka*, every remaining line of the poem participates in one or the other of the two patterns, and the overall metrical strategy of the five lines (2 through 6) is precisely that of the limerick: A,A,B,B,A.

A great many poems exhibit prosodic patterns and strategies far more extensive, and complex, than those shown above.[20] Consider again, for example, the "two mothers" poem (*Sabhā* 734). As we have just seen, the final two lines participate in a closural parallelism, but in fact, this is only one of three separate patterns in the eight-line poem, including a most unusual *first*-foot pattern of three lines' duration:

| | | | | |
|---|---|---|---|---|
| | 1 | ∪∪∪∪–∪∪–∪– | /–∪∪∪∪––// | (A) |
| | 2 | –∪–∪––∪– | /∪∪–∪∪––// | (B) |
| (C) | 3 | ∪∪∪∪∪∪∪∪–∪–/ | ∪∪∪∪––∪∪// | |
| (C) | 4 | ∪∪∪∪∪∪∪∪–∪–/ | –∪∪∪∪–∪∪// | |
| (C) | 5 | ∪∪∪∪∪∪∪∪–∪–/ | ∪∪–∪∪––// | (B) |
| | 6 | ∪∪––∪∪–∪– | /∪∪–∪∪––// | (B) |
| | 7 | –∪–∪∪∪–∪– | /–∪∪∪∪––// | (A) |
| | 8 | –∪∪–∪∪–∪– | /–∪∪∪∪––// | (A) |

But if interpretation of such complex patterns is more interesting, it is also more hazardous, and infinitely more cumbersome, than interpretation of simple "focus" or "closure" patterns. I have presented elsewhere[21] an analysis of the three interlocking patterns in "two mothers," as well as an analysis of a still more intriguing poem—*Sabhā* 704, the "horoscope" poem (translated in Part Two). The latter is perhaps the best example of the pitfalls of such analysis. It is a comparatively long poem (fourteen lines) and the subject matter itself is somewhat dry for any but the astrologically inclined. In the original, however, this thematic flatness is more than offset by a series of interlocking prosodic games, of contracts kept, half-kept, and violated in clever ways. Patterns of meter join with those of alliteration; the poem entertains us with a display of prosodic fireworks, brass bands, and acrobatics, while the astrologer drones his way toward a startling (and prosodically buttressed) conclusion. It is, in short, a fascinating study for the prosodist; unfortunately, however, there appears to be no way even to illustrate, much less to explain,

20. There are also, it should be noted, a great many in which no patterns exist; the phenomenon is widespread, but by no means universal.

21. "Poems to the Child-God," Ph.D. dissertation (University of California, Berkeley, 1974), pp. 111–133.

so complex a pattern without making unreasonable demands on the reader's patience. In the case of the "horoscope" poem, an analysis of metrical patterns in a single eight-line segment required fifteen pages; even the comparatively simple "two mothers" involved six pages of prosodic commentary.

The problem is that we simply have no ready vocabulary, no descriptive short cuts, for analysis of this sort; with the tools currently available, a prosodic analysis of any sophistication must be a slow, blow-by-blow affair. And yet the patterns are there, and are of considerable structural importance; we can hardly ignore them. What is needed is an analytical framework that treats prosodic phenomena in terms of function, rather than merely of taxonomy. The first step in developing such a framework must, I fear, be the grueling process of gathering prosodic data on a very large corpus of poems, not only poems by Sūr but ideally poems by all major poets in the *pada* tradition. In addition to exploring the functions of metrical parallelism, we might also inquire into the validity of the concept "metrical norm" for Indian verse. For the classical prosodist, there were rules (to be followed with none but the rarest of exceptions) or there were no rules; the concept of a statistical norm (akin to the iambic in English verse), against which variation would be both permissible and perceptible, appears never to have become a part of the theory (as opposed to the practise) of Indian verse. And yet, as I have argued elsewhere,[22] the poetry itself clearly demonstrates the existence of such a norm. (In the case of the *sāra* meter, for example, it may be established with statistical certainty that the verse of Sūr and Tulsī operates on the basis of a four-*mātrā* foot and an anapestic norm and that the poets, consciously or not, exploited this norm by, among other things, returning to it with great regularity in the last variable foot of most lines.[23])

22. "The Persistent Anapest: Norm and Deviation in Medieval Hindi Prosody." Unpublished paper.

23. I have shown in the paper mentioned in note 22 that the "feet" of *sāra* are best represented as (in terms of *mātrā*): (2)(4)(4)(4)(2)/(2)(4)(4)(2)//. By the last unregulated foot, then, I mean the last four-*mātrā* foot.

But the study must not stop with metrics: we must also have a great deal more information than is at present available on the relationship between *chanda* and *tāla*—between, that is, meter as dictated by the syllables of the poem and rhythm as interpreted by an individual style of performance. In the realm of prosody, perhaps more than anywhere else, the student of literature and the musicologist must eventually join forces. In short, what is needed is nothing less than a major reappraisal of medieval North Indian metrics, one that goes beyond classification to an examination of the *rhetoric* of prosody. While the classical tradition may not provide us with such a tool, it most certainly encourages us in the search. Indian poetics has long regarded poetry as the union of sound and sense; one day we must take that definition seriously, and begin to examine, with all the rigor of the *ālaṃkārika*, just how it is that Sūr and his fellow poets effect that union.

## Chapter V

# MISERS OF SOUND AND SYLLABLE: SUMMING UP

> Let us inspect the Lyre, and weigh the stress
> Of every chord, and see what may be gain'd
> By ear industrious, and attention meet;
> Misers of sound and syllable. . . .
>
> —Keats[1]

"Interpretation," laments Susan Sontag, "amounts to the philistine refusal to leave the work of art alone."[2] It is a perennial accusation: that the critic, like Śvetaketu with his fig, dismantles first the fruit to find the seed; and then the seed, to find—nothing. There are a few such philistines who claim to see, as Śvetaketu's father saw, within that final "nothing" the subtle essence of it All; but all too often, goes the argument, they have simply rendered the fig inedible.

Yet even as Sontag condemns the interpreter, she pardons the formalist. "What would criticism look like," she asks, "that would serve the work of art, not usurp its place?" Her answer:

> What is needed, first, is more attention to form in art. If excessive stress on *content* provokes the arrogance of interpretation, more extended and more thorough descriptions of *form* would silence. What is needed is a vocabulary—a descriptive, rather than prescriptive, vocabulary—for forms.[3]

Finally, in a footnote, she defines the area of greatest need:

> One of the difficulties is that our idea of form is spatial (the Greek metaphors for form are all derived from notions of space). This is why we have a more ready

1. John Keats, sonnet XVII, *Poetical Works*, H.W. Garrod, ed. (London, 1956), p. 371.
2. Susan Sontag, *Against Interpretation*; quoted in *Literary Criticism: An Introductory Reader*, ed. Lionel Trilling (New York, 1970), p. 614.
3. Sontag, p. 617.

vocabulary of forms for the spatial than for the temporal arts.[4]

Form—temporal, sequential form—has been our concern for the past four chapters. No work of criticism can be wholly free of the "arrogance of interpretation," but at least a conscious effort has been made here to avoid all reference to "symbols," or to "the deeper/underlying/inner meaning of the poem." The meanings of Sūr's poems have been clear to many people for four centuries. What the critic has to offer is, at best, a clearer vision of *how* the poem succeeds in meaning what it means; of how the words of common speech can be so uncommonly arranged.

That there *is* uncommon care apparent in the ordering of Sūr's words has been a major, if largely implicit, thesis of this book. It is by no means a radical thesis, but it is certainly at odds with the prevalent image, in the West at least, of *bhakti* poetry as a spontaneous outpouring of devotional fervor, a rebellion against the fetters of traditional form no less than the fetters of traditional thought. Charlotte Vaudeville characterizes Sūr's verse in particular as "chansons tombées des lèvres d'un improvisateur de génie."[5] Speaking more generally of the contrast between regional *bhakti* literature and that of Sanskrit, van Buitenen notes: "Though there is in this poetry and song much that is Sanskritic in imagery and expression, its basic character is more vital than polished, more vivid than refined";[6] and Dimock, making what is essentially the same comparison, finds poetry in the regional languages to be "more fervid, more direct, less sophisticated."[7] The resulting portrait is certainly appealing, and is not in any real sense inaccurate; yet I think we must be careful not to allow the mystique of spontaneity to conceal what may be merely another form of sophistication.

4. Sontag, p. 617n.
5. Charlotte Vaudeville, trans. and ed., *Pastorales par Soûr-Dâs* (Paris, 1971), p. 46.
6. J.A.B. van Buitenen, in *The Literatures of India: An Introduction*, ed. Edward C. Dimock et al. (Chicago, 1974), p. 21.
7. Edward C. Dimock, *The Literatures of India*, pp. 3–4.

In particular, we must be careful not to accept uncritically the *bhakti* poets' self-image, a point that has been made most cogently by A.K. Ramanujan in his discussion of Basavaṇṇa, a Vīraśaiva poet who proclaimed:

> I don't know anything like timebeats and metre
> nor the arithmetic of strings and drums;
>
> I don't know the count of iamb and dactyl.
> My lord of the meeting rivers,
> as nothing will hurt you
> I'll sing as I love.[8]

"But then," Ramanujan cautions, "'spontaneity' has its own rhetorical structure; no free verse is truly free."[9] However pleasing the romantic vision of a song wholly spontaneous, the illusion of spontaneity is seldom achieved by any but the meticulous craftsman.

Sūr's case is no different. The poet suppresses Lakṣmaṇa's name until a last, crucial line; he leads an unsuspecting audience to the brink of demonic assault, then leaves them to fend for themselves; a dry horoscope becomes a prosodic kaleidoscope, coming to rest precisely at the moment of the one significant prophecy; the "natural" progressions of *nakhaśikha* and *daśāvatāra* frame themselves neatly in final delicate reversals; rhetorical figures tease us with misleading precision through all but the last couplet of a poem. While a standard by which to measure "degree of structure" has yet to be devised, clearly Sūr's poetry *is* unitary in structure; it *does* make contracts, its conclusions *are* implicit in its premises.

To a limited extent, of course, these conclusions are implicit in the shape of the mythos itself: the fact of an oft-told tale at once constrains and enables Sūr's verse. His "omniscient audience" approaches any retelling of the Kṛṣṇa tale with the expectation of a specific set of events in a specific order; the poet must confine narrative innovation to the interpolation of detail. The "bedtime-story," for example,

8. A.K. Ramanujan, trans., *Speaking of Śiva* (Baltimore, 1973), p. 37.

9. Ramanujan, p. 38.

may achieve so great an effect within so few lines only because it moves in the small open spaces between the bars of convention. Had we not known all the characters of both *mythoi,* and the web of real and fictive, marital and metaphysical relationships that bind them, the poem would have been impossible—that is, we would not have understood it. Had the poet tampered in any major way with the story that we knew, the poem would, again, have been impossible—that is, we would have rejected it. Kṛṣṇa's utterance of the suppressed name surprises, but it does not shock our sensibilities; it is appropriate; we applaud the poet for making us "discover" that which we already know.

At the level of narrative structure, then, the characteristic shape of Sūr's poems of epiphany is a progression from generalized description of a stage in the mythos (a child's bedtime story; a ball-game on a riverbank), to the revelation of a well-known episode in the mythos (the abduction of Sītā; the defeat of Kāliya). When we move from the level of narrative to that of rhetorical figures, the poet's stamp appears as a preference for metonymy over metaphor: a preference, that is, for the relationship of part and whole, rather than the relationship of like and like. At times this metonymic linkage is explicit: a child's umbilicus, cut and bound in rough twine by a village midwife's hand, becomes the Navel, the lotus-seat of Brahmā on the world's first day. More often metonymy comes garbed as metaphor: simile dissolves to synecdoche, "seems" gives way to "is." The Gopīs hover a half-step short of truth when they observe that Kṛṣṇa "resembles" Śiva. The gods "mistake" Kṛṣṇa's idle twirling of a butter-churn for a re-enactment of the primal Churning. Kṛṣṇa and Balarāma, spawned from two hairs of a single god, are "like" the *soma*-drunken Aświns when they stagger on toddler's legs. When Kṛṣṇa, eighth *avatāra* of Viṣṇu, balances a butterball on his teeth, it is "as if" the earth yet trembled atop the tusks of the Boar—who was, of course, *avatāra* number three. At every instant the syntax-ordered world of Sūr's verse threatens to collapse into a unity beyond the taxonomies of speech.

The poems' prosodic structure also belies the illusion of spontaneity. Sūr emerges from our study as a careful wordsmith, carving fine verse from the soft stone of a most unpromising verse-form. The *pada*'s conventions are few; its form provides little in the way of audience expectation for the poet to exploit, by fulfillment or violation. Given a form so loose, the poet must tighten it from within; he must manufacture his own "rhetoric of spontaneity," *and must teach its conventions to the audience as the poem proceeds.* Other poets may use alliteration merely as ornament; Sūr uses his to establish patterns of expectation, and thus sets us up for the rhetorical force of an expectation fulfilled or frustrated—the comfort of a clock-chime, or the panic of a missed heartbeat. Again, convention does not recognize a prosodic foot; so Sūr must invent one, superimposing on the lines of his poem a repeated pattern of long and short syllables, the pattern continuing just long enough to make its interruption perceptible. Other poets may use syntactic parallelism as a principle of paratactic generation; Sūr knows both the value of parataxis, and its limits: he interrupts a pattern bluntly, to add focus to a line; or subtly, to presage closure or effect a transition.

To be sure, these efforts are not always successful: the simplicity of the *pada* form invites casual versifying, and it must be admitted that the *Sūrsāgar* contains, in its five thousand *padas*, a great many examples of sheer doggerel. But if we judge a poet by the quality of his successes, rather than by the quantity of his failures, then Sūr's verse must strike us with the structural tightness he was able to impose upon the *genre.* It is tempting to suggest that Sūr, working within a form too loose, arrived at a conclusion not far from that of Keats, who found his chosen form too tight:

> . . . Misers of sound and syllable, no less
> Than Midas of his coinage, let us be
> Jealous of dead leaves in the bay wreath crown;
> So, if we may not let the Muse be free,
> She will be bound with garlands of her own.[10]

10. Keats, sonnet XVII.

We move now from close analysis of Sūr's craft, to a more leisurely appreciation of his art. Part Two of this book presents a sampling of poems from the *Sūrsāgar*, unencumbered by critical comment, accompanied only by the briefest of explanatory notes. Before I relinquish the reader entirely to the poet and his verse, I should like to exercise the critic's prerogative one last time, and urge that the reader keep in mind, while approaching each new poem, three principles central to all that has been said in the preceding chapters.

The first principle is that of the "omniscient audience." Each poem should be approached not as a new tale, but as an old tale retold. The poetry of the *Sūrsāgar* was never intended for an audience unfamiliar with the mythos; it will not work for such an audience. If the poetry is to reach the Western reader, that reader must keep in mind the broad outlines of the tale. (Those outlines are presented, briefly, in the Introduction; further details are included in the short introductions preceding each section of the poems.)

The second principle is that of sequential perception. Here, the cautionary note is simple: read slowly. The educated reader consumes the printed page at a rate so rapid as to lose much of the sense of the sequence of linguistic events. These poems were meant not to be read, but to be sung; and while the translations will not, alas, permit that mode of performance, they should at least be read at a pace approximating that of an oral rendering. There should be time for each line to make its impress on the mind, and to shape our expectation of what is to come, before we move to the next.

The third point to be kept in mind is that the intention of this poetry is devotional; it was intended to generate in the audience an emotion (or, better, a complex of emotions) toward a god whom poet and intended audience fervently believed to be the source and substance of all that is. This intention must often be kept consciously in mind, because it is not always apparent in the poems themselves; and the latter observation brings us back, full circle, to the central thesis of this book, and to the principle by which the poems so far discussed have been selected.

The focus of this study has been the "epiphanies." Not all of Sūr's poems fit this category, a fact that will become more apparent in Part Two, in which I have attempted to present a balanced cross-section of Sūr's work. Indeed, the other sort of poem—that which shows on its surface little in the way of devotional intention—is the sort that has become most closely associated, in the minds of many, with the name Sūrdās. That same conventional wisdom which stresses the quality of "spontaneity" in *bhakti* poetry in general, tends to stress for Sūr's verse in particular a quality we might best term "softness." In the writings of those sympathetic to the poet, the quality often emerges as "tender" or "pastoral": witness, for example, the title of Vaudeville's volume of translations, "*Pastorales* par Soûr-Dâs," or van Buitenen's characterization of Sūr as "best known for his tender poems about Kṛṣṇa the child."[11] Sūr's detractors employ terms opposite in valence, but contributing to much the same image. We have already seen Dwivedi's slighting reference to Sūr's "little world of sweet dreams";[12] a more thoughtful case for the opposition is made by Pundit Rāmcandra Śukla, whose brilliant and acerbic advocacy of Tulsī appears elsewhere in this study. Śukla finds that the softness of Sūr's work serves to weaken its devotional impact:

> *Śakti, śīla,* and *saundarya* (roughly, "power, propriety, and beauty"): of these three attributes of God, Sūr has treated only *saundarya,* that which evokes love. In Hindi literature, it is Goswāmī Tulsīdās who has treated the other two attributes as well, thereby doing full honors to the popular form of God.[13]

To a certain extent Śukla's comparison is justified, and with it, the conventional wisdom. If we confine ourselves to the context of the printed page, much of Sūr's poetry does indeed seem dominated by a "pastoral simplicity," sometimes exquisite, sometimes merely cloying. Divorced

11. J.A.B. van Buitenen in *The Literatures of India,* p. 21.
12. See Chapter I.
13. Rāmcandra Śukla, *Sūradāsa* (Benares, 1948), p. 156.

from a ritual context of performance—a temple, an image of the deity with priests in attendance, and an audience prepared to worship—the song of *vātsalya* is often simply sweet.

Here, then, is at least part of the importance of the several hundred poems from the *Sūrsāgar* that I have dubbed the "epiphanies": they have the strength to outlive any one context of performance, to convey a sense of power even when divested of all ritual trappings. The epiphanies carry their temple with them; god shares the stage with child, awe with tenderness, *śakti* with *saundarya*. As for *śīla*—propriety, ethics, sermonizing—it has no place in these verses; their purpose is not to instruct, not to make a Donne-like assault through the door of reason, but simply to be experienced. Like the verse below, in which "tininess" expands suddenly into a divine umbrella, Sūr's epiphanies are intended not to tell us the way to Sūr's god, but to take us there:

> With your tiny little face, and your tiny arms and legs,
>   with a tiny bit of butter on your tiny little hand;
> You talk a tiny bit, and you fret a tiny bit,
>   and you're a tiny bit delighted at the tiniest little
>     thing.
> Your tiny little cheeks and your tiny little teeth
>   form a tiny little smile that
>     captivates us all.
> Just a tiny, oh a tiny little closer,
>   Lord, let Sūr approach,
> And with a tiny bit of grace, grant me
>   a tiny bit of shelter.[14]

14. *Sabhā* 768.

PART TWO

# *Poems to the Child-God*

# A WORD ON THE POEMS

The poems of the *Sūrsāgar* tell a story; the sequence of events in that story provides one obvious principle by which to arrange the poems. This is by no means the only order employed. Over the past four centuries, a variety of editors and compilers have arranged the verses to suit a variety of purposes. There are collections that group together those *padas* appropriate to each of the twelve months, and others that arrange the verses to suit the eight daily "offices" of Vallabhite ritual. But in the present anthology, as in many others, it is the tale that dictates the arrangement.

A narrative ordering of the verses seems particularly appropriate to the needs of those readers for whom Kṛṣṇa is a recent or casual acquaintance. Through reading the *Sūrsāgar* as if it were a novel or a biography, such a reader may approach Sūr's own vision of the life and character of Kṛṣṇa. But there is a risk here as well: for it is as certain as such things can be that the work was never intended to be read as a connected narrative.[1] Here again we come up against the problem of the "omniscient audience." The Indian audience receives a "new" Kṛṣṇa-poem much as one would receive an anecdote about an old friend. Such a tale needs but a word or two of preface, and it will inevitably be measured against everything we already know of the man. It may be amusing, or endearing, or revealing (or preposterous, or offensive, or merely trite) depending upon the degree to which it at once confirms, and yet casts new light upon, the character we already know.

For the reader unfamiliar with the tradition of Kṛṣṇaite verse, then, this collection must serve a double function, and this in turn requires a rather demanding double vision on the part of the reader. On the one hand, here lies the tale of

Kṛṣṇa, to be enjoyed as any other story. On the other hand, here lies a body of poems, each of which presupposes that the reader knows the tales told by all the others. It is a challenge, to be sure: the poems may be "translated," but the Western reader must still be willing to effect a self-translation of sorts, and move to meet the poems half-way.

In the pages that follow, three things have been done to assist the reader in this self-translation. First, the poems have been divided into convenient sections,[2] with each section prefaced by a summary of the relevant portion of the Kṛṣṇa-mythos, as well as a brief discussion of those aspects of the tale that are distinctive to the *Sūrsāgar.* Second, each poem has a brief set of notes; the notes are listed together, by section and poem number, at the end of Part Two. Finally, at the end of the book there is a glossary of terms that will be unfamiliar to some readers. Beyond this, the reader is on his own. He must stretch, across time and language and dogma and poetic convention, across all the dimensions of that gulf separating sixteenth-century Brindāban from here and now, to hear a poet's dialogues with his audience and with his god.

## MAṄGALĀCARAṆA: *Benediction*

I bow before Lord Hari's lotus feet
By whose grace the lame leap mountains
    and the blind see all;
The deaf hear, the mute speak,
    the beggarman strolls beneath a parasol of silk.
The Lord of Sūrdās, full of mercy:
    I bow again and again at his feet.

## I. NANDANANDANA: Nanda's Son

Scenes from the first two years of Kṛṣṇa's earthly life account for perhaps a hundred fifty *padas* in the *Sūrsāgar*. The figure can only be approximate, for it is sometimes difficult to assign individual *padas* an exact place in the chronology of Kṛṣṇa's life; indeed, one often suspects the poet of being deliberately vague on the subject. More traditional accounts, such as the *Bhāgavata Purāṇa*, underline Kṛṣṇa's divinity by accelerating his development: he is only seven, for example, when he persuades the cowherds of Braj to abandon their traditional worship of the Vedic god Indra—a thoroughly adult feat of rhetoric, even if we ignore the miraculous sequel. Sūr could hardly contradict the "authoritative" version of the tale; but he could and did avoid, in all but a few instances, any explicit references to Kṛṣṇa's age. A child who grew up too fast would have left little room for developing the irony of a child who seems, but is not, like any other of his age.

It is a child in every way normal who appears in many, perhaps most, of the poems of Kṛṣṇa's infancy. Hindi critics have often proclaimed these, the *padas* of "pure" *vātsalya*, as the finest poems about children to be found in any literature of the world, and the claim may not be all that extravagant; the world's adult poets tend to be preoccupied with adults. But Sūr's psychological realism is not the focus of the present study. The poems selected here for translation are intended not only to confirm the poet's undisputed sensitivity to the nuances of child behavior, but also to establish his genius for juggling the two halves of a paradox.

The paradox is nowhere more apparent than in the poems of infancy: the younger the child, the wider must be the chasm between earthly appearance and cosmic reality. Something like a fifth of the poems in this section of the *Sūrsāgar* expand upon the irony of a god trapped in an infant's body, a god who must learn to crawl in the dust of a world he created. The weakness of mortal flesh, however, disappears in moments of crisis, and a considerable number of verses depict the child's battles with an assortment of demonic would-be assassins sent by Kaṃsa. First comes Pūtanā, she of the glib tongue and poisoned nipples; Kṛṣṇa sucks the murderous wet-nurse dry (poems 3–5). Sakaṭāsura attacks in the unlikely form of a cart (6); Tṛṇāvarta, in the form of a whirlwind (11–13). Śrīdhara—"brahmin by caste, but butcher by deed" (9)—appears to have been the poet's own creation: he is mentioned in none of the earlier texts, and his comic-opera encounter with Kṛṣṇa (who spares his life because "it's not *nice* to kill a brahmin") bears the stamp of that same irreverent wit that emerges later in the "bee-songs."

Among the most intriguing of the infancy poems are those in which the ever-watchful gods, misconstruing some innocent action performed by the child, prepare for an early apocalypse. Kṛṣṇa lies on his back and sucks his toe (7); the gods recall a similar scene, reported by the sage Markaṇḍeya, who was once granted a terrifying interview by a chortling, toe-sucking infant Viṣṇu, who lay on a broad banyan leaf afloat—and utterly, utterly alone—in the primal Sea of dissolution. The Sea looms again in their minds when Yaśodā rocks the child to sleep—for when Viṣṇu closes his eyes in sleep, the curtain falls on the drama of Creation (10). Two poems in the present section allude to the churning of that same Sea, a monumental enterprise undertaken by gods and demons, through which they recovered a number of treasures long lost to the world (21, 23); the first article so retrieved was the moon (21). Finally, the child Kṛṣṇa is "mistaken" by the Gopīs, in a moment of near-revelation, for Śiva, the Destroyer himself (25).

But while the gods tremble at the realization that the continued existence of the universe is subject to an infant's whim, the infant himself seems blissfully unaware of the extent of his powers. Even when he disposes of his demon assailants, he does so in play. Demons, like all else in creation, are merely Kṛṣṇa's toys: his to make, his to break.

## *Ḍhāḍhī: The Singer*

1. Nanda, with a happy heart
I came from Govardhana;
When I heard that your son was born
I rose and came running.

Troupes of singers and beggars
gathered from afar when they heard.
Some were spread along the road, waiting,
for many days;
Some wore ornaments of gold and jewels,
and marvellous clothes of many kinds,
When they came upon me in the road
like a procession marching before a king.

Nanda, you are greatly generous!
You give whatever you are asked;
Who else in these Three Worlds
has won fame such as yours?
Yet if you gave me a fortune, I would not be content,
I would not go without seeing the child.

Nanda, hear my plea,
then will I leave gladly!
Give me the one thing
I have come to beg:
Let Yaśodā's son stand on his feet
and come here, to this courtyard, to play;
And when I have heard Mohan* laugh
and speak a word
I shall go home.
I am the Singer of your house;
Sūrdās is my name.

## *Jhūlnā: The Cradle*

2. Kānha's* cradle, *ré*!

He built it and brought it, the carpenter, *ré*!
  and set it to swing for you;
    the baby's cradle, *ré*!
He asked for a fortune, the carpenter, *ré*!
  Father gave him two;
    the baby's cradle, *ré*!

And how is it built, your cradle, *ré*?
  And how did they make the cord?
    The baby's cradle, *ré*!
Adorned with jewels is my cradle, *rí*!
  and silken is the cord;
    the baby's cradle, *ré*!

Rocking now in the cradle, *hó*!
  and now on Father's knee;
    the baby's cradle, *ré*!
Rocked by all the women, *hó*!
  and watched by Sūr so happily,
    the baby's cradle, *ré*!

## *Pūtanā-vadha: The Slaying of Pūtanā*

3. So deceitfully, Pūtanā came to Braj
At the King's command;
Her form so lovely, her nipples painted
  with poison.
She kissed the child's face, and gazed at his eyes,
  and clasped him to her breast:
"You're so lucky, Nandarānī,
  to have the boy Kanhāī.*. . ."

4. "Just give me Gopāl for a second, my friend!
Let me have a good look at his face,
then I'll give him right back, my friend!
So soft his flower-like hands and feet,
I just love those lips, those teeth, that nose,
my friend!
His dangling locks, the jewels at his throat—
he's the beauty of a million Kāmas, my friend!
I think about him night and day;
*I've* never known such fortune, my friend!
Treasure of the Vedas, and of the sages all;
you're just so lucky to have him, my friend!
He whose form, in the eyes of the world,
shames a million suns and moons, my friend!"

Yaśodā, Sūr dotes on your son,
the Gopīs' darling
and Pūtanā's foe.

5. . . . so she took him by the hand, and suckled him;
and Kṛṣṇa knew her.
"Lord, O Lord make him let me go,"
she shrieked as she ran from the house
And fell all shrivelled upon the earth
as if bitten by a snake;
Thus do the faithful still sing the tale,
O Lord of Sūrdās!

## *Sakaṭāsura: The Cart-demon*

6. The Demon took up the *pān*,
pledged an oath to the King,
and left with his head bowed low
though the pride swelled in his heart;
and he took on the form of the Cart.

The Braj-folk started
  as the thunderous sound drew near.
They looked to the sky
to the four quarters
to the ten directions
  and man and woman, they were numb with fear

as the Demon came to the cradle where the Lord lay,
clasping his foot,
busily sucking his big toe.
Laughing, chortling, a radiant child
but of course this child well knew
the demon who'd foolishly come as a foe:
  a tiny little kick, a great and fearful sound
  and the Cart was hurled to the ground.

Sūr's Lord, and Nanda's darling;
he saved the lives of all the folk in Braj
  when he slew the Demon—in play, as a jest—
  and did away with that troublesome pest.

7. Taking foot in hand, he sticks his toe in his mouth;
The Lord lies alone in his cradle
  playing happily by himself.
Śiva thinks; Brahmā ponders;
  the seas surge against the Banyan-tree;
The clouds assemble, thinking the flood come 'round at last;
  the Lords of the Quarters assemble the earth-bearing
    elephants;
The sages are terrified; the Earth trembles;
  the Serpent spreads his hundred hoods in alarm.
The people of Braj know nothing of these things,
    but Sūr understands:
      He is thrusting with his foot at the Cart.

8. Yaśodā joyfully plays with Śyām.
"Oh when will he crawl upon his knees!"
she prays of Brahmā;
"Oh when will I see his first two teeth
with these two eyes of mine!
Oh when will I hear the first words
spoken by his lotus-mouth!"
She kisses hand and foot and lip and brow,
his hanging locks she kisses;
How can Sūr describe such a scene?
Where will he find the skill?

## *Śrīdhara-aṅga-bhaṅga: The Mutilation of Śrīdhara*

9. Brahmin by caste, but butcher by deed
was Śrīdhara.
He spoke thus to King Kaṃsa:
"Lord, here am I,
your obedient servant;
Let me slay this Nanda's son!"

Said Kaṃsa, "So be it! Go,
let there be no delay!"
And so Śrīdhara came
to the house of Nanda
And Yaśodā bowed low at his feet.

"At your service, my Lord," she said;
"Will you eat? Shall I bring
Water from the holy river Yamunā?"
So she left for the river,
and Śrīdhara said to himself:
"Now hasn't this turned out well indeed!"

The Brahmin's mind was bent on murder;
but the Child knew.

"Now it's not nice," thought Hari,
"to kill a Brahmin;
So I'll just mangle him a bit!"

The Brahmin came near;
the child took him by the hand
threw him down
seized his throat
twisted his tongue
and smashed a jar of butter on his head!

He smeared the butter on the Brahmin's face,
then lay in his cradle again;
and just as his mother
returned with the water
this innocent Kṛṣṇa began to cry!

Yaśodā saw that her son lay crying,
and "Brahmin!" she cried in rage,
"What is this evil thing you've done?"
From the Brahmin's mouth
not a word did come;
what a tale he could tell if he'd still had a tongue!

She threw the Brahmin out of the house,
and took her son upon her lap;
then all the folk in the land of Braj
did gather round to gaze;
and so sings Sūr in Hari's praise!

*10.* Yaśodā puts Madana Gopāla* to sleep
And the Three Worlds tremble at the sight,
even Śiva and Brahmā are deceived.
His sleepy eyes,
black beneath their drooping lids,
Are like a pair of bees, each trapped at dusk
in the night-closing petals of a flower.
Breath ripples through his torso
as waves through the churning Sea;

Brahmā mourns his lotus-throne
as the child's navel sinks with every breath.
Śyām runs a hand through his lovely locks,
scattering them in disarray,
O Sūr, as if the Serpent
spread its thousand hoods above the Lord.

### *Tṛṇāvarta-vadha: The Slaying of Tṛṇāvarta*

11. Nanda's wife shone lovely in her joy
Seated in her courtyard,
her son Sāraṅgapāṇī* in her lap
As Kaṃsa, great in pride,
recalled the demon Tṛṇāvarta
and sent him forth. . . .

12. Yaśodā daydreams:

"When will my little one crawl upon his knees,
when will he plant his two feet upon the earth?
When will I see his first two teeth,
when will he lisp his first word?
When will he call Nanda "father,"
when will he call me "mother"?
When will he catch my skirt
and babble angry words at me?
When will he first feed himself
with his own two tiny hands?
When will he laugh and talk with me,
his beauty dissolving all my cares?"

She left Kṛṣṇa alone in the courtyard,
left to work in the house;
And a whirlwind arose,
and the clouds began to growl. . . .
Sūr says:
The people of Braj heard this sound
and froze in fear where they stood.

13. . . . then came the great whirlwind,
and all Gokul thought:
Now this is the end of the world.
The evil one swept Gopāl* high into the sky;
but the Child knew him.
He crushed the demon's throat,
and stopped the demon's breath,
till the blood streamed down from the demon's eyes.

And then little Kṛṣṇa,
as he played there in the sky,
dashed the demon down upon the stones.
(The Braj-girls ran to the grove where he fell,
and clasped the child to their breasts;
Kissing him, fondling him, they took him home.
There were celebrations in every house in Braj;
and all gave Sūr's little Lord their jewels to wear,
and all gave him water to drink.)

14. "A great astrologer has come to your house,
hearing of the birth of your son;
He has drawn up a most thorough horoscope,
and would like to tell you about it."

"In this auspicious year, month of *bhādra*,
on the eighth, a Wednesday,
Dark phase of the moon, Rohiṇī the star, midnight—
Wonderful! It's worth a celebration!
His ascending sign is Taurus, with a high moon;
he will know much joy of the flesh.
His sun is in Leo, the fourth house;
he will ever be triumphant.
In his fifth, Virgo, is Mercury;
he will father many sons.
In his sixth, Libra, are Saturn and Venus conjoined;
his enemies will flee before him.

He will marry girls both high and low,
  for *Rāhu* is in the seventh.
In the house of Fate, in Capricorn, is Mars;
  his glory will be great.
In the house of Wealth, in Pisces, is Jupiter;
  the nine gems will fill his home.
In the house of Deeds the lord is Saturn;
  his body will be black."

The first and the eternal, the Lord transcending all,
  the dweller in every soul;
Thus did you descend,
  O Lord of Sūrdās!

*15.* He eats his butter and sulks;
His eyes inflamed, a frown on his brow,
  he yawns again and again.
Now he crawls with tinkling anklets,
  his body covered with dust;
Now he bends and tugs at his hair,
  and a tear comes to his eye.
Now he babbles baby-talk;
  now he speaks out, "Father!"
Seeing the beauty of Sūr's Hari
  his mother won't leave him for the blink of an eye.

*16.* Kṛṣṇa crawls, crowing with glee
In the jewel-studded courtyard of Nanda,
  chasing his own reflection.
He sees his form reflected,
  and reaches to grasp it with his hand;
He laughs, and then stares in wonder
  at the mirrored gleam of his teeth.

His flower-like hands and feet
  are mimicked in the golden floor,
    as if a lotus blossomed from each and every gem
      to pedestal each tiny hand and foot.
Seeing the childish glee on his face,
  Yaśodā calls Nanda time and again;
Then drawing Sūr's Lord beneath her bodice,
  time and again she gives suck.

*17.* In the jewel studded courtyard of Nanda
  the two Brothers are at play.
The White and the Black, such a pair they make!—
  Balarāma and Kanhaiyā.*
Lovely locks dangling,
  yellow *bindu* on their brows,
The lion-claw necklace agleam on their breasts,
  lifting the sorrow of the saints;
And Yaśodā and Rohiṇī together,
  devoted mothers both,
Snapping their fingers to make them dance,
  thinking the children their sons.
The blue and yellow silks
  are pleasing to the eye;
Sūraja sings the praises
  of the joy of children at play.

*18.* He tries to come outside.
It's so easy now
  to crawl within the courtyard,
    but the doorstep stops him every time.
He trips and falls,
  can't get across;
    it's all such an enormous task.
Once he measured the Earth in a mere three steps;
  now he's stopped at the borders of his very own house.

And Balarāma says to himself,
"What an act he's putting on!"
(The infinite glories
of the Lord of Sūrdās
are a delight to his devotees.)

*19.* Yaśodā delights in watching him walk.

Clumping along on faltering feet,
showing off when he sees his mother,
He walks as far as the doorstep,
but returns again and again;
Stumbles and falls, but can't quite cross—
and the gods are made to wonder:

For he makes in a second a million worlds,
and destroys in a second a million more;
Yet he sits in the lap of a cowherd's wife
as she teaches him to play,
And she leads him by the hand
across that doorstep
step by step by step.

The sight of the Lord of Sūr
stuns the minds of gods and men.

*20.* What happened to that strength of yours, God?
The strength by which you plunged as the Fish into the sea,
took back the Vedas, and slew the ancient demon;
The strength by which you took the mountain
on your Tortoise-back,
and thus contrived to churn the sea;
The strength by which you took upon your Boar's-tusks
the Earth, as if it were a flower;
The strength by which you split Hiraṇyakaśipu's breast,
and bestowed a wealth of kindness on your devotee;

The strength by which you once trapped Bali,
  and measured the Earth in just three steps;
The strength by which you took form
  to place upon the Brahmin the *tilak* of your protection;
The strength by which you cut off Rāvaṇa's heads,
  and made Vibhīṣaṇa king at last;
The strength by which you broke the pride of Jāmbavat;
  the strength by which you heard the plea of Earth.
Sūrdās says: Now you can't even cross the threshold
  of your house!
    You just stand there; Lord, you don't *know*!

21. With a clatter Hari put on the necklace
  And it was like a pair of moons, both poised
    above a new-formed, rain-dark cloud.
  Once he bore the Mountain and the Tortoise,
    the gods and the demons and the Snake,
      with never a moment's fear;
  Now the Gopīs must help him bear the weight
    of the gold he wears so proudly on his arms.
  Sūr's Syām peers into the jar of curds,
    and face will not part from reflected face:
  As if two moons emerged from the Churning,
    as if illumined by the light of his laugh.

22. Look, see the state of the Stateless One!
    What a form he's taken for himself!
  He whose home is the Three Worlds,
    what a dump he's landed in!
  Whose umbilicus bore Brahmā,
    fulfilling all his yogic vows,
  His umbilicus the Braj-girl seized
    and sliced, and tied with twine!

The face which Śiva gazed upon in meditation,
 making it the object of his veneration,
Is kissed by the woman Yaśodā
 embracing her nursing child!
Those ears which hear the cries of mankind,
 and speed Him from Garuḍa's back to their relief—
Yaśodā leans near those very same ears
 and coos and sings and whispers.
The nourisher of the cosmos, the lifestaff of all,
 frets about a little butter.
With a million vast worlds in his every hair
 he lies in a narrow cradle.
The arm that saved Prahlāda
 and tore open Hiraṇyakaśipu's breast—
Yaśodā grabs that very same arm
 and says: "Hold still now, love!"
He whose vision gods and sages sought in vain,
 and Śambhu fixed ever in his mind,
*He*, O Sūr, is right here in Braj,
 a playful cowherd in Gokul!

*23.* When Mohan* grasped the churn
At the touch of hand to curds, clay jar and churning-cord,
 the Sea, the Mountain, and the Serpent knew fear.
Sometimes he measures the world in three steps;
 sometimes he can't cross the doorstep.
Sometimes the very gods cannot reach him;
 sometimes he plays with Nanda's wife.
Sometimes he's not content with the whole Sea of Milk;
 sometimes he delights in simple butter and curds.
Not even Śeṣa can tell the tale
 of the *līlā* of the Lord of Sūrdās.

*24.* The buttered bread gleams in Hari's hand
As if a petaled lotus, knowing the moon its foe,
clutched the nectar cupped in its heart.
He stuffs it into his lotus-mouth,
and bears a simile so stout:
As when the Hog raised the earth with all its mountains
upon the very tips of his tusks.
Naked, laughing, he grasps his topknot
and dances 'round his father.
Let Sūr eat the leavings of his Lord,
so beautifully smeared with spit!

*25.* "Sisters, take a look at Nanda's son!
With his dusty, matted locks
Hari's made himself look like Hara!
That necklace of blue silk and gems—
for a minute I thought it a snake!
Hari shakes his rattle and laughs;
Hara beats his drum and dances.
Gopāl* wears a garland of lotus—
how shall I describe it?
It's like the elephant's trunk resting at
Hara's throat—
*that's* the look it has!
That string of pearls
gleams on Śyām's black body, like—
Like Gaṅgā, fearing Gaurī
and clinging to Hara's neck!"
Seeing the lion-claw pendant at his breast,
the women wonder anew:
It was like the young moon, slipped from the brow
to the breast of Tripurāri.
The Limbless saw the limbs and paused,
taking Nanda's son for Hara;
May you live forever in the heart of Sūr,
O image of Śyāma-Śiva!

26. On seeing Hari's face in the morning
Yaśodā is cheered, Nanda delighted,
As the heart is pleased at the sight of a lotus
unfolding in the rays of the day-making sun.
His mother uncovers that face as she wakes him:
"Get up now, my darling, my little sweet-potato!"

And he rises like the full moon
bursting from the foam
when the Gods churned the Milky Sea.

He whom Śiva, Śeṣa, Brahmā and the rest
proclaim with the Vedic "Not this, not this!"
That same Gopāla* —
now listen, Sūr!—
that full and perfect Bliss has come to Braj.

## II. MĀKHANCOR: The Butterthief

Once Kṛṣṇa learns to talk, he is by turns guileful and naive. Sūr manages to extract much the same sort of dramatic irony from each of these poles: the audience turns from laughing with Kṛṣṇa, to laughing at him. An officious brahmin makes a ritual food-offering to a god he assumes is elsewhere (10); when Kṛṣṇa obligingly eats the offering, the brahmin is outraged—and the audience joins in Kṛṣṇa's mirth at the absurdity of this blustering priest, who will never know how near he came to the Lord he professes to serve. But when brother Balarāma taunts Kṛṣṇa with his color, suggesting that no one so black could really be Yaśodā's son, the blade of irony is reversed: it is a tearful Kṛṣṇa who now plays the fool, and the audience shares in Balarāma's smug awareness of Kṛṣṇa's true origins (8). Some of the best of such poems achieve a disturbing, and effective, ambiguity as to the direction of this irony. When Kṛṣṇa asks for the moon as a toy (5), and Yaśodā appeases him with its reflection in a bowl of water, our first reaction is to applaud the mother's cleverness —but then we are nagged by the question: was the request really so unreasonable, coming from this particular child?

It is during this period of his life that Kṛṣṇa occasionally (but briefly) allows his parents to glimpse the reality underlying his *līlā*. In the most famous of these epiphanies, Kṛṣṇa eats a handful of mud, and Balarāma tattles; confronted by Yaśodā, Kṛṣṇa denies the offense and invites Yaśodā to inspect his mouth. What she sees there is well known to the Indian audience; and the poem included here (11), in a masterful bit of understatement, coyly refrains from describing Yaśodā's vision. But in another *pada*, Yaśodā herself supplies the details:

> . . . he showed me his mouth,
> and there were the Centers of the Three Worlds,

Heaven and Hell and Earth!
  Forests and mountains hovered in his mouth;
And when I saw the rivers
  and Mount Sumera,
    I was astounded. . . .

(*Sabhā* 874)

Nanda is granted a similar vision, in an episode apparently invented by Sūr. Kṛṣṇa mischievously interrupts his father's worship (of Viṣṇu!) by popping the god's image into his mouth; when Nanda looks around for the missing god, he finds far more than he had lost (13). But in the most effective of these verses, Kṛṣṇa's self-revelation is an accident: Yaśodā innocently chooses the tale of Rāma for a bedtime-story, and a sleepy Kṛṣṇa becomes overly involved in the events of his own previous incarnation (6).

As the child becomes mobile, the stage of his *līlā* widens from home to village. The poems recounting his adventures as the Butterthief of Gokul may well be the most popular in the entire *Sūrsāgar.* They require little in the way of explanation, except perhaps a reminder that the child's insistence on eating butter from every house but his own, as well as the ambivalence of the Braj-girls' response to his pilfering, both prefigure the later, more adult relationship between village women and village rake.

The role of Balarāma in these poems is noteworthy: Kṛṣṇa's "brother" and co-incarnation often serves the poet as an all-knowing narrator and stage-manager. It is Balarāma who reminds us that Kṛṣṇa is not really Yaśodā's son (8), and who reminds Kṛṣṇa that he of all children has nothing to fear from the bogey-man (9); it is likewise Balarāma who sets the stage for the "mouth epiphany." The poet uses this brotherly omniscience to similar effect in the final episode of the Butterthief sequence. Yaśodā, stung by the milkmaids' repeated accusations that her son is a thief, punishes him by tying him to a heavy mortar. In doing so, we are told, Kṛṣṇa's mother is actually serving her son's purpose: Kṛṣṇa has decided to free two mythic brothers, doomed by an ancient curse to stand as trees in the village. Once bound, Kṛṣṇa drags the mortar between the trees, uprooting them and thus breaking the curse, whereupon the two brothers bow as devotees before the child (23). But even as Yaśodā sets events in motion by tying her son to the mortar, Balarāma smiles a knowing smile and muses, to no one in particular:

. . . Who can bind this one,
and who may set him free?
Nobody knows
but he. . . .

1. Hari stole butter for the very first time.
He fulfilled the furtive longings
of the women of the village,
then he ran off through the narrow lanes of Braj.
And Hari thought to himself:
"I'll go to every house in the land!
I've taken birth in Gokul
for the fun of it;
I'm going to eat *everyone's* butter!
Yaśodā thinks I'm just an ordinary child;
Oh will I have a time with the Gopīs!"

So lovingly says Sūr's Lord:
"These Braj-folk
are mine."

2. Yaśodā sits in the courtyard, churning butter;
Hari stands laughing, his tiny teeth agleam.
It is a sight to steal away the mind,
a beauty beyond describing:
Like a troupe of heavenly nymphs, adorned
to tempt a sage from the labors of his mind.
The mother says, "Dance!
Mohan,* dance and I'll give you butter!"
His tiny feet pound and stamp upon the earth,
his anklebells ring.

Sūr sings the praises of his name,
  earth and heaven resound with his fame;
    but the Lord of the Three Worlds dances
      for his butter.

3. "Mother, when will my topknot grow?
  How many times I've drunk my milk,
    and it's *still* so small!
  You keep saying it'll grow like brother's,
    it'll get long and thick, you say;
  And if I comb it, and braid it, and wash it,
    then it'll drag along the ground
      like a big black snake.
  You keep feeding me plain old milk,
    you never give me butter-and-bread!"
  (Sūrdās says: Live long, you brothers,
    Hari and Haladhara!)

4. The two boys frolic as one.
  Footsteps stumbling,
    swinging their dust-drawn limbs,
  They toddle along the road, anklebells tinkling,
    shrieking each to each,
  Like a pair of tender goslings
    enraptured with their own new speech.
  At a tiny waist, a gold-belled belt
    gleams a slivered gleam,
  As gold upon a touchstone
    leaves a thin and gleaming slash.
  Earrings glitter in lovely ears;
    a lotus-pair, swaying, swaying,
  As when Bāsava sent the sacrifice
    at the Life-poet's command.
  Locks of hair stray across a face,
    doubling its beauty,
  As when the crescent moon was embraced
    by the son of Siṃhikā.

Now they dash to the door,
  now to father Nanda's side;
Their Gopī-mother takes the hand of Sūr's own Lord
  and kisses him.

5. Again and again, Yaśodā coaxes:
"Come, Moon!
  Moon, my little one's calling you!
He's going to eat
  honey and fruit and nuts and sweets,
    and he might give you some too!
He'll play with you in his hand,
  and he won't even drop you once;
Just come down and live in this bowl of water
  I've got here in my hand. . . ."
She set the bowl upon the ground,
  and took him and showed him the moon;
And Sūr's Lord laughed
  and dipped his two hands
    again and again and again.

6. "Listen, son, and I'll tell you a lovely story."
The lotus-eyed was overjoyed;
  the clever gem made sleepy sounds.
"Daśaratha was a king, of the line of Raghu,
  and he had four sons.
The greatest, named Rāma,
  wed the daughter of Janaka.
On his father's oath he left the kingdom,
  went into the forest with brother and bride.
Then as he, the noble one, lotus-eyed,
  ran after the golden deer
Rāvaṇa stole Sītā away"—
  Nanda's son heard, and awoke, and arose:

"My bow, my bow!" shouted Sūr's Lord,
"Lakṣmaṇ!
Give me my bow!"—and his mother drew
back in awe.

7. Wake up, wake up, Gopāl!*
Child, you mustn't sleep so much;
morning's the best part of the day!
All the little boys in the village
come by to see you, and then leave,
Like a string of black bees, all waiting
for a lotus-bud to bloom.
If you don't believe me, Sūr's Lord,
my little black *tamāla*-tree,
Then just wake up
and open your eyes
and come and see for yourself!

8. "Mother, Brother's always teasing me!
He says, 'Yaśodā bought you,
who says she gave you birth?'
What can I do? I'm so mad
I can't go out and play.
Again and again he asks:
'Who's your mother,
who's your father?
White is Nanda, and Yaśodā white;
how come *you're* so black?'
The other boys all snap their fingers
and laugh to see me dance.
You sure know how to beat *me*,
but you never get mad at Brother!"
Yaśodā heard Mohan's* angry words
and was amused.

"Listen, Kānha*: your brother's a liar,
he's a scoundrel from birth!
I swear by the cows we live by:
I *am* mother,
you *are* son."

9. "Don't go far to play now, Love,
a bogey-man's come to the woods!"
Kṛṣṇa laughed and asked:
"Who *sent* the bogey-man?"
"Such a little thing you let scare you now!"
laughed brother Balarāma.
"You slept on the serpent Śeṣa in the seven nether worlds;
have you forgotten all that now?
When Śaṅkhāsura took the four Vedas,
and hid them in the sea,
In the form of a fish you slew him;
where was your bogey-man then?
You bore mount Mandara beneath the ocean,
churned the sea for the gods and demons;
In tortoise-form you bore the earth;
you didn't see the bogey-man there!
When Hiraṇyākṣa wanted war,
and the pride rose in his heart,
You took the form of the boar, and slew him,
and raised the earth upon your tusks!
When you took upon yourself that terrible form,
and rescued Prahlāda,
Rending Hiraṇyakaśipu with your claws,
you didn't see the bogey-man there!
You tricked Bali when you came as a dwarf,
and crossed the earth in just three steps;
He placed your sweat in the sacred vessel,
and touched your sacred feet!

When they slew the sinless sage
  and took away Kāmadhenu,
Twenty-one times you swept the Kṣatriyas from the earth;
  you didn't see the bogey-man there!
In the form of Rāma when you slew Rāvaṇa
  he of ten heads and twenty arms,
When you burned all Laṅkā to a crisp—
  you didn't see the bogey-man there!
For the sake of your *bhakta* you came to earth
  and purged it of all its demons;
The Vedas forever sang *'Neti!'*
  of this *līlā* of the Lord of Sūrdās!"

*10.* A Brahmin from a great house came to Braj.

As he went from door to door, he proclaimed:
  "I heard that a son was born to Nanda,
  and I rose and ran straight here."

When at last he arrived at Nanda's door,
  Yaśodā was overjoyed;
She washed his feet and sat him down,
  then prepared her house for a proper feast.

"Eat whatever you please," she said,
  and the Brahmin was pleased indeed:
"At last," he thought, "God has been good;
  blest is Yaśodā to bear such a son!"

So she milked the cow, and brought the milk,
  which the Brahmin eagerly took
To mix the *khīr*, the *ghī* and the sweets
  as an offering on Kṛṣṇa's behalf;
  and he fixed his mind on the Lord.

When at last the Brahmin opened his eyes,
  what should he see but little Kanhaiyā,*
    eating the god's own food!
"Yaśodā, come see what your son has done!
  He's polluted that which must be pure!"

Humbly the woman folded her hands
  and begged the Brahmin's pardon,
    as she sent afresh for the foods she would need,
      the honey, *ghī,* the milk and the rest;
Sūr's Śyām, leave that Brahmin alone!
  why must you always be such a pest?

*11.* "Mohan,* won't you spit out the mud?"
"You're always doing these disgusting things,"
  said his mother, with a stick in her hand.
But he wouldn't obey;
  he played a clever trick:
He opened his mouth,
  and he showed her,
  and the Play unfolded. . . .
A long while later she opened her eyes.
  The curtain of illusion had parted.
Sūr, Yaśodā saw, and was bewildered;
  she could say nothing;
  no sweet words,
  no scolding;
  nothing.

*12.* Nanda worships; Hari watches.
He rings the bell and bathes the image;
  he adorns it with sandalwood paste.
On a leaf-plate he spreads an offering of food;
  he circles it with the flame.
And then Kānha* says:
  "Father, you made the offering,
    but God didn't eat a thing!"
Nanda looks at his wife and exclaims,
  "Did you hear what Kānha said!
Fold your hands, Sūr's Śyām,
  show respect for the gods,
    and the gods will keep you well!"

13. Yaśodā stands near and watches;
The sight of Śyām's childish play
floods her mind with love.
As Nanda performs the rituals of worship,
seated in deep meditation,
Kānha* stealthily snatches the image
and pops it into his mouth.
"Now," he thinks, "let's all just see
how great this 'god' really is!"
Nanda opens his eyes; looks all around;
alarmed, amazed, he asks:
"Where did my god go? Who took him?"

Then Yaśodā points at her son's face:
"Let's take a look in your mouth, Kanhāi.*
Why did you put the god in your mouth?
You've melted it now, it's ruined!"

And so he spread wide his mouth
and the Three Worlds were there revealed;
and when Nanda peered inside
O Sūr, he was stunned,
he was speechless.

## *Prathama mākhan-corī: The First Buttertheft*

14. Śyām went to the Gopī's house.

He peeked through the door; nobody home.
He looked all around; he crept inside;
And the Gopī heard him coming,
and she hid.
Śyām sat himself down by the butter-churns,
alone in the empty, silent house.
He found the butter-jugs and began to eat
until
in a jewel-studded pillar
he glimpsed his own reflection,

and struck up a clever conversation:
  "Today's the first time I ever stole;
  it's good to have a friend along!"
So he fed himself,
and tried to feed his reflection—
but the butter dropped to the floor.
He asked:
  "What's wrong?
  You can have the whole pot if you want,
  but don't drop it like that; it's good!
  It's fun, feeding you like this;
  now tell me, what do *you* think?"

At this the Braj-girl laughed aloud;
Sūr's Lord turned around, and saw her face
and that famous Foe of Mura ran away.

*15.* "Take him home, Yaśodā!
You're the daughter of a fine family;
  it's a fine way you've taught your son to talk!
Oh, it wouldn't be so bad
  if he'd eat my butter by himself,
    but he always brings along his friends.
And when I tried to catch him—well!
  what can I say about *that*?
As soon as he saw me, he ran off and hid,
  so I went in and lay down;
Then he snuck up behind me and grabbed my braid,
  and he tied it to the bed!"

"Listen now, mother, let me tell you about *her*.
  She called me in,
And made me pick out all the ants
  that had fallen in her butter-jar;
Then she left me alone
  to look after the house
    while *she* went and slept with her man!"
Sūr says, Yaśodā laughed at the tale
  while the Gopī hid her face in shame.

*16.* "Now they're just lying, these girls!"

"He's five years old
give or take a day or two;
he's not *old* enough to steal!
It's all an excuse for them to come see him,
these lying little peasant-girls!
They blame the blameless!
What makes them think
that God isn't going to blame *them*?
Why, how could Kṛṣṇa's tiny arms even reach that high?
And how could he get back so soon?"

"*We'll* tell you how:
He stood on top of a big stone mortar,
and hoisted his friends on his back!
If you don't believe it, Yaśodā,
just come along with us,
come see it with your very own eyes!
You don't even *try* to control this child,
this Lord of Sūrdās!"

And his mother did indeed begin to wonder.

*17.* "Mama, I didn't eat the butter!"

"It was all just a trick the other boys played:
*they* smeared it on my face!
Go look for yourself!
The butter-jar's hanging 'way high on a hook;
Tell me how I could reach it
with my tiny little hands?"

So said Kṛṣṇa
as he wiped the butter from his face,
and tried to hide the plate behind his back.
But Yaśodā just dropped her stick, and smiled,
and took him into her arms.

So the Lord once again showed the power of his *bhakti*,
as his childish antics charmed his mother's mind;
Sūr says, even Śiva and Brahmā
can never know Yaśodā's joy!

*18.* Yaśodā bound Śyām to the mortar
Then she left him outside, alone,
and set about her work in the house.
And she muttered, as she churned the butter:
"Why should he steal butter
from one house after another
When he can get all he wants right here at home?
And then they say he hits the girls,
and runs away. . . .
You! Balarāma!
Get along with you too!"
And Sūr's Śyām, still bound to the mortar,
was watched by every woman in Braj.

*19.* "A fine mother's heart you've got, Yaśodā!
Your lotus-eyed son you've tied to the mortar
for the sake of a little butter!
A treasure beyond the reach of gods and sages,
a treasure beyond the wildest dream—
You had it right here, sitting in your house;
you've forgotten it now in your pride!
There once was a time you would run to embrace
any mother's son you saw crying;
This time it's the son of your very own house!
Why now are you being so cruel?
He keeps looking at you
with those tearful eyes,
does your little son Kanhāi.* . . .
What can I do? What oath can I swear?
I beg you: let him go!"

(Defender of the gods, demons' bane,
he whom the Three Worlds fear;
"Not this, not this!" sing the Vedas forever
of this *līlā* of the Lord of Sūrdās.)

*20.* Just say the word,
and *I'll* supply the butter,
If that's the reason you won't let him go,
won't drop that stick in your hand!
Listen, woman: Don't be this way.
Look at his face, all contorted with fear,
Like a lotus that wilts
in the Moon's chill rays.
You seized this charming little child by the arm,
and brutally you bound him to the stone!
So now the tears rain down
from the eyes of Sūr's Śyām
like pearls from the face of the Moon.

*21.* Haladhara saw Śyām, and smiled to himself.
"Who can bind this one, and who may set him free?
Nobody knows but he. . . .
He alone creates, he alone destroys;
his praises are sung by the Serpent's thousand tongues!
And yet he contrives this clever ruse
to shatter the trees, and free the Twins.
Destroyer of demons,
Ferry for the faithful,
Saviour of the fallen is he called;
But the Lord of Sūrdās,
for the sake of *bhāva-bhakti*,
has sold himself into Yaśodā's power."

22. And then Śyām conceived the plan.
The women had all returned to their homes;
his mother had set about her work;
So, unseen, he dragged the great stone
between the Twin Trees,
and the leaves began to tremble at his touch.
He felled both trunks
and they crashed to the earth,
where the sons of Kubera emerged;
To each he clasped two hands in greeting,
and thus displayed his four arms.
(Sūr, blest is this Braj
that gave birth to Hari,
destroyer of the woes of the world.)

23. Blest be Govinda* who came to Gokul!
Blest, blest be Nanda,
blessèd night and day;
blest Yaśodā who bore Śrīdhara!*
Blest, blest the child-play
on the Yamunā bank;
blest the forest where he grazes the cows!
Blest be this time,
blest be the Braj-folk,
blest, blest the flute
with its honeyed notes;
Blest, blest the anger
and the scolding blest;
Blest be the butter
and blest Mohan, who ate it!
And Blest, O Sūr, be the mortar
to which Govinda,
for our sake,
let his blessèd arms be bound.

## III. GIRIDHARA: The Mountainbearer

The move from Gokul to the forest of Brindāban marks a significant broadening of scale in the Kṛṣṇa story. The stage, of course, has expanded: Kṛṣṇa runs with the older boys now, driving the herds out into the woods and pasturelands each morning. He returns to the village only at dusk, a time of day known in Hindi poetry as *godhūli,* the time of "cow-dust"; nothing is so characteristic of evening in rural India as the haze of dust floating above the returning herds (2).

But a more dramatic manifestation of this increase in scale is the increasingly ominous threat posed by Kṛṣṇa's demonic antagonists. As the child grows, so do his enemies. Kṛṣṇa as an infant, confined to Nanda's house, slew demons whose threats were confined to the child alone. Kṛṣṇa the Butterthief slew no demons; but his one feat of supernatural strength, uprooting the Yamalārjuna trees, resulted for the first time in the salvation of someone other than himself. In the third stage of his development, Kṛṣṇa the Cowherd conquers demons (and gods) who threaten the whole of Brindāban.

There are a considerable number of these episodes, but few, apparently, which Sūr found of literary interest; the rest—such as the enormous forest-fire, which Kṛṣṇa extinguishes by the simple expedient of swallowing it (8)—the poet dispatches in a perfunctory *pada* or two. There are only two of the heroic episodes from the Cowherd period over which the poet lingers; between them they constitute a coming of age for the young god, a full and public display of his more-than-human powers.

The first of these is the defeat of Kāliya, a monster-serpent living in a deep pool of the river Yamunā, where he threatens the herds and people of Brindāban with his poison. Sūr's version of the tale is far longer and more involved than that found in classical texts—Sūr brings Kaṃsa into the episode through a somewhat bizarre twist in the plot—but the poems translated here require little in the way of background. Two of them involve the prelude to battle: Kṛṣṇa has a prophetic nightmare, in which he sees himself pushed into the dread pool (5); the actual plunge comes as the result of a suspenseful game of ball at the river's edge, leading to a fight between Kṛṣṇa and another child, and climaxing with Kṛṣṇa jumping into the water—from motives which, in Sūr's version, are surprisingly complex, and not entirely heroic (6). The sequel follows more or less classical lines: Kṛṣṇa engages the serpent in battle and defeats it, finally performing a dramatic dance atop its many hoods; then, responding to a plea from the serpent's wives, Kṛṣṇa spares its life in a famous act of mercy (7).

Kṛṣṇa's most spectacular feat of strength, the lifting of Mount Govardhana, held a special importance for Sūr. The sect of Vallabha, in whose service Sūr is said to have written and recited his verse, was centered at Govardhana; its ritual focused on the icon of Śrīnāthjī, a figure of the child Kṛṣṇa balancing the mountain atop one hand. The tale involves a marvellous contest between Kṛṣṇa, by now fully aware of his own divinity, and the Raingod Indra, leader of the Vedic pantheon. Kṛṣṇa persuades the cowherds that their devotion to Indra is misplaced: the god does nothing for them, he argues; they would do better to worship the cattle that provide their livelihood, and the hills and forests that give them pasturage (13). He convinces them to take the food-offering prepared for Indra, and deliver it instead to the mountain called Govardhana. (In some of Sūr's poems on the Govardhana episode, the child adds an element of persuasion not found in the classical versions of the tale: the god of the mountain, he claims, came to him in a dream.)

But in fact it is to Kṛṣṇa himself, not the mountain, that the villagers unwittingly address their worship: the child appears in the guise of the spirit of the mountain, and himself consumes Indra's feast (14). Indra is furious (and, in Sūr's version, comically petulant); using his power as raingod, he attempts to drown the impudent cowherds in a great deluge (15). It is this that occasions the lifting of Govardhana: for seven days the child holds the mountain as an umbrella above his people and their herds, until Indra is forced to acknowledge Kṛṣṇa's supremacy. But while Indra is fully persuaded, the cowherds, still locked in Kṛṣṇa's *māyā*, are less so. One moment they beg Kṛṣṇa to extricate them from the calamity —for which, after all, he is responsible (16); the next, however, they show genuine doubt concerning his ability to perform the miracle unaided (17); and Kṛṣṇa, once the episode is over, is quick to obscure his true role (18).

Interspersed between the idyls of the young cowherd, and the miracles of the young god, we catch our first glimpse of the young but precocious lover. Sūr portrays the great romance of Rādhā and Kṛṣṇa as beginning with a chance childhood meeting (9). The poet apparently envisioned Rādhā as the daughter of a family with some pretensions—whether to caste or class is never really clear; in either case, there is considerable irony evoked by the use of the sacred dual name, Rādhā-Kṛṣṇa, as a taunt flung at Rādhā by her disapproving mother (10).

The poems in this section include two other episodes that show the changing nature of Kṛṣṇa's relations with the women of the village. The first of these is the classic *cīraharaṇa* episode, in which Kṛṣṇa steals the clothes of the herdsgirls—the Gopīs—as they bathe in the Yamunā. From his perch in a tree on the riverbank, Kṛṣṇa refuses to return the clothes until the women come out of the concealing water, and raise their concealing hands in supplication (11). In the second episode, Kṛṣṇa and his band of friends waylay the Gopīs on their way to market, and demand a toll to be paid (they say) in milk (12). Both episodes include some poems containing a didactic element, with Kṛṣṇa revealing to the Gopīs a portion of his divinity, and lecturing them on the path of *bhakti*, but they also provide the poet an opportunity to engage the child and his future mistresses in mildly scandalous (and delightfully idiomatic) banter.

1. "I want to milk, teach me to milk!
How to hold the bucket between my knees,
how to lead the calf to the teat;
How to tie the feet with a rope,
how to hold the cow still;
How the stream of milk
rings loud in the bucket;
tell me of all these things!"

"Evening's coming on, Kanhaiyā*;
you might get hurt by the cows,"
The cowherds tell Sūr's Śyām;
"Get up and milk the cows
in the morning."

2. He drives the cattle home from the woods
At dusk, his dark face dappled
with dust from the cattle's hooves.
By the peacock-feather in his hair, a black curl dangles
like a bee that's reached its goal:
It sips the nectar of his lotus-face;
it clings; it refuses to fly.
At his breast he wears a necklace
of pearls, a feast for the Goose of the Creator.
The Lord runs with the sons of cowherds,
one with them in color and caste,
one with them in stature and age.
(Sūrdās dotes on this *līlā* of his Lord:
a man may sing its praises and live.)

3. This same Hari drapes a blanket 'round his shoulders
and goes barefoot to drive the herds to graze.

Lord of the Three Worlds
Lord of the Four Quarters
Lord of man and woman

Lord of bird and beast
feared
by Sun and Moon;
He fills the meditations of Śiva and Brahmā;
He soothes the triple sorrows of his devotees;
  and for their sake
    he takes on a human form.

Sūrdās says,
He of whom the Vedas sing "Neti!"
  wanders now from grove to grove.

4. Sleep came to Śyām and he slumbered.
His mother arose and laid them both down,
  then busied herself in her work.
She bid the others be silent,
  calling each softly by name;
And none dare speak loudly
  lest Balrām and Mohan* awake.
Śiva, Sanaka and the rest, none reach the goal,
  though they meditate morning and night;
But the Lord of Sūrdās, *brahmaṇ* eternal,
  sleeps now in Nanda's house.

## *Kālīdamana: The Defeat of Kāliya*

5. Then the child Kṛṣṇa jumped out of bed:
"Mother, where are you?
  Why did you leave me alone?"
Nanda awoke, and Yaśodā awoke,
  and they called him to their side.
"You were asleep, what woke you up?"
  they asked as they lit the lamp.
"In my dream, somebody pushed me
  and I plunged into the Yamunā-dah!"
Yaśodā said to Sūr's Śyām:
  "Don't be afraid, my love."

6. He tore himself free in anger
As his friends all stood and watched,
and he ran to climb the *Kadamba*-tree.
The gang clapped their hands and laughed:
"Śyām, you ran away! He's got you scared!"
Śrīdāmā ran home, crying
"I'm going to tell Yaśodā!"
"Friend, friend!" Śyām called him back.
"Here, come and get your ball!"
Sūr's Śyām tucked the yellow cloth between his knees
and plunged into the deep!

7. When Śyām stretched long his limbs
And the Snake knew its own body bursting,
it cried out "Mercy, mercy!"

This cry the Lord of Mercy heard,
and drew back at once;
For this was the cry of Draupadī
when he once spun long her sari;
And this was the cry of Gajarāja
when he left Garuḍa to save him;
And this was the cry of the Pāṇḍavas
when he saved them from the flames;
This cry the Lord could not bear,
so merciful is he.

Sūr's Lord made small again his limbs
seeing the Serpent so shattered.

## *Dāvānala-pāna: The Swallowing of the Forest-fire*

8. Amazed at the sight, the people exclaim:
"Earth and sky alike were aflame,
fire spreading in great, bounding strides;

There was no rain; no-one brought water;
  what made it stop?
It burst so fiercely upon the forest!
  Why did it go out?"

"Oh, you know these grass-fires,"
  laughed Gopāl*;
"They're over almost before they've begun."

Listen, Sūr, to the difference
  between what the Lord *does*, and what the Lord *says*;
    such are the games the Lord plays.

## *The Meeting of Rādhā and Kṛṣṇa*

*9.* Śyām the Black says:
  "Who are you, white girl?

  Where do you live,
    who's your father,
      why haven't I seen you in the streets of Braj?"

  "And why should I come to Braj?
  I always play at my father's house;
  And I always hear of this Nanda's son
    who runs around stealing butter."

  "What could I steal from you?
    Come on, let's go
                play."

  The Lord of Sūr,
    Sovereign among lovers,
      seduced simple Rādhā with his words.

*10.* "Why do you keep going to *their* house?"

  When she's home her mother scolds her,
    but she's not a bit afraid.

"Rādhā-Kṛṣṇa, Kṛṣṇa-Rādhā,
It's all over Braj,
it's so shameful!
You're the daughter of the great Vṛṣabhānu;
but *that* one has no caste, no rank.
Stay away from Gokul!
Haven't you had your fill
of shame?"

The mother lectures the daughter,
but the daughter wavers not;
she only smiles.

### *Cīra-haraṇa: The Clothes-Stealing*

11. Kṛṣṇa, give us back our clothes!
You carried them into that *kadamba* tree
and left us here, naked, in the water!
We can't come out like this,
we'd be so ashamed;
You can keep our blouses,
and keep our garlands,
just throw us back our skirts!
Oh don't keep saying that same shocking thing—
"Women,
come out naked!"
Sūr's Śyām, show a little pity;
it's getting cold.

### *Dāna-līlā: The Gift*

12. Don't ask for things we'll never give you!
Every time you catch a girl alone in the woods,
you run to block her path;
On road, and riverbank, and narrow trail,
you plague us with your silly patter!

Who ever taught you you could ask for a thing like this!
Well, we can tell
you won't be content
'til we've told you a thing or two:
You just can't have the thing you want,
but you can have all the milk you can drink!
First go get it, Mohan,*
from somebody else,
and then *we* might give you a call!
Now stop being such a naughty little boy
with us, Sūr's Śyām!

## *Govardhana-līlā: The Episode of Mount Govardhana*

*13.* "Believe what I say!
If you care for the Land of Braj,
then worship Govardhana!
No matter how much you take from your cows,
*they'll* go on giving you milk;
What did *Indra* ever do for you?
He's a crutch; give him up!
If you hope to get everything
you've ever prayed for,
then listen to what I say,"
Said Sūr's Lord to the herdsmen,
"for I swear what I say is true."

*14.* "That Mountain looks so much like Śyām . . .
So hungrily it feasts,
stretching out its thousand arms;
And this child standing here, holding Nanda's hand—
he's the very same form as the Mountain!"

To little Rādhā her friend, Lalita, says:
"See the Form!

The same earrings,
the same garland,
the same yellow mantle;
The Mountain's splendour is as the beauty of Śyām,
Śyām's beauty is matched by the Mountain!"

There was a woman, Badaraulī,
a servant in Vṛṣabhānu's house,
who set out an offering of food;
The Mountain stretched its arm
down into the house,
and took it.

Little Rādhā stood stunned by the beauty of it all,
as little Śyām fixed his eyes upon her;
The Beloved succumbed to the glances of desire
cast sidelong by the Lord of Sūrdās.

## *Indra's Revenge*

*15.* These Braj-folk have forgotten me!
A fine thing! The offerings for *my* sacrifice;
they gave it all to the Mountain!
The insolent little beasts!
I don't know what's got into them;
Why, I'm the Lord of thirty-three *crores* of Gods,
and they know it, and still they ignore me!
Well I won't leave a cowherd on the face of this Earth,
for they didn't deliver my due.
Listen, Sūr:
when *I* begin to strike
what help is that Mountain going to be?

*16.* "Now *you* save us, Nanda's son!
It was you who told us
not to worship the Raingod;
well, it's a hard rain falling out there now.

The Braj-folk look to you
as a *cakora* looks to the Moon:
don't let us down."

"Listen:
Don't be afraid,
don't close your eyes,
just watch me pick up that Mountain
on the tips of my fingers.
Yes, Indra in his pride has brought down the floods,
has massed the black clouds on every side,"
Declared Sūr's Lord,
"but I'll protect you;
you'll never feel a drop of that rain!"

17. "Oh don't let that Mountain
fall off of Śyām's hand!"
One thought in the mind of every man in Braj,
and it strikes a mighty fear in their hearts.
The herdsmen race to prop the Mountain with their staffs,
leaping and plunging in their haste,
For the Mountain is mighty, and Śyām so frail.

But seven days he bore it on his hand,
until the heavens rained themselves dry;
And thus the son of Nanda saved the herdsmen and their wives
from the rain that streamed down from Indra's clouds,
A rain so hard it tore from their roots
the two tree-cursed sons of Kubera;
Thus the Lord of Sūr broke Indra's pride,
and saved the land of Braj by the strength of his hand.

18. "Your arms are so strong!"
Says Yaśodā to Kṛṣṇa,
glancing time and again at his arms.
"It didn't hurt a bit,"
he says;
"The cowherds helped
And so did my father Nanda; together,
they braced the Mountain
with their staffs.
How could *I* lift Govardhana,
huge and heavy as it is?"

Sūr's Lord explained himself so,
but his mother gazed yet in awe. . . .

## IV. MURALĪDHARA: The Flutebearer

In this section we leave behind Sūr's special province—Kṛṣṇa's childhood—and move into the much-travelled territory of the loves of Kṛṣṇa and the Gopīs. The theme was a favorite (perhaps *the* favorite) among the poets of medieval North India, but if Sūr added little that was truly novel, he handled the traditional material with extraordinary skill.

These poems need less glossing than most—unless, of course, we succumb to the temptations of allegorical interpretation. There is indeed an esoteric core to Kṛṣṇa's erotic *līlās*, and there are *padas* (although seldom the better ones) in which Sūr explicitly addresses the metaphysical aspects. But there are many others in which the mystery is allowed to remain, simply, a mystery. Whatever else they may imply, these are love poems; I think we do them no injustice by reading them as such.

The affair follows a classic sequence: attraction, union, separation. If we disregard the verbal foreplay of earlier episodes, the sequence begins with the flute-songs. Kṛṣṇa plays a plain, bamboo flute: a cowherd's toy—but then Kṛṣṇa is no ordinary cowherd. His flute is irresistible; it charms everything in the forest of Brindāban (1); above all, it charms the Gopīs (2).

For a time they resist its pull; they even come to resent it, and for two good reasons. First, the flute is a threat. The Gopīs are married women, they have parents, in-laws, reputations; they can see where the flute must lead them. But at the same time they are jealous: the flute spends more time at Kṛṣṇa's lips than they do; indeed, sometimes it seems that Kṛṣṇa has become a slave to his own music (3, 4, 6).

On a night of the full moon in autumn, the flute's song becomes too much to bear. The women leave their husbands' beds, and gather in a grove on the Yamunā bank; there they dance, with Kṛṣṇa, in the *rāsa-maṇḍala*. The dance is a favorite theme of painters as well as poets. At its center stands Kṛṣṇa, alone or accompanied by Rādhā. He plays his flute, and to its music turns the surrounding circle of dancing figures. Half of them are fair-skinned Gopīs; the other half—and here lies a part of the mystery—are duplicates of that same, cloud-dark Kṛṣṇa who stands at the circle's hub. He both dances and directs the dance, and each of the Gopīs believes that he dances with her and her alone (9, 10).

The night (or is it more than one?) is long and eventful. Between bouts of love, moonlit chases, and an occasional discourse on the meaning of the mystery, Kṛṣṇa and the Gopīs relax in the cooling waters of the Yamunā (11). Sūr complicates the traditional story with a somewhat mysterious wedding between Rādhā and Kṛṣṇa but it is destined to be a brief union. The *rāsa-līlā* is the climax of Kṛṣṇa's life in Brindāban. Soon he departs for Mathurā, to take up at last that task which ostensibly prompted his incarnation: the slaying of Kaṃsa.

The Gopīs' suffering in his absence is presented for the most part in a stylized, classic fashion. The fevers of *viraha*, of love-in-separation, followed a course set by convention long before Sūr's day. Metaphors extended nearly to breaking-point were characteristic of the genre (13, 14). Yet even in the rather clichéd realm of *viraha* Sūr found a loophole, a clear space for creation. He seized upon an episode from the *Bhāgavata*, the mission of Uddhava to the Gopīs, and expanded it into what was to become a genre in Hindi verse, the so-called *bhramargīt* or "bee-songs."

The episode begins when Kṛṣṇa, now in Mathurā, sends his friend Uddhava to Brindāban, with messages for those whom Kṛṣṇa has left behind. Uddhava, a somewhat over-earnest *paṇḍit*, patiently (and naively) attempts to console the Gopīs with the argument that since Kṛṣṇa is in fact the supreme Lord, and therefore the dweller in every soul, he can never truly leave them. The proper remedy for the suffering of *viraha* is, he says, to "abandon the *saguṇa*, think on the *nirguṇa*" (15)—that is, to cease thinking of Kṛṣṇa as an embodied god, and think of him rather as the formless, all-encompassing soul of the universe.

Sūr's Gopīs spread their scathing reply over some seven hundred extraordinarily witty poems, all contributing to more or less the same message: Uddhava is a fool (16); abstractions are no substitute for flesh (17); the Gopīs have no interest in enlightenment, they just want their man back. Failing that, they find the agony of love in separation infinitely preferable to any dispassionate philosophy preached by a bookish *paṇḍit*. Uddhava, come to convert the Gopīs, is himself converted to the path of *bhakti*; he abandons his mission and returns to Mathurā. The Gopīs remain in Brindāban, waiting as before, for a Kṛṣṇa who never returns to his life as a cowherd in the land of Braj (18).

1. When Hari puts the flute to his lips

The still are moved and the moving stilled;
Winds die, the river Yamunā stops,
crows fall silent and the deer fall senseless;
bird and beast are stunned by his splendor.
A cow, unmoving,
dangles a glassblade from her teeth;
Even the wise can no longer
hold firm their own minds.

Sūrdās says: Lucky the man
who knows such joy.

2. Honeybee, Kṛṣṇa's flute is honey-sweet.
We hear, and our very breath is immersed in love
like a wick immersed in oil,
shining hot and bright,
And the moths see the flame,
and destroy their greedy bodies;

Like a fish who yearns for a sliver of meat,
  and seizes a bamboo hook;
    a crooked thorn,
It twists in the heart
  and then will not come out.
As a hunter sounds a horn
  and draws a herd of deer;
Aims an arrow,
  looses it,
    and threads their hearts upon the shaft.
As a *ṭhag* lures a pilgrim
  with *laḍḍūs* sweet with wine,
Makes him drunk and trusting,
  takes his money and his life;
Just so, Honeybee,
  Hari takes our love by deceit.

Sūr's Lord tore up the sweet sugarcane
  and planted a garden of longing.

3. The flute has become everything to him!
Now you just try to drive her away,
  she who's taken Nanda's son in her power!
Sometimes on his lip,
  sometimes on his hand he lays her,
    sometimes he clasps her to his heart and sings;
Sometimes he plays himself into a trance
  and she lies there dangling from his lips.
She for whom he's so lost his senses,
  how will you get her away from him?
Sūr's Śyām's forgotten us all;
  now how could he forget *her*?

4. So Hari clings to his flute!
   Why not?
So she casts a sudden spell
   when he draws her to his lips!
      Why not?
So he cups her in his hand!
   So she makes him bow his neck!
      Why not?
So she locks his body in *tribhaṅga*,
   and she robs him of his mind!
      Why not?
So he'll ever be her slave! Why not?
   He *is* a cowherd,
      she *is* a flute;
He never lets her go, Sūr's Śyām,
   as he pipes his grazing herds from grove
      to grove.

5. Sisters, hear the tale of her ancestry!
Thus was her father, and her mother thus,
   see now this her *karma*:

They come when the rains fall
   full upon the earth,
      filling pond and river,
(Though the *cātaka* despairs
   of a single drop);
The Earth gives birth to them all,
   yet herself stays ever virgin.
They are born in her,
   and die in her,
      but bear her yet no love!

In such a family was this bitch born—
   let me sing you her praises!
Sūr says,
   May the hearing cheer you
      as I am cheered in the telling.

6. Gopāl* does love that flute,
Sisters! Though she makes our Nanda's-son
dance so many dances;
Makes him stand upon one foot,
and orders him about,
Bends his tender body to her will,
crooks his waist at her command—
He's a slave now, our wise man; a cripple!
She bows the neck of Him who bore the Mountain!
Lying couched upon his lip,
she compels his fingers to caress;
Furrowed brow, wide-eyed and nostrils flared,
she turns his wrath on us
And thinking him happy
even for a second, Sūr,
she shakes him head to toe.

7. Śyām, I might as well tell you:
I can't bear this talk
that travels from house to house.
My father takes up his sword, enraged;
my brother runs out, bent on murder;
and my mother—
She says I'm a disgrace to my sex,
she prays that no-one on this earth
give birth to another girl.

I beg of you one thing only:
don't come again to these streets;
But if you come, O don't let the honeyed notes of that flute
reach my ears.
By thought and word and deed, I swear to you,
my heart and mind both cling to you;
O Lord of Sūrdās, you are the Dweller in my heart;
why can't you let it be content?

8. Your lover is in your power, my friend,
As the shadow is held close
in the power of the body.
Your love is beyond explaining!
As the *cakora* is in the power
of the Autumn moon,
and the *cakravāka* in the power of the Sun;
As the bee is in the power of the tightly closed lotus,
so is Śyām,
all-knowing,
in your power.
As the *cātaka* is in the power
of the raindrop out of *svāti*,
as the breath is in the power of the body;
So is Sūr's Lord so completely in your power;
look into your heart
and know.

9. Black tresses tangle in earring
Yellow cape catches on nosering
within a single garland, two bodies entwine.

Breath clings to breath
Eye clings to eye
black cloud enshrouds a brighter beauty.

They dance, each surpassing the other;
They embrace, each delighting in the other;
"*Tā! Tā! Thei! Thei!*" they cry out the *tāl*.

Sūr's beloved Lord
In the great Circle of his lovers
takes the border of a woman's skirt
to wipe the sweat from his limbs.

*10.* O Mother!
It was like lightning flashing
cloud to black cloud,
Lightning 'midst cloud and cloud amidst lightning:
Śyām gleaming black amidst the fair girls of Braj!
And the jasmine scent on the Yamunā bank,
heavy in the Autumn eve;
The forms of our bodies lit by the moon,
its liquor in every limb;
Passion's dance, led by passion's prince,
and the village-girls roused to joy!
And he,
Form of all forms,
a black cloud,
clouding our minds with his bliss. . . .
We danced like birds,
like parrot and peacock and sparrow and finch;
darting, like the fish;
stately, like the elephant;
O Sūr, which of us can say
what it was like with Mohan?
Enchantresses
enchanted
by the Enchanter.

*11.* Rādhā raises lovely splashes in the River.
Saffroned breasts slip from her bodice,
across them her hair hangs wet;
Blue-stoned earrings dangle at her cheeks.
Her hips sway slowly, like an elephant's;
a girdle swings loosely at her tiger-thin waist.
The Play goes on, in the waters of the Yamunā;
immersed in love, swamped with passion,
She rests her lovely neck on the arm of Nanda's son
and delights in her own good fortune.

(The hosts of gods, delighted, rain flowers
  and the kettle-drums of heaven sound with joy;
Sūr's Syām and Syāmā play out their passion
  and thrash the River's surface into waves.)

*12.* I will go with the dark one.

What is to happen, may it happen now.
I care not for fame or shame,
  I fear
    no-one.
Let them be angry! What can they do?
I'll give up my life at the first word from them!
Yes, I'll throw it all away,
I'll keep only my vow:
  Oh when will I plant again
    the seed of his love?

Sūr, what is this fragile earth?
  I will enter my beloved's house in the sky.
What is this Braj but a pond to play in?
  I will worship Nanda's son,
    and know a fuller joy.

*13.* My eyes have sown a creeping vine of separation

And watered by the streams of my tears,
  my friend,
    its roots sink all the way to Hell.
It spreads,
  as is the way with vines;
    its shadow grows dark and dense;
How can I control it now,
  my friend,
    when it spreads all through my flesh?

Who knows what lies
in another's heart?
My vine keeps changing
from one moment to the next;
When Sūr's Lord left,
he left behind the bitter fruit of his love.

14. Yamunā looks so black and sunken,
O Traveller! Tell Hari
how his River burns with fever.
She slips to the earth
from her mountain-bed;
waves tremble across her body.
The sands are arrayed
like powdered drugs upon her shores;
sweat flows from her in streams.
Her hair lies strewn
as reeds upon the riverbank,
her unkempt *sari* soiled with rivermud;
Grieving, she wanders aimlessly,
like the black bees that drone above her banks
day and night;
Day and night, the cries of waterfowl
echo her own.
Sūr's Lord,
as is the River
so are we.

15. "Gopīs, hear Hari's message!
Meditate, concentrate within yourselves;
this is his command!
Eternal is he, completely indestructible,
contained within the bodies of all.
Without knowledge of truth there can be no liberation;
it is gained by singing *Veda* and *Purāṇa*.

Abandon the *saguṇa,* think on the *nirguṇa*
with all your mind,
with all your soul;
By that device pass beyond separation;
thus will you meet *Brahm.*"

Hearing Uddhav's cruel message
the Gopīs were saddened.
Sūr says: Who can drive away separation?
Who can drown without water?

*16.* That bitch Yoga, she won't sell in Braj!

Who will give pearls for radish-leaves?
That's how it'll be,
Udhau,
With this trade of yours!
Oh it's big enough for the bellies
of those you bought it from;
But who will abandon the grape
for the bitter *nīm*-fruit?
Sing us the praises of Sūr's dark lord;
Who will tend this *nirgun* of yours?

*17.* "In what land does this *nirgun* live?
Explain *that* to us, Uddhava!
No,
we're not laughing at you,
tell us truly:
Who's his father,
who's his mother,
who's his woman,
who's his slave?
What's he look like,
what's he wear,
what pleasures does he seek?

Don't fool us poor,
  simple milkmaids,
Or it'll be bad *karma* for you!"

Uddhava was struck speechless,
  says Sūr,
    it just totally destroyed his mind.

*18.* In this pain
My body will thrash itself to death.

Will my lovely black cloud, oh sister,
  never come to embrace me again?
Will he and his friends, my lovely one,
  never show me their supple-limbed grace again?
Will my Mohan* never put flute to lips,
  never take my mind away,
    never call my name again?
Will he never go with me
  to the overarching wood again,
    never send the messenger
      to call for me again?
Will he never take my arm in passion again,
  never fall at my feet
    and drive away my sulk again?

For this alone
  does the breath stay in this
    clay shell of a body:
Will Hari ever let me see him again?

(Sūrdās does not give up, does not
  abandon life, for this:
    the Beloved will come to Braj
      again.)

## V. SŪRAPRABHU: Sūr's Lord

Not all the *padas* in the *Sūrsāgar* concern the Kṛṣṇa-līlā. Of those that do not, a few are addressed to Viṣṇu's other incarnations: the one included here (4) relates an episode in which Rāma, the seventh *avatāra,* wins the hand of Sītā by breaking a famous bow. It is an unusual poem; the bow-breaking episode served other poets as a vehicle for extolling Rāma's might, but Sūr finds it rather an opportunity to describe Sītā's Rādhā-like concern for the young hero.

The remainder of the poems in this section are *vinaya-pada,* poems of "prayer" or "petition." Like Tulsī's famous *Vinaya Patrikā,* these verses purport to be humble poems of petition, addressed to an all-merciful god by an unworthy sinner. Sūr, however, exhibits a constitutional inability to stay as solemn as the material seems to demand. We have seen elsewhere that Sūr delights in playing with his audience; this is no less true when the audience happens to be God himself. In the best of these poems, the poet undercuts the posture of humility by declaring himself the greatest sinner in history, the king of all sinners everywhere. He flaunts his sin before Kṛṣṇa, promising new excesses of debauchery; he dares Kṛṣṇa to put his powers of salvation to the ultimate test: if the Lord can save Sūr, then he can truly save anyone.

It is a delightfully outrageous ploy, calculated to seize God's attention by any means possible, to storm the doors of salvation by sheer rhetorical force. But in the last poem of the section, the strategy changes: Sūr stalks his god, lulls him with flattery—then pounces through a moment's chink in the Lord's armor.

1. Now I have danced too much, Gopāl!*
Robed in anger and desire,
  a garland of passions at my throat;

The bells of illusion encircle my ankles
and chime sweet sounds of slander.
My mind, become a drum dusted by delusion,
beats an inchoate cadence,
Echoes through my body its tones of longing,
played to a dozen different beats.
With the sash of *māyā* bound at my waist,
and the *tilak* of greed on my brow,
I summon up a thousand artful steps,
across sea and solid land,
beyond Time.

Vanquish all this,
Sūr's sinful ignorance,

O Nandalāl.*

2. Today I will surpass them all,
surpass those sinners one by one!

It's you or me, Kṛṣṇa;
and I'll fight, trusting in my strength,
For I am a sinner of seven generations;
fallen, I will be freed!
Now I want to dance naked!
I shall strip you
of your honor—
Why do you flinch? O I've got you now,
Hari-hard-as-Diamond!
Sūr the Fallen will rise only, Lord,
when laughingly you give him
the flowers of your grace.

3. Kṛṣṇa,
Turn back my cow!
Day and night she strays from the path;
she is strong and I cannot hold her.

Ever hungry, never filled, she tramples her way
through the fields and forest of Veda.
She drinks at the eighty *ghāṭs*
yet her thirst is never quenched;
I give her food of the six flavors,
and yet she is not pleased.
She eats the evil and forbidden,
beyond describing,
And she eats the sky and the mountains,
eats the river and the forest
and is not filled.
With her blue hooves she churns the earth
of the fourteen worlds;
What world then can hold her?
Red-eyed, cruel and arrogant,
she fears no-one,
Fighting even the Three Strands,
goring gods and men,
Bearing away men's minds
on the white horns atop her brow.
All the sages try to stop her—
try, and then tire;
Tell me then,

How can Sūr control her,
O Source of All Grace?

4. She gazes at Rāma's body.
"Keep him safe, for me,"
she prays to Brahmā.
"My father's so terribly strict
about this thing with Śiva's bow;
but Rāma's just a boy!
Why should *he* bear the burden of that bow,
Sisters,
I ask you: Why?"

Knowing Sītā's doubts, Sūr's Lord
took the bow upon his fingertips. . . .
At its breaking, the great kings there assembled all
scattered and hid,
as the stars flee the rising sun.

5. Hari-Hara-Śaṅkara, *namo namo*!
Serpent-sleeper, serpent-wearer;
nectar-giver, poison-drinker.
Blue-throated, blue-hued;
lover, Love's slayer.
Crowned by the crescent moon, crowned by
the moon-spotted
peacock-feather;
Yamunā's beloved, Gaṅgā's bearer.
Adorned in cattle's dust or corpse's ash;
bull-rider, cattle-grazer.
Never born, nothing desiring, none opposing: this is
the One;
these, the many incarnate.
Sūr says:
They are the same
in form and name and attribute;
only their followers create distinctions.

6. With your tiny little face, and your tiny arms and legs,
with a tiny bit of butter on your tiny little hand;
You talk a tiny bit, and you fret a tiny bit,
and you're a tiny bit delighted at the tiniest little
thing.
Your tiny little cheeks and your tiny little teeth
form a tiny little smile that
captivates us all.
Just a tiny, oh a tiny little closer,
Lord, let Sūr approach;
And with a tiny bit of grace, grant me
a tiny bit of shelter.

# EPILOGUE: THE LAST POEM

Sūr was blind: on this, at least, do all commentaries on Sūr's life agree; and all exhibit a fascination with the paradox of the blind seer. As the eye dims, does the ear grow sharper? Do patterns of sound rise up to compensate for the loss of patterns seen? Or does the mind make patterns of its own in the darkness, unseen by the man of normal vision? "He does have eyes," Akbar is made to say, "but they are with God." Such is the explanation offered in the *Caurāsī vaiṣṇavan kī vārtā.* The text returns to the theme in the final scene of Sūr's life. Viṭṭhalnāth, Vallabha's son and successor and Sūr's own *guru,* approaches the poet's deathbed:

> *And then Viṭṭhalnāth asked: Sūrdās-jī, where are your eyes now? And Sūr answered, with a poem:*
>
> Drunk with the colors of this joy
>   my eyes dart like birds;
> They are lovely now, so clear, so sharp;
>   this cage will not hold them a second more.
> They flutter about my head;
>   snared, they thrash
>     in the gold ring at my ear.
> Sūr's eyes are trapped in the vision of His darkness,
>     else they'd fly off
>       now.
>
> *As he said this, Sūrdās left his body and entered the* līlā *of his Lord. Afterwards, Viṭṭhalnāth gathered his disciples and returned to Govardhana.*

# NOTES TO PART TWO

## *A Word on the Poems*

1. There is a tradition that views the *Sūrsāgar* as a Hindi translation of the *Bhāgavata Purāṇa,* and therefore a more or less connected narrative. This is not, however, a view shared by any significant number of scholars—although it should be noted that Brajeśvar Varmā, offering what is decidedly a minority position, argues that *certain* episodes of the *Sūrsāgar* were indeed intended to be read as continuous narrative. (*Sūradāsa: jīvana aura kāvya kā adhyayana,* Allahabad, 1950.) Varmā's arguments are provocative, and have some merit; but even Varmā does not make similar claims for the greater part of Sūr's work.
2. Compilers of verses from the *Sūrsāgar* have traditionally devised their own categories and subcategories. I have taken advantage of this customary freedom here. The section titles are in each case epithets of Kṛṣṇa.

## *Maṅgalācaraṇa: Benediction:*

*Sabhā* 1.

## *I. Nandanandana: Nanda's Son*

1. *Sabhā* 653; Caturvedī p. 86.
2. *Sabhā* 665; Caturvedī p. 105. Line 4 of the Caturvedī version ("and how is it built" etc.) is lacking in the *Sabhā* edition. Caturvedī argues convincingly for its inclusion. I have taken some liberties with the translation—rendering "Nanda" as "Father," *lākh* (literally "a hundred thousand") as "a fortune," etc.—in an attempt to retain as far as possible the lullabye quality of the original.

3. *Sabhā* 670; Caturvedī p. 128. I have split the verse (the other half appearing below as Number 5) to provide a narrative framework for Number 4, which is by far the most interesting poem in the Pūtanā series.
4. *Sabhā* 673; Caturvedī p. 130. For discussion of the verse, see Chapter II.
5. *Sabhā* 670; Caturvedī p. 128. See note 3 above.
6. *Sabhā* 680; Caturvedī p. 137. The original consists of four rhymed couplets. The meter is much too long to retain the couplet-structure in English; each of the four *stanzas* of the translation, however, corresponds to a couplet in the original. See Glossary under *pān*. The King is Kaṃsa.
7. *Sabhā* 681; Caturvedī p. 120. The poem is a spectacular example of the "rediscovered episode" (Chapter II). Kṛṣṇa's pose is interpreted in three different ways within the same poem. To the people of Braj, there is nothing unusual: they see only a child sucking his toe. The gods, however, remember the last time Kṛṣṇa-Viṣṇu adopted this pose (see introduction to this section), and assume that the iconographic pose portends another *pralaya*, universal dissolution. But in the final line, we discover that the truth lies somewhere in between: Kṛṣṇa is really drawing back his baby-foot to give Sakaṭāsura his deathblow. This last line has occasioned some confusion. While the *Sabhā* edition includes it in the Sakaṭāsura poems, Caturvedī does not; Dhīrendra Varmā gives a Hindi prose translation of the last line, but does not comment on its connection with the Sakaṭāsura episode, although he gives a lengthy entry on Sakaṭāsura in his glossary which would appear to refer to this poem (*Sūrsāgara-Sāra, saṭīka,* Allahabad, 1972). Pandey and Zide have translated the line as "Sūrdās says that he knows what will happen and so is worried"—a translation that bears no visible relationship to the Hindi text. (S.M. Pandey and N.H. Zide, trans., *The Poems of Sūrdās,*

xeroxed instructional material, South Asia Language and Area Center, University of Chicago, 1962). See Glossary under *pralaya*; *Banyan*. I have rendered *sahasau* as "a hundred"; literally it is "a thousand," but what is significant is "a very large number," and the alliteration of "hundred hoods" at least partially captures the texture of the original line (*seṣa sakuci sahasau* etc.).

8. *Sabhā* 692; Caturvedī p. 131.
9. *Sabhā* 675; Caturvedī p. 132. The original consists of sixteen short couplets; each stanza of the translation corresponds to two couplets of the original.
10. *Sabhā* 683; Caturvedī p. 112. The comparison of eyes to black bees trapped in the night-closing lotus may seem extravagant, but is in fact something of a cliché. The original stretches the comparison even farther (I have toned it down somewhat for the Western audience): the eyes are not simply "black," but "black, white, and red (cornered)." For the other similes, see Glossary under Kūrma (for Churning); Brahmā; and Śeṣa (for "Serpent"). The latter, it should be noted, is here not a threatening but a protective figure.
11. *Sabhā* 696; Caturvedī p. 145. Here as in the Pūtanā series, I have split a long narrative verse and used it to "bracket" a more interesting poem. The other half of this verse is to be found in 14 (below).
12. *Sabhā* 694; Caturvedī p. 142. For discussion of the poem, see Chapter I.
13. *Sabhā* 696; Caturvedī p. 145. See note 11 (above). The last line is somewhat obscure.
14. *Sabhā* 704; Caturvedī p. 152. My thanks to George Saliba, an authority on astrological systems, for assistance in deciphering the terminology of this verse. I have elsewhere discussed the prosodic aspects of the poem (Chapter IV); the original provides a virtuoso display of metrical and alliterative patterning, building up to the final

prophecy: that Kṛṣṇa will be "black." There is, I think, more than a little irony in the form of this final "prophecy." In the *Bhāgavata* version, the sage Garga's ceremonial naming of the child (clearly the episode referred to here) also mentions Kṛṣṇa's color—"This your son took a body in three successive *yugas*, each time of a different complexion, white, red, and yellow. Now he is dark-complexioned." (N. Raghunathan, trans., *Srimad Bhāgavatam*, Madras, 1976, vol. II, p. 191). Sūr, however, innovatively links the prophecy with the planet Saturn—associated in Indian astrology *and* folklore with two things: the color black (al-Beruni, *Elements of Astrology*, trans. R. Ramsay Wright, London, 1934, p. 240), and bad luck (cf. the Hindi proverb *sanīcar ānā*). Kṛṣṇa, the astrologer intones, has the "bad luck" to be born black! For another instance of Sūr's satirical treatment of Kṛṣṇa's dark complexion, see Chapter III.

15. *Sabhā* 718; Caturvedī p. 172.
16. *Sabhā* 728; Caturvedī p. 194. The verse is heavily alliterative (e.g., line 1: *kilakata kānha ghuṭurubani āvata;* line 6, *kari kari pratipada pratimani basudhā. . . ).*
17. *Sabhā* 734; Caturvedī p. 201. For discussion, see Chapter III.
18. *Sabhā* 743; Caturvedī p. 214. For an explanation of the "three steps," see Glossary under Vāmana.
19. *Sabhā* 744; Caturvedī p. 215. For discussion see Chapter I.
20. *Sabhā* 745; Caturvedī p. 216. The poem is in the form of a *daśāvatāra stotra*, a sequential praise of the ten incarnations (here cut short at number eight) of Viṣṇu. For discussion see Chapter III. For the tales of individual incarnations, see Glossary under Matsya; Kūrma; Varāha; Narasiṃha; Vāmana; Paraśurāma; Rāma. Also see Jāmbavat.
21. *Sabhā* 759; Caturvedī pp. 237, 251. For discussion see Chapter III. See Glossary under Kūrma.

22. *Sabhā* 746; Caturvedī p. 217. For discussion see Chapter IV. See Glossary under Brahmā; Śiva; Garuḍa; Narasiṃha.
23. *Sabhā* 762; Caturvedī p. 253. For discussion see Chapter III. See Glossary under Kūrma; Vāmana; Sea.
24. *Sabhā* 782; Caturvedī p. 273. For discussion see Chapter III. See Glossary under Varāha.
25. *Sabhā* 788; Caturvedī p. 245. For discussion see Chapter III. See Glossary under Śiva; Kāma. The point of the poem is that the Gopī almost—but not quite—realizes the truth declared in the final line: Śiva (Hara) and Kṛṣṇa (Hari, Śyāma) are ultimately one and the same.
26. *Sabhā* 822; Caturvedī p. 326. For discussion of the central figure, see Chapter III. See Glossary under Kūrma, Neti.

## *II. Mākhan-cor: The Butterthief*

1. *Sabhā* 886; Caturvedī p. 412.
2. *Sabhā* 764; Caturvedī p. 256. "Nymphs . . . to tempt a sage": a common motif in Indian mythology is that of the human sage who, by virtue of asceticism and meditation, achieves power rivalling that of the Gods—who retaliate by sending a woman to seduce the sage, and thus destroy the source of his power.
3. *Sabhā* 793; Caturvedī p. 283. "Haladhara": Balarāma.
4. *Sabhā* 802; Caturvedī p. 301. The poem is a masterpiece of alliteration: for example, the first three lines of the original ("The two boys . . . each to each"): *biharata bibidha bālaka saṅga/ḍagani ḍagamaga pagani ḍolata, dhūri dhūsara aṅga/calata maga, paga bajati paijani, parasapara kilakāta.* The "earrings" simile is probably the most obscure in the *Sūrsāgar.* It apparently alludes to the episode in which Indra (Bāsava, Vāsava) attempted to prevent the Aśvins—the radiant twins, children of the

Sun—from partaking of the *soma* sacrifice. In retaliation, the sage Cyavana (the Life-poet?) called forth a demon named Mada ("intoxication"), and Indra was forced to relent. Hence the highly complex linkage: the earrings (golden, like the Aświns) are "swaying"—as, we may assume, were the Aświns when they finally imbibed the intoxicating *soma*. For an explanation of the Siṃhikā simile, see Chapter III. See Glossary under Siṃhikā; Rāhu.

5. *Sabhā* 809; Caturvedī p. 309. The motif is a common one in Indian literature: a child asks for the moon, to play with (or to eat), and is tricked into accepting its reflection in a bowl of water.
6. *Sabhā* 816; Caturvedī p. 317. The narrator is Yaśodā. For discussion see Chapter II.
7. *Sabhā* 825; Caturvedī p. 329. The speaker is Yaśodā.
8. *Sabhā* 833; Caturvedī p. 371. For discussion see Chapter III.
9. *Sabhā* 839; Caturvedī p. 365. The poem follows the pattern of a *daśāvatāra stotra* (see note on poem number 20 of the preceding section): each heroic event mentioned by Balarāma was performed by Viṣṇu-Kṛṣṇa in an earlier incarnation.
10. *Sabhā* 866; Caturvedī p. 388. The point is that "little Kanhaiyā" is in fact (but wholly unknown to the Brahmin) the very Lord for whom the offering was intended.
11. *Sabhā* 872. For discussion of the famous "mud-eating" episode, see Chapter I.
12. *Sabhā* 879; Caturvedī p. 404.
13. *Sabhā* 880; Caturvedī p. 405.
14. *Sabhā* 883; Caturvedī p. 409.
15. *Sabhā* 940; Caturvedī p. 469. The implication is that Kṛṣṇa *did* tie the Gopī's braid to the bed—while the Gopī was otherwise occupied with her husband.
16. *Sabhā* 910; Caturvedī p. 439. The speakers are Yaśodā, and the Gopīs who have come to complain to her about Kṛṣṇa's thievery.

17. *Sabhā* 952; Caturvedī p. 483.
18. *Sabhā* 997. There are no Caturvedī readings for this and subsequent poems; only one volume of the Caturvedī edition was completed. For discussion of the "mortar-binding" episode, see Chapter I.
19. Sabhā 981. In this and the following poem, the speakers are the Gopīs who, seeing Kṛṣṇa punished by Yaśodā for stealing their butter, now regret having complained in the first place.
20. *Sabhā* 972. The lotus closes its petals at night, and bears a traditional enmity toward the moon. The reference to "pearls" in the last line is somewhat obscure.
21. *Sabhā* 998. "Haladhara": Balarāma.
22. *Sabhā* 1001. For an explanation of the episode, see Glossary under *Kubera.*
23. *Sabhā* 1002. The speakers are Kubera's sons, now released from their tree-forms; but it is only in the last line that we *realize* who is speaking.

## *III. Giridhara: The Mountainbearer*

1. *Sabhā* 1019.
2. *Sabhā* 1035. The poem is striking in its use of alliteration (e.g., line 2: "*sandhyā samaya sāṃvare mukha para,* . . ." and the final line: ". . . *jīvata jana jasa gāe*").
3. *Sabhā* 1071.
4. *Sabhā* 1133.
5. *Sabhā* 1135. For discussion of this poem, and of the episode in general, see Chapter II. See Glossary under *Kāliya.*
6. *Sabhā* 1157. For discussion, see Chapter II.
7. *Sabhā* 1174. The middle section, set off typographically in the translation, is framed by epanaphora in the original. The lines of this section, lines 3 through 7 of the original ("This cry . . . This cry"), begin:

   *yaha bānī . . .*
   *yahai bacana . . .*

*yahai bacana . . .*
*yahai bacana . . .*
*yaha bānī . . .*

Thus the lines beginning *yaha bānī*, "This voice/cry," contain Kṛṣṇa's reaction to the cry on *this* occasion, and at the same time frame the three lines of a "flashback," all of which begin with *yahai bacana*—synonymous with *yaha bānī*. The three *yahai bacana* lines range backward (and *forward*) over Viṣṇu-Kṛṣṇa's history, as the cries of Draupadī, Gajarāja, and the Pāṇḍavas (see Glossary) echo through time as a single cry for mercy, manifest now in the plea of Kāliya.

8. *Sabhā* 1216. In the common version of the episode, frequently seen in paintings, Kṛṣṇa instructs his companions, ringed in by the fire, to cover their eyes so that they will not see him draw the fire into his mouth and extinguish it.
9. *Sabhā* 1291.
10. *Sabhā* 2326. For discussion see Chapter III.
11. *Sabhā* 1406.
12. *Sabhā* 2080. "You just can't have. . . .": the original plays on the multiple meanings of *rasa*: aesthetic (or sexual) pleasure, and fluid (*gorasa*, "milk"): *jo rasa cāhau, so rasa nāhiṃ, gorasa piyau aghāī*—"The *rasa* you want, not that *rasa*; drink your fill of *gorasa*."
13. *Sabhā* 1439. See Glossary under Govardhana; also see introduction to this section.
14. *Sabhā* 1455. Throughout the poem, Kṛṣṇa is in fact in two places at once. In his child-form he stands beside Nanda, to all appearances a simple spectator; but at the same time he has taken on the enormous form of the spirit of the mountain.
15. *Sabhā* 1469. See Glossary under Indra.
16. *Sabhā* 1483.
17. *Sabhā* 1491.
18. *Sabhā* 1583.

## IV. *Muralīdhara: The Flutebearer*

1. *Sabhā* 1238.
2. *Sabhā* 4450.
3. *Sabhā* 1855.
4. *Sabhā* 1898. For a description of the *tribhaṅga* pose, see Chapter III. "He *is* a cowherd, she *is* a flute": *vai ahīra, vaha benu.* The Gopīs refer to Kṛṣṇa as an *Ahīra,* a cowherd by *caste.* The implication is: he's *only* a cowherd, she's *only* a flute, so why should we care, anyway?
5. *Sabhā* 1875. The poem is more or less a riddle, for which the answer is: the cursed *bamboo* flute.
6. *Sabhā* 1273. For discussion see Chapter III.
7. *Sabhā* 2302. The speaker is Rādhā.
8. *Sabhā* 2687. The speaker is a Gopī, addressing Rādhā. For a note on the metaphysical implications of the Rādhā-Kṛṣṇa relationship, see Introduction. See Glossary under Cakora; Cakravāka; Cātaka.
9. *Sabhā* 1767. *Tāl*: musical beat, rhythm; often *spoken* in very rapid, stylized syllables that represent the various sounds of the *tabla.*
10. *Sabhā* 1666. "Parrot and peacock and sparrow and finch": I have taken considerable liberties in substituting English bird-names, for reasons of euphony.
11. *Sabhā* 1778.
12. *Sabhā* 2286. The speaker is Rādhā.
13. *Sabhā* 3864.
14. *Sabhā* 3809. The speakers are Gopīs, sending a (tactfully oblique) message of their longing to Kṛṣṇa, who has now left for Mathurā.
15. *Sabhā* 4120. See Glossary under *nirguṇa; brahm;* Uddhava.
16. *Sabhā* 4282.
17. *Sabhā* 4249. Uddhava's point was that the ultimate reality is *nirguṇa*—without qualities, without form, undifferentiated. The Gopīs intentionally misunderstand,

insisting that God *must* have form, and origins, and desires.

18. *Sabhā* 4025.

## V. *Sūraprabhu: Sūr's Lord*

1. *Sabhā* 153. See Glossary under *māyā*.
2. *Sabhā* 134. "Surpass those sinners": the word "sinners" does not appear in the original, but is clear from context. "Hari-hard-as-Diamond": a play on words: *Hari-hīrā*.
3. *Sabhā* 56.
4. *Sabhā* 467. For discussion see Chapter II.
5. *Sabhā* 789. "Hara" and "Śaṅkara" are both epithets for Śiva. The pairs ("serpent-sleeper, serpent-wearer," etc.) each establish a correspondence between an epithet or attribute of Kṛṣṇa, and one of Śiva. "Never born, nothing desiring, none opposing—this is the One": Śiva, the prototypic *yogī*; "these, the many incarnate": Viṣṇu-Kṛṣṇa. See Glossary under Śiva.
6. *Sabhā* 768.

## *Epilogue: The Last Poem*

*Sūradāsa kī vārtā*, p. 101. I have taken considerable liberties with this translation, but only in the direction of compressing, as nearly as possible, the *sense* of the original into something approaching its compactness. The critical word is *anjana*, a black substance applied around the eyes for medicinal and cosmetic purposes. This is what I have rendered as "the vision of His darkness": there is a play on (1) the eyes of the poet being "trapped" in the black ring of *anjana*; (2) the blackness of the *anjana* being like that of Kṛṣṇa; (3) the healing quality of the *anjana*—in this case for one who was blind, but will now See.

## GLOSSARY

*avatāra*: "Descent," or incarnation, of Viṣṇu.

Balarāma, Balrām: Kṛṣṇa's "brother" and co-*avatāra*. See Introduction.

Bali: See Vāmana.

Banyan Tree: The World-Tree; in some Purāṇic cosmogonies, the only element of creation that survives during periods of *pralaya*. In one famous tale, Viṣṇu in the form of a toe-sucking child is depicted as lying on the leaf of the Banyan, afloat in the Sea of Dissolution.

Bāsava (Vāsava): An epithet of Indra.

*bhakta*: A devotee; one who practises *bhakti*.

*bhakti*: Devotion to a personal god. See Introduction.

*bindu*: A mark on the forehead, which may serve (depending upon the substance employed) cosmetic, medicinal, or religious functions.

Bliss: One of the three attributes of *brahmaṇ*: *sat*, "existence"; *cit*, "consciousness" or "sentience"; *ānanda*, "bliss." The latter is considered the primary attribute by devotees of Kṛṣṇa.

Boar: See Varāha.

*brahm*: See *brahmaṇ*.

Brahmā: The Creator. See *trimūrti*.

*brahmaṇ*: The supreme reality; the one absolute Being from which all other existence derives. In some sects (including that of Vallabha), Kṛṣṇa is considered to be the "true form" (*svarūpa*) of *brahmaṇ*.

Braj (Vraja): A strip of land along the Yamunā river which includes the major holy places associated with the life of Kṛṣṇa: the city of Mathurā, where Kṛṣṇa was born; and the village of Gokula and forest of Brindāban where Kṛṣṇa passed his childhood and youth among the cowherds. See Introduction.

Brindāban (Vṛndāvana): The forest. See Braj.

*cakora*: A species of partridge which is fabled to live on moonbeams.

*cakravāka*: A species of bird doomed by a curse to separation from its mate during the hours of darkness.

*cātaka*: A bird which is fabled to live solely on raindrops. In the local tradition referred to by Sūr, the *cātaka*'s taste appears to have been still more specialized: only those raindrops falling when the constellation *svāti* is on the horizon (raindrops that are also fabled to produce pearls) would do.

Churning: See Kūrma.

crore: 10 million.

Daśaratha: The father of Rāma.

*ḍhāḍhī*: A class of itinerant bards who perform at weddings and other festive occasions.

Draupadī: The wife of the Pāṇḍavas, the heroes of the *Mahābhārata.* In a crucial gambling match, Draupadī was won by enemies of the Pāṇḍavas, who attempted to complete her humiliation by undressing her in public. Draupadī called out for Kṛṣṇa, whom she considered her relative. He performed a miracle on Draupadī's behalf: her captors attempted to unwind her clothing, but the cloth proved to be infinite in length.

Dwarf: See Vāmana.

Fish: See Matsya.

Flood: See *pralaya.*

Gajarāja: An elephant, saved from a crocodile by Viṣṇu, to whom he was devoted.

Gaṅgā: The river Ganges, commonly represented as passing through the hair of Śiva before falling to earth; in this form it is sometimes spoken of as Śiva's second wife, or as co-wife/rival to Pārvatī (Gaurī).

Garuḍa: The eagle-mount of Viṣṇu.

Gaurī: "The fair one"; an epithet of Pārvatī, the consort of Śiva.

*ghāṭ*: Embankment of a river, usually with steps leading to a bathing place.

*ghī*: Clarified butter; a substance prized for both its flavor and its ritual purity.

Gokul (Gokula): The village of the cowherds. See Braj.

Goose: The mount of Brahmā. Fabled to feed on pearls.

Gopāla: Same as Govinda.

Gopīs: The herdsgirls of Braj, including Yaśodā and Rādhā.

Govardhana: A mountain near Brindāban, which Kṛṣṇa persuaded the cowherds to worship in place of Indra, and which he subsequently lifted above their heads to protect them against Indra's wrath, in the form of torrential rains.

Govinda: "The Cowherd"; an epithet of Kṛṣṇa.

Haladhara: "The Plowman"; an epithet of Balarāma.

Hara: "The Destroyer"; an epithet of Śiva.

Hari: An epithet of Viṣṇu in general, and of Kṛṣṇa in particular.

Hiraṇyakaśipu: See Narasiṃha.

Hiraṇyākṣa: See Varāha.

Hog: See Varāha.

Indra: The chief god of the Vedic pantheon, serving the functions of both war-god and rain-god. Later considered to be king of those who reside in heaven (*svarga*). See also Govardhana.

Jāmbavat: A character involved in the tales of two of the *avatāras* of Viṣṇu: (1) Jāmbavat led an army of bears to assist Rāma in the invasion of Laṅkā; (2) Kṛṣṇa battled Jāmbavat to obtain the *syamantaka* jewel.

Janaka: King of Mithilā; father of Sītā. See Rāma.

*kadamba*: A species of tree. Two episodes in the Kṛṣṇa tale involve Kṛṣṇa climbing into the branches of a *kadamba* overhanging the river Yamunā. In the first of these, he leaps from the *kadamba* into the river to do battle with Kāliya; in the second, he steals the clothes of the Gopīs as they bathe, carries them up into the tree, and refuses to return them until the Gopīs agree to leave the water.

Kāliya: A giant serpent who inhabited a pool in the Yamunā, and threatened the people of Braj with his venom. Kṛṣṇa defeated Kāliya but, moved by pleas for mercy from the serpent and his wives, spared his life.

Kāma: The Love-god. Kāma once attempted to play matchmaker between Śiva and Pārvatī; Śiva, angry at having his meditation disturbed, opened his third eye and burned Kāma to a crisp, whence his epithet *anaṅga*, "the Limbless."

Kāmadhenu: "The Cow of Wishes." See Paraśurāma.

Kaṃsa: The evil king of Mathurā, whose destruction was the ostensible motivation for the Kṛṣṇa-incarnation; Kṛṣṇa's archenemy. See Introduction.

Kānha, Kanhaiyā: Hindi variants of the name Kṛṣṇa.

*karma*: The accumulated merit or demerit of an individual's past lives, which will in turn determine the state of the individual's future birth.

*khīr*: A sweet gruel of milk and rice.

Kṣatriya: The "warrior" or "princely" caste, second (after the Brahmins) in the hierarchy of the four *varṇas*.

Kubera (Kuvera): The god of wealth. His twin sons, Nalakūbara and Maṇigrīva, were caught by the sage Nārada in the midst of a drunken orgy, and were condemned to stand as trees (the Yamalārjuna trees), until freed by Kṛṣṇa.

Kūrma: The Tortoise, second incarnation of Viṣṇu, who figures in the episode of the Churning of the Milky Sea. In the latter enterprise, the gods and demons churned the ocean in an attempt to recover a number of important articles, including the Moon and *amṛta*, the nectar of immortality. For this purpose Mount Mandara was used as the churn, twirled by a churning-cord consisting of the world-serpent, Śeṣa or Vāsuki, pulled on one end by the gods and on the other by the demons. It was the task of Viṣṇu in the form of Kūrma the Tortoise to provide with his back a firm supporting base, at the bottom of the Ocean, for Mount Mandara.

*laḍḍū*: A ball-shaped sweetmeat.

Lakṣmaṇ (Lakṣmaṇa): The brother of Rāma.

Laṅkā: The realm of the demon-king Rāvaṇa; usually identified with Ceylon (now officially known as Śrīlaṅkā). See Rāma.

*līlā*: The divine "Play" or "Sport" of Kṛṣṇa. Individual episodes in the Kṛṣṇa-*līlā* are also known as *līlās*: e.g., the *dān-līlā, kālī-daman-līlā*, etc. Also see Introduction.

Limbless: *anaṅga*; see Kāma.

Mādhava: "Descendant of Madhu"; an epithet of Kṛṣṇa.

Mandara: See Kūrma.

Mathurā: The city in which Kṛṣṇa was born.

Matsya: The Fish, first incarnation of Viṣṇu. In the version of the story employed by Sūr, Viṣṇu became incarnate as Matsya to rescue the Vedas from the demon Śaṅkhāsura.

*māyā*: Creative power, power to create illusion. A word with many different meanings in different philosophical systems; it may generally be defined as that illusory force (often personified as a goddess) by which the "world of name and form" is created.

Milky Sea: The abode of Viṣṇu during periods of *pralaya*. Also see Kūrma.

Mohan (Mohana): "The Enchanter"; an epithet of Kṛṣṇa.

Mountain: See (1) Govardhana; (2) Mandara.

Mura: A demon who was slain, along with his seven thousand sons, by Kṛṣṇa, whence Kṛṣṇa's epithet Murāri, "the Foe of Mura."

*namo namo*: "Obeisance"; a highly respectful salutation (Sanskrit; more correctly *namo namaḥ*).

Nanda: Chief of the cowherds at Gokul, and foster-father to Kṛṣṇa. See Introduction.

Nandalāl: "Nanda's Darling"; an epithet of Kṛṣṇa.

Nandarānī: "Nanda's Queen"; Yaśodā.

Narasiṃha: The "Man-lion," fourth incarnation of Viṣṇu. The demon Hiraṇyakaśipu persecuted the worshippers of Viṣṇu including Hiraṇyakaśipu's own son, Prahlāda. A boon granted the demon by Brahmā ensured him against being slain by man or by beast, by day or by night, inside or outside; Viṣṇu circumvented all these restrictions by appearing in the form of a half-man, half-lion (neither man nor beast), at the moment of sunset (neither day nor night), from a pillar on the very threshold of the demon's house (neither inside nor outside), and ripped the demon to pieces with his claws.

*neti neti*: "Not so, not so"; an Upaniṣadic formula for stating the ineffability of *brahmaṇ*; i.e., all that can be said of the ultimate reality is "it is not this, not this; it is beyond all labels."

*nirgun* (*nirguṇa*): "Without attributes"; a phrase used to describe the unqualified, undifferentiated *brahmaṇ*; opposed to *saguṇa*, "with attributes," used to describe a qualified and differentiated *brahmaṇ*, and in particular to describe a god such as Kṛṣṇa.

"Not this": See *neti*.

*pān*: A preparation of betel leaf. "To take up the *pān*": refers to the practise of a king calling together his followers when some feat of valor was demanded. *Pān* was placed on a tray; a hero volunteered for the task at hand by "taking up the *pān*."

Pāṇḍavas: Five brothers who are major figures in the epic *Mahābhārata*, the central story of which concerns the struggle between the Pāṇḍavas and the Kauravas. Kṛṣṇa (as an adult, and long after leaving Braj) sided with the Pāṇḍavas, and served as both charioteer and military adviser to the great archer Arjuna, to whom (in what is undoubtedly the best-known portion of the *Mahābhārata*) he delivered his famous battlefield sermon, the *Bhagavad-gītā*.

Paraśurāma: "Rāma-of-the-Axe," the sixth incarnation of

Viṣṇu. A Brahmin, Paraśurāma was the sworn enemy of the Kṣatriya caste; he is said to have "cleansed the earth" of Kṣatriyas twenty-one times. His hostility on one occasion was engendered by the kidnapping, by a Kṣatriya king, of the mythical cow Kāmadhenu.

Play: See *līlā*.

Prahlāda: See Narasiṃha.

*pralaya*: The periodic dissolution of the world, commonly represented as a great flood.

Purāṇa: Literally "Old," "handed down from the past"; any of a number of historical-mythological-theological texts (traditionally eighteen in number) which embody the teachings of the major sects of later Hinduism. The most important from the standpoint of the medieval Kṛṣṇa-*bhakti* movement is the *Bhāgavata Purāṇa*.

Pūtanā: A demoness, sent by Kaṃsa to slay Kṛṣṇa. Taking on the form of a beautiful woman, and smearing her nipples with poison, Pūtanā approached Yaśodā and, through flattery, persuaded Yaśodā to allow her to suckle Kṛṣṇa. The child not only proved immune to the venom, but in fact sucked the very life-breath from Pūtanā, at which point she reverted to her previous, and hideous, form. The villagers chopped her into pieces and cremated her on an enormous bonfire.

Rādhā: A Gopī, Kṛṣṇa's favorite, and by far the most important single character, aside from Kṛṣṇa himself, in the Kṛṣṇa-*līlā*. She is in many sects held to be Kṛṣṇa's own *śakti*, or "power," "creative energy"; in Kṛṣṇa-*bhakti* literature, she is the paradigm of the soul longing for reunion with God.

Raghu: A mythical ancestor of Rāma, whence one of the latter's most common epithets, Rāghava, "descended from Raghu."

Rāhu: A demon held responsible for lunar eclipses. At the time of the Churning of the Milky Ocean, Rāhu was one of the demons who joined the gods in an effort to retrieve *aṃrta*, the nectar of immortality. The moon saw

Rāhu stealing a sip and informed Viṣṇu, who promptly cut off Rāhu's head—but not before the *amṛta* had reached his throat, thus making his *head* immortal. The disembodied head of Rāhu now circles through the heavens, chasing after and periodically devouring the tattle-tale moon, only to have the moon escape each time through his severed gullet; hence the eclipses. Rāhu also represents the "ascending node" in astrological terminology.

Rāma: The seventh *avatāra* of Viṣṇu. The overwhelming majority of Vaiṣṇavite worship is addressed to one of two *avatāras*, Rāma and Kṛṣṇa. Rāma was the hero of Vālmīki's Sanskrit epic, the *Rāmāyaṇa*. The story has been recast by hundreds of later writers, one of the best-known versions being the Hindi *Rāmcaritmānas* of Tulsīdās. For understanding the poems presented here, a few prominent features and episodes of Rāma's life are essential: (1) Rāma is the eldest of four sons of King Daśaratha of Ayodhyā. (2) His closest companion throughout life is his brother Lakṣmaṇa. (3) Rāma marries Sītā after winning her in a trial of strength set by Janaka, Sītā's foster-father. Janaka is in possession of the bow once used by Śiva in destroying the Triple Cities (see Tripurāri). Janaka announces that Sītā will marry the man who can string that bow. No-one else is able to lift it; Rāma lifts, strings, and breaks it, all in a single motion. (4) As a result of a rather complicated palace intrigue, Daśaratha, with extreme reluctance, sends Rāma into the forest for fourteen years of exile. Rāma is accompanied by Lakṣmaṇa and Sītā. While in the forest the latter is abducted by Rāvaṇa, demon-king of Laṅkā. The remainder of the tale centers on the search for Sītā, and the great battle in which Rāma and Lakṣmaṇa, aided by an army of monkeys and bears led by Hanumān, destroy Rāvaṇa and his armies and free Sītā.

*rasa*: A word whose meanings range from "juice, liquid substance" through "vital essence" to "ultimate aesthetic and/or sexual gratification." In Sanskrit poetics, the eight (or nine) *rasas*—the erotic, the compassionate, the heroic, etc.—signify the various emotional states into which a work of art might endeavor to lead its audience. For discussion of the medieval theological emendation of the system see Chapter I.

Rāvaṇa: The ten-headed demon-king of Laṅkā, and arch-enemy of Rāma.

Rohiṇī: The "mother" of Balarāma. Balarāma is actually conceived in the womb of Devakī, as is Kṛṣṇa himself; Balarāma, however, is transplanted while still a fetus into the womb of Rohiṇī. Rohiṇī, like Devakī, is a wife of Vasudeva; but unlike Devakī, who is imprisoned in Mathurā, Rohiṇī lives in safety in the house of Nanda, chief of the cowherds of Gokula. Rohiṇī and Nanda's wife, Yaśodā, raise Balarāma and Kṛṣṇa together, all the while believing the children to be their true sons.

Śambhu: An epithet of Śiva.

Śaṅkhāsura: See Matsya.

Sāraṅgapāṇi (Śārṅga-pāṇi): "Holder of the (bow) *Sāraṅga* ( = Śārṅga, made of horn); an epithet of Viṣṇu.

Sea: The sea mentioned in these poems is generally the Milky Ocean, atop which Viṣṇu is commonly represented as spending the intervals between cycles of creation, asleep on the back of the serpent Śeṣa. The *churning* of the Milky Sea is an event frequently alluded to (see Kūrma).

Serpent: See (1) Śeṣa; (2) Kāliya.

Śeṣa: King of the serpents; his back is Viṣṇu's resting-place in intervals between cycles of creation. Frequent reference is made to the hoods of Śeṣa's thousand heads, spread protectively over his sleeping master. Śeṣa enters the Vaiṣṇavite mythos in a variety of ways. In many versions of the Kṛṣṇa tale, Balarāma is said to be an incarnation of Śeṣa; Śeṣa (or Vāsuki) is used as the churning-cord in the churning of the Milky Ocean. Also see Sea; Kūrma.

Siṃhikā: A demoness; the mother of Rāhu. Siṃhikā lives in

the ocean between Laṇkā and the Indian mainland; she waylays flying travelers by seizing their shadows and pulling them down into her jaws. Her most famous intended victim was Hanumān, the ally of Rāma, who slew her.

Sītā: Wife of Rāma.

Śiva: The Destroyer (see *trimūrti*). The iconography of Śiva is frequently mentioned in Sūr's poems: his rather gruesome appearance is often contrasted with the benevolent aspect of Kṛṣṇa, while at the same time the two are metaphysically identified as aspects of a single godhead. Śiva is associated with asceticism, and is often depicted as a *yogī*, with matted hair (through which descends the River Gaṅgā), body covered with ashes and entwined with a cobra. One poem in the present collection alludes to Śiva's frenzied dance in which he wears the skin of an elephant-demon he had slain; the destruction of the universe is also associated with Śiva's dance, which is performed to the accompaniment of a small, hand-held drum. As a *yogī*, he is disturbed only at great risk; see Kāma. His mount is the Bull, Nandī.

Snake: See (1) Śeṣa; (2) Kāliya.

Śrīdhara: (1) An epithet of Viṣṇu; (2) an evil Brahmin sent by Kaṃsa to kill Kṛṣṇa.

Sumera: Mount Meru, a mythical peak in the Himalayas, considered to be the navel of the earth.

Sūraja: "Sun"; another name employed by Sūrdās.

*svāti*: See Cātaka.

Syām (Śyāma): "The dark one"; an epithet of Kṛṣṇa.

Śyāmā: An epithet of Rādhā.

*tāl*: "Beat" or "rhythm"; musical term.

*ṭhag*: Thug, a highwayman, often one who killed and robbed in the name of the goddess Kālī.

Three Strands: According to certain schools of philosophy, the three basic constituents of all creation: *rajas*, "physical activity, passion"; *tamas*, "inertia"; *sattva*, "clarity."

Three Worlds: Heaven, Earth, and Hell; collectively used in the sense of "the whole universe."

*tilak*: See *bindu*.

Tortoise: See Kūrma.

*tribhaṅga*: The "three bends" pose, the stance taken by Kṛṣṇa when he plays the flute. For a full description, see Chapter III.

*trimūrti*: The "triple figure," the three gods among which Hindu tradition divides the functions of the universe: Brahmā the creator, Viṣṇu the preserver, and Śiva the destroyer. They are frequently spoken of as three facets of a single deity. In Vaiṣṇavite texts, Brahmā is depicted as emerging from a lotus in Viṣṇu's navel. In practise, only Śiva and Viṣṇu are objects of worship; Brahmā is frequently portrayed as something of a buffoon, who, once his work of creation is completed, has little to do but make trouble for the other gods, and in particular for Viṣṇu.

Tripurāri: The "enemy of the Triple City"; an epithet of Śiva, alluding to an episode in which he ended a thousand years of tyranny by destroying the "triple city" from which the demons had ruled the Three Worlds.

Tṛṇāvarta: A demon, sent by Kaṃsa in the form of a whirlwind, who attempted to kill the infant Kṛṣṇa, but was himself killed by the child.

Twin Trees: See Kubera.

Uddhau, Uddhava: A rather pedantic philosopher; a friend of Kṛṣṇa's, whom the latter sent back from Mathurā to Brindāban ostensibly to carry messages of consolation to those whom Kṛṣṇa had left behind.

Vāmana: The "Dwarf," fifth incarnation of Viṣṇu. A generous demon named Bali had won control of the Three Worlds. Viṣṇu approached him in the form of a Brahmin dwarf, and asked for a reasonable boon: as much land as he could cross in three steps. The boon granted, the Dwarf grew to cosmic proportions; in the three steps he covered earth, sky, and the heavens, which thus reverted to the control of the gods. At the same time he rewarded Bali's generosity by leaving to him control of Hell.

Varāha: The "Boar," third incarnation of Viṣṇu. The earth was stolen by a demon named Hiraṇyākṣa, and carried beneath the ocean; Varāha plunged into the sea, rooted the earth out from the sea-bottom, then slew Hiraṇyākṣa.

Vāsuki: See Śeṣa.

Vedas: The four earliest, and in theory most sacred, of Hindu texts. While nominally considered to be the infallible source of all divine law, in practise the Vedas played a rather minor role in popular medieval Hinduism.

Vibhīṣaṇa: Brother of Rāvaṇa. See Rāma.

Viṣṇu: The Preserver (see *trimūrti*). For many Hindus, Viṣṇu is the supreme god, from whom all other gods emanate. He is most commonly worshipped in the form of two of his ten *avatāras* or incarnations, Rāma and Kṛṣṇa. For the devotees of Kṛṣṇa, the subordination of Kṛṣṇa to Viṣṇu is often reversed and Kṛṣṇa himself is considered to be the true form of the godhead; among Western scholars, it is common to indicate the complex and ambiguous relationship between the two by using a joint name, Viṣṇu-Kṛṣṇa. In the poetry of Sūrdās, Viṣṇu is most commonly mentioned through the tales of his first eight incarnations; see Matsya, Kūrma, Varāha, Narasiṃha, Vāmana, Paraśurāma, and Rāma. The eighth incarnation is usually considered to be Kṛṣṇa himself, except when Kṛṣṇa is treated as the supreme godhead in his own right, in which case Balarāma is often listed as the eighth. The ninth and tenth incarnations—Buddha and Kalki—are of little importance in Sūr's poetry.

Vṛṣabhānu: The father of Rādhā.

Yamalārjuna: See Kubera.

Yamunā: One of the major rivers in North India; the cities of Delhi and Mathurā are both situated on its banks.

As the river which runs through the land of Braj, it is the river most sacred to the devotees of Kṛṣṇa.

Yaśodā: Kṛṣṇa's "mother," and one of the major characters in the *līlā*. The wife of Nanda the cowherd, Yaśodā was chosen to be the foster-mother of Kṛṣṇa, who was actually born to Devakī. On the night of his birth, Kṛṣṇa was switched with Yaśodā's new-born daughter; through a magic spell, the exchange was made without Yaśodā's knowledge, and Yaśodā raised Kṛṣṇa in the belief that he was her own son. See Introduction.

# BIBLIOGRAPHY


ARCHER, W.G., *The Loves of Krishna in Indian Painting and Poetry*, New York, 1957.

*Le Bhāgavata Purāṇa*, ed. and French trans. Eugene Burnouf, Paris, 1898.

BHĀRADVĀJ, Jagdīś, *Kṛṣṇa-kāvya meṃ līlā-varṇana*, New Delhi, 1972.

BRYANT, Kenneth E., "*Sant* and *Vaiṣṇava* Poetry: Some Observations on Method," *Sikh Studies: Working Papers from the Berkeley Conference*, ed. Gerald Barrier and Mark Juergensmeyer, monograph of the Graduate Theological Union, Berkeley, 1978.

BURKE, Kenneth, *Counter-Statement*, London, 1953.

——, *The Philosophy of Literary Form*, New York, 1957.

CATURVEDĪ, Jawāharlāl, *Sūradāsa: adhyayana-sāmagrī*, Mathura, 1959.

CHAMBERS, A.B., "The Meaning of the 'Temple' in Donne's *La Corona*," *Journal of English and German Philology* 59 (1960).

COPE, Jackson I., "The Rhythmic Gesture: Image and Aesthetic in Joyce's *Ulysses*," *English Literary History* 29 (1962).

DAVIE, Donald, *Articulate Energy*, London, 1955.

DE, Sushil Kumar, *Early History of the Vaiṣṇava Faith and Movement in Bengal*, Calcutta, 1942.

DIMOCK Edward C., *The Place of the Hidden Moon: Erotic Mysticism in the Vaiṣṇava-Sahajiyā Cult of Bengal*, Chicago, 1966.

——, and Denise Levertov, trans., *In Praise of Krishna: Songs from the Bengali*, New York, 1967.

—— et al., eds., *The Literatures of India: An Introduction*, Chicago, 1974.

DONNE, John, *The Divine Poems*, ed. Helen Gardner, Oxford, 1952.

DWIVEDI, Ram Avadh, *A Critical Survey of Hindi Literature*, Varanasi, 1966.

EMERY, Clark, *The World of Dylan Thomas*, Miami, 1958.

FISH, Stanley, *Self-Consuming Artifacts: The Experience of Seventeenth-Century Literature*, Berkeley, 1972.

——, *Surprised by Sin: The Reader in Paradise Lost*, Berkeley, 1971.

FRYE, Northrop, *Fables of Identity: Studies in Poetic Mythology*, New York, 1963.

GAUTAM, Manmohan, *Bhramaragīta kā kāvya-vaibhava*, Delhi, 1967.

GEROW, Edwin, *A Glossary of Indian Figures of Speech*, The Hague, 1971.

GONDA, J., *Aspects of Early Viṣṇuism*, Utrecht, 1954.

GOPINATHA RAO, T.A., *Elements of Hindu Iconography*, New York, 1968.

GROWSE, F.S., *Mathura: A District Memoir*, Allahabad, 1883.
GUPTA, Jagdīś, *Braja-bhāṣā Kṛṣṇa-bhakti kāvya*, Allahabad, 1968.
HARIRĀYA, *Sūrdās kī vārtā*, ed. Premnārāyaṇ Ṭaṇḍan, Lucknow, 1968.
INGALLS, Daniel H.H., trans., *Sanskrit Poetry from Vidyākara's "Treasury,"* Cambridge, Mass., 1968.
JAKOBSON, Roman, and Morris Halle, *Fundamentals of Language*, The Hague, 1956.
JINDAL, K.B., *A History of Hindi Literature*, Allahabad, 1955.
JOŚĪ, Mahādevśāstrī, ed., *Bhāratīya saṃskṛtikośa*, Poona, 1974.
JOYCE, James, *Stephen Hero*, New York, 1944.
JUNG, C.G., and C. Kerényi, *Essays on a Science of Mythology: The Myth of the Divine Child and the Mysteries of Eleusis*, Princeton, 1963.
KABĪR, *Kabīra-bījaka*, Śukdev Sinha, ed., Allahabad, 1972.
KELLOGG, S.H., *A Grammar of the Hindí Language*, 3rd edition, London, 1938.
LEISHMAN, J.B., *The Monarch of Wit: An Analytical and Comparative Study of the Poetry of John Donne*, London, 1965.
MACCAFFREY, Isabel, *Paradise Lost as "Myth,"* Cambridge, 1959.
MACFIE, J.M., *The Ramayan of Tulsidas; or, The Bible of Northern India*, Edinburgh, 1930.
MAUD, Ralph, *Entrances to Dylan Thomas' Poetry*, Pittsburgh, 1963.
MIŚRA, Gaurīśaṅkar, *Sūra-sāhitya kā chandaḥ-śāstrīya adhyayana*, Allahabad, 1969.
MISRA, Janardan, *The Religious Poetry of Sūrdās*, doctoral dissertation, Königsberg, 1939.
MĪTAL, Prabhu Dayāl, *Aṣṭachāpa paricaya*, Mathura, 1949.
MOYNIHAN, William, *The Craft and Art of Dylan Thomas*, Ithaca, N.Y., 1966.
NATHAN, Leonard, "Conjectures on a Structural Principle of Vedic Poetry," *Comparative Literature* 28, 2 (Spring, 1976).
NOWOTTNY, Winnifred, *The Language Poets Use*, New York, 1962.
O'FLAHERTY, Wendy Donniger, *Hindu Myths*, Baltimore, 1975.
OLSON, Elder, *The Poetry of Dylan Thomas*, Chicago, 1954.
PANDEY, S.M., "Mīrābāī and Her Contributions to the Bhakti Movement," *History of Religions* 5:1 (1965).
______, and Norman Zide, *The Poems of Sūrdās*, xeroxed instructional material, Chicago, 1962.
______, and ______, "Sūrdās and His Krishna-*bhakti*," in Milton Singer, ed., *Krishna: Myths, Rites, and Attitudes*, Chicago, 1966.
QUEARY, Louis B., *Contracts and Structure in Macbeth, Antony and Cleopatra, and Coriolanus*, Ph.D. dissertation, University of California, Berkeley, 1973.
RAMANUJAN, A.K., trans., *Speaking of Śiva*, Baltimore, 1973.
SAID, Edward W., *Beginnings: Intention and Method*, New York, 1975.

Śarmā, Harbaṃślāl, *Sūra aura unakā sāhitya*, Aligarh, 1958.
______, ed., *Sūradāsa*, Delhi, 1973.
Śarmā, Munśīrām, *Sūradāsa kā kāvya-vaibhava*, Kanpur, 1965.
Śarmā, Yajñadatta, *Sūra-sāhitya aura siddhānta*, Delhi, 1955.
Śāstrī, Ved Prakāś, *Śrīmadbhāgavata aura Sūrasāgara kā varṇya viṣaya kā tulanātmaka adhyayana*, Agra, 1969.
Sloan, Thomas O., and Raymond B. Waddington, eds., *The Rhetoric of Renaissance Poetry*, Berkeley, 1974.
Smith, Barbara Herrnstein, *Poetic Closure: A Study of How Poems End*, Chicago, 1968.
Sontag, Susan, *Against Interpretation*, New York, 1961.
Śukla, Rāmcandra, *Sūradāsa*, Varanasi, 1948.
Sūrdās, *Sūrasāgara*, ed. Jawāharlāl Caturvedī, Calcutta, 1965.
______, *Sūrasāgara*, eds. Jagannāth Dās "Ratnākar" et al., Nāgarī Pracāriṇī Sabhā, Varanasi, *saṃvat* 2029.
Ṭaṇḍan, Premnārāyaṇ, ed., *Brajabhāṣā Sūra-kośa*, Lucknow, 1962.
Thomas, Dylan, *The Collected Poems of Dylan Thomas*, New York, 1957.
Tindall, William, *A Reader's Guide to Dylan Thomas*, New York, 1962.
Tiwārī, Śaśi, *Sūra ke Kṛṣṇa: eka anuśīlana*, Hyderabad, 1969.
Tomar, Kaṇikā, *Brajabhāṣā aura Brajabuli sāhitya*, Varanasi, 1964.
Tulsidas, *Kavitavali*, ed. Satīś Kumār, Delhi, 1972.
______, *Kavitāvalī*, trans. F.R. Allchin, London, 1964.
Varma, Dhīrendra, *Sūrasāgara sāra saṭīka*, Allahabad, 1972.
Varmā, Vrajeśvar, *Sūradāsa: jīvana aura kāvya kā adhyayana*, Allahabad, 1950.
Vaudeville, Charlotte, *Kabīr*, Oxford, 1974.
______, trans. and ed., *Pastorales par Soûr-Dâs*, Paris, 1971.
Vidyāpati, *Vidyāpati-gīta-saṃgraha*, ed. Subhadra Jha, Varanasi, 1954.
Wellek, Rene, and Austin Warren, *Theory of Literature*, New York, 1949.
White, Charles S.J., "Kṛṣṇa as Divine Child," *History of Religions* X:2 (1970).
Wilson, Frances, ed. and trans., *The Love of Krishna: The Kṛṣṇakarṇāmṛta of Līlāśuka Bilvamaṅgala*, Philadelphia, 1975.
Wilson, H.H., *Religious Sects of the Hindus*, Calcutta, 1958.
Wimsatt, W.K. Jr., and Monroe C. Beardsley, *The Verbal Icon: Studies in the Meaning of Poetry*, Lexington, Ky., 1964.
Wimsatt, W.K. Jr., and Cleanth Brooks, *Literary Criticism: A Short History*, New York, 1957.

# INDEX

Page references in *italic* indicate subject matter within poems.


Affective fallacy, 23*n*
*Āīn-i-Akbarī*, x
Akbar: brought political stability, 4; possible associations with Sūr, x, 1, 3, 209; Vallabhite legends concerning, 2-3 and *n*
*Alaṃkāra, upamā* and *utprekṣā* as, 76
*Alaukika. See Laukika*
Allama Prabhu, 75
Alliteration: examples of in Sūr's verse, 214*n16*, 215*n4*, 217*n2*; homorganic, 74*n*; as ornament, 113, 138; as preclosural cue, 56; as traditional prosodic category, 126; in translation, xvi; used to establish patterns of expectation, 138; used to reinforce metrical parallelism, 128, 131
"Amnesia": of audience, 38-39, 48, 55; of cowherds narrative necessity, 38
*Amṛta*, churned from Kṣīrasāgara, 73
Anapestic norm, of *sāra* meter, 132
Antiphanes, on narrative resources of tragic and comic poets, 59
Archer, W.G., on "amnesia", 38
Aristotle, on structure, 43
Asceticism, emphasized in Brahmanical systems, 5
Audience: "amnesia" of, 48; experience poetry sequentially, 41, 100; intended for *Sūrsāgar*, xiii; led to "forfet" Kṛṣṇa's divinity, 38-39; led to participate in narration, 29, 47; as locus of poem, 23; misled by poet, 50-51, 54, 64-65; "omniscient", 45-48, 60-61, 65, 136-137, 139, 145; as "privileged spectators," 107, 112; suspicious of rhetoric, 105
*Avatāras*: animal, 13, 16; collectively form "biography" of Viṣṇu/Kṛṣṇa, 51-52; sequence of as structural principle, 52-53, 60; of Viṣṇu, 8
*Avatāras*, Kṛṣṇa-mythos interlocks with tales of: all (*daśāvatāra*), 52-53, 99-104; Kūrma, 85, 86-87, 88-89; Narasiṃha, 116; Rāma, 53-57, 85, 102-3, 170-71; Varāha, 78. *See also* Buddha; Kalkī; Kṛṣṇa; Kūrma; Matsya; Narasiṃha; Paraśurāma; Rāma; Vāmana; Varāha

*Baghanakha*, tiger-claw necklace of Kṛṣṇa, *80*, *86-87*, 87-88 and *n*, *111*, *115*, 116, *160*, *162*, *164*
Balarāma: always aware of Kṛṣṇa's divinity, 39*n*, 107, *161*, 162, 166, 167-68, *172-73*, *179*; fair in color, 8, 111, 160; incarnation of Śeṣa, 8; mentioned in poems, *169-70*, *171*, *178*, *179*, *185*; reminds Kṛṣṇa of divinity, 39*n*; serves poet as all-knowing narrator, 107, 167-68; teases Kṛṣṇa, 52-53, 107-9, 166, *171*, *172-73*; transplanted to Rohiṇī's womb, 9
Bali, deceived by Vāmana, *53*, *99*, *162*, *172*
Bāsava. *See* Indra
Basavaṇṇa, on spontaneity, 136
"Bedtime-story" (poem): discussed, 53-60, 167; Sanskrit version, 54*n*; Sūr's version, *170-71*.
*Bhagavad gīta*, Kṛṣṇa's role in, 7, 10
*Bhāgavata Purāṇa*: as source for Kṛṣṇa mythos, 10-11 and *n*, 35, 149; episode of Uddhava and Gopīs in, 194; revelations of Kṛṣṇa's divinity in, 35-39; and *Sūrsāgar*, 35*n*, 39*n*, 211*nl*
*Bhakti*: contrasted with ascetic systems, 5; Kṛṣṇa lectures Gopīs on, 183; movement, 4-5; Uddhava converted to, 195
*Bhakti* poet, conventional image of, 94-95, 135-36

*Bhakti* poetry, "folk" quality of, 94–95, 104–105
*Bhaṇitā*: as convention of *pada*, 101; as preclosural cue, 51, 57, 67
Bhāradvāj, Jagdīś, on Sūr's poetry, 28, 29, 34
*Bhāva*: in Hindi criticism, 22–24, 34–35; in *rasa* theory, 22. *See also* *Sakhya*; *Śṛṅgāra*; *Vātsalya*
*Bhramargīt*: description of, 194–95; examples of, *202–4*; simile in, 76
Blindness. *See* Sūr; Milton
Boar. *See* Varāha
"Boar" (poem), *77*, *77–78*, 128
"Bogey-man" (poem), *52–53*
Brahmā: born from Viṣṇu's navel, *118*, *157*, *162*; as Creator, 7–8; prayed to, *68*, *155*, *207*
*Brahman*, Kṛṣṇa identified with, 11, 89, 108, 129, *185*, 195, *203*
Brahmins: Kṛṣṇa's conflicts with, 150, *155–56*, 166, *173–74*; Paraśurāma defender of, *162*
Braj, land of, 3, 4–5
Braj *bhāṣā*: ascendancy of, 3–5; dialect of Hindi, 14; language of *Sūrsāgar*, ix, 3–4
Braj renaissance, 4–5
Brindāban: cowherds move to, 10, 181; restoration of, 3–4
Buddha: as incarnation of Viṣṇu, *93*, 100; of little interest to Sūr, 52
Burke, Edward: on "psychology of information," 46
Butter, Kṛṣṇa fond of, *72*, *73*, *77*, *156*, *159*, *163*, *164*, *167–69*, *175–80*, *187*
Butter-thief, Kṛṣṇa, 61, 73, 77, 167, *168*, *175–80*, 181, *187*

Caitanya, role in Braj renaissance, 4, 5
*Cakora*, feeds on moonbeams, *191*, *199*
Caste: Balarāma teases Kṛṣṇa about, 109; of Kṛṣṇa, 109, 219*n4*; system opposed by *bhakti* movements, *1*, 4
*Cātaka*, *197*, *199*
Caturvedī, Jawāharlāl, xi, xii
*Caurāsī vaiṣṇavan kī vārtā*, as source for Sūr's life, x, 1*n*, 209
Chambers, A.B., on Donne's "Temple," 59
*Chanda*. *See* Prosody
*Chappai*, six-line verse form, 61
Chiasmus, syntactic, 83
Child-god: irony of, 6, 12–13, 52, 149; in Western mythology, 60
Child-poems, importance of in *Sūrsāgar*, xiii, 6
Churning. *See* Kṣīrasāgara
Closural strategy: in "bedtime-story" poem, 55, 56–57; closing of "frame" as, 74; problems in, 100–1; return to norm, 124, 130; in "Tṛṇāvarta" poem, 47–48; use of rhyme in, 49–50
Closure: defined, 44; distinguished from "stopping," 44–45; and formally required stopping point, 64, 67; as simultaneous fulfillment of several contracts, 65. *See also* closural strategy
Cloud, Kṛṣṇa compared to, *86*, 88, 109, *162*, 194, *199*, *200*
Contract: in "bedtime-story" poem, 55, 56; defined, 43*n*, 44; effect of violating, 29; "fine print" in, 51, 103; for predictable sequence, 99; and prosody, 131; thematic, formal, syntactic, 64–65; for *vātsalya*, 77; weak, 66
Convention: of *chappai*, 63; as "language," 40; mythology as aspect of, 40; in similes, 87, 88; in treating theme of love-in-separation, 194. *See also* *Pada*, conventions of
Couplet, as structural unit, 81–82, 91–93, 94, 118–120. *See also* Simile-couplets
Cowherds: deceived by Kṛṣṇa's *māyā*, 183; forget Kṛṣṇa's divinity, 38; "help" in lifting of Govardhana, *191–92*; as Kṛṣṇa's companions, *184*; Kṛṣṇa raised among, 10; move to Brindāban, 10, 18; persuaded by Kṛṣṇa to worship Govardhana, 149, 182, *189*
Cunningham, J.V.: on tradition, 60

*Dāna-līlā*, 188–89
Daśaratha, father of Rāma, *53*, *55*, *170*
*Daśāvatāra stotra*, 52, *52–53*, *99–100*, 100–104
Davie, Donald, on syntactical structures in poetry, 114

De, Sushil Kumar, on works of Rūpa Goswāmin, 21
Deceit: of *Braj-līlā*, 112; by Kṛṣṇa, 61
Demons: compared in Sūr's and Tulsī's verse, 17; sent by Kaṃsa, 10, 159-51, 181. *See also* Forest-fire demon; Hiraṇyākṣa; Hiraṇyakaśipu; Pūtana; Sakaṭāsura; Tṛṇāvarta
Demythification, function of, 109
Devakī, mother of Kṛṣṇa, 8-9, 108-9
Devotional intention of Sūr's verse, not always apparent, 139
Diminution, shortening of unit of repetition, 120
Dimock, Edward C.: on *bhakti* literature, 135; on *bhāvas* of *bhakti*, 21-22
Distance, control of, 58, 62, 120
Donne, John, "Temple," 57-60
Doubt, concerning omnipotence of gods: on part of audience, 71; on part of characters, 69-71; on part of Kṛṣṇa, 70-71
Dramatic irony, 37, 81, 106-7, 112
Draupadī, *186*
Duṣyanta, 106
Dwārakā, 10, 104
Dwarf. *See* Vāmana
Dwivedi, Ram Avadh, criticizes Sūr's poetry, 23

Earth: appeals to Viṣṇu in form of cow, 8, *100*, 104; raised by Varāha, *77*, *78*, *99*, *161*, *164*, *172*; Viṣṇu measures in three steps, *162*
Eliot, T.S., "Marina," 113
Enjambment, rare in Hindi poetry, xv
Enumerative structure, in medieval English lyric, 105. *See also* Paratactic structure
Epanaphora: beginning consecutive lines with same word, 74, 101-2, 104; in conjunction with rhyme, 119; as "frame," 217-218*n*7; pronominal, 119, 120
Epiphanies: importance of in Sūr's verse, 140-41; poems of revelation and ironic contrast, xiv, 25; recreate cycle of distraction and revelation, 39; and reversal, 35; in tradition of Sanskrit *subhāṣita*, 42
Epiphany: "editing" by critics, 29-35; process of active remembering, 47; relationship between religious and aesthetic, 24-25; relationship to *vātsalya*, 34-35; as revealed to Yaśodā, 36; as used by Joyce, 24-25
Erotic sentiment, most pleasing to Kṛṣṇa, 14. *See also Śṛṅgāra*
Expectation, effect of violating, 28-29, 50-51. *See also* Contract

Fish: *See* Matsya
Fish, Stanley: on "affective fallacy," 23*n*; on Milton's similes, 79, 80, 90
Flashback, strategy of, 100
Flute: attracts Gopīs, 95, *180*, 193-94, *195-6*, *197*, *204*; Gopīs jealous of, 95, 98, 193, *196-98*; Kṛṣṇa learns to play as cowherd, 10
Flute songs, 95
"Folk" quality, of bhakti poetry, 94-95, 104-5
"Foot," in Hindi prosody: defined, 81*n*; of Hindi meters, 125-6, 127; not recognized by convention, 138; of *sāra* meter, 132*n*
Forest-fire demon, 181, *186-7*, 218*n8*
Frye, Northrop, on difference between criticism and experience of literature, 40-41

*Gajagāminī*, xiv-xv
Gajarājā, *186*
Gaṅgā, and Śiva, *80*, *164*, *208*
Garuḍa, *118*, *163*, *186*
Gaurī, consort of Śiva, *80*, *164*
Gautam, Manmohan, on Sūr's similes, 76
Generalization, of Kṛṣṇa, 28-29
Gerow, Edwin, on notion of *upamā*, 78
*Gīta-govinda*, 52
*Godhūli*, 181
Gokula, 3, 9, 167
Gopinatha Rao, T.A., describes icon of Kṛṣṇa-with-flute, 96
Gopīs: attracted by flute, 193-94, *195-96*, *197*, *204*; clothes stolen by Kṛṣṇa, 183, *188*; debate with Uddhava, 194-95; fair in color, 194, *199*, *200*; jealous of flute, 95, 98, 193, *196-98*; love affair with Kṛṣṇa, 183, *188'89*, 193-95, *195-204*; suffer

longing, 194–95, *195–96*, *201–2*, *204*; unaware of Kṛṣṇa's divinity, 81, 82, 98, 150, *164*; as "victims" of dramatic irony, 107
Govardhana: Kṛṣṇa as spirit of, 182, *189–90*; Kṛṣṇa lifts, 98, 183, *191–92*; Kṛṣṇa persuades cowherds to worship, 149, 182, *189*; seat of Vallabha sect, x, 182, 205; site of Śrīnāthjī temple, x
Growse, F.S., 4
Gupta, Jagdīś, on impediments to *rasa*, 34*n*
Gupta, M.P., xi

Hanumān, 85, 102
Hara, epithet of Śiva, *80*
*Harivaṃśa*, as source for Kṛṣṇa mythos, 10–11 and *n*
Hindi, *bhakti* poetry in, 14–17
Hiraṇyakaśipu, slain by Narasiṃha, *52*, *99*, *110*, *115*, *118*, *161*, *163*, *172*
Hiraṇyākṣa, slain by Varāha, *52*, *172*
"Horoscope" (poem): metrical patterning of, 131; poem, *158–59*
Hyperbole, in Sūr's similes, 78
Icon: held by Vallabhites to be *svarūpa*, 89; of Kṛṣṇa with flute, 96–98
Illusion: of parataxis, 104–5; of spontaneity, 136. *See also māyā*
Incarnation, irony of, 12–13
Indra: attempts to drown cowherds, 182–83, *190–91*; opposed by Kṛṣṇa, 149, 182–83, *189–92*; prevents Aśvins from sharing in sacrifice, *169*, 215–16*n4*
Ingalls, Daniel H.H., on epiphany in Sanskrit poetry, 40
*In medias res* beginning, 63, 66
Intentional fallacy, 23*n*
Interpretation: allegorical, 193; arrogance of, 134–35

Jakobson, Roman, on metaphoric and metonymic poles, 90
Jāmbavat: ally of Rāma, 102–3; recognizes Kṛṣṇa as Viṣṇu, 103, *162*
Janaka, father of Sītā, 53, *170*
Jayadeva, author of *Gīta-govinda*, 52
Jest, as core of Sūr's poetry, 17–18
Jindal, K.B.: on child poems, 30–31 and *n*, 32–33; compares Sūr and Tulsī, 69*n*
Joyce, James, on epiphany, 24–25, 26, 35, 40

Kabīr: question of identity, ix; stresses *nirguṇa* nature of Rāma, 14*n*; uses metrical parallelism, 127; uses paratactic structure, 93, 94
Kālī, as cult figure, 4
Kālidāsa, author of *Śakuntalā*, 106
Kāliya, Kṛṣṇa's battle with, 66–68, 67*n*, 69–70, 181–82, *185–86*
Kalkī: of little interest to Sūr, 52; tenth *avatāra* of Viṣṇu, 100
Kāma: burned by 'Siva, *80*, 84; mentioned in poems, *80*, *153*, *164*
Kāmadhenu, *53*, *173*
Kaṃsa, King: in Kāliya tale, 182; Kṛṣṇa's archenemy, 8; sends demons to slay Kṛṣṇa, 10, 150, *152*, *153–54*, *155*, *157*; slain by Kṛṣṇa, 10, 194
*Kavitāvalī* of Tulsīdās, 61
Keats, John, on constraints of conventional form, 138
Kellogg, S.H., on Hindi prosody, 125
Kerényi, C., on child-god in Western tradition, 60
Kṛṣṇa: complex character in Sūr's verse, 7, 70, 182; dark color of, 10, 108–9, 111, *159*, *160*, 166, *171*, *184*, 194, *199*, *200*, *201*, *209*, 213–14*n14*, 220
Kṛṣṇa, tale of: 8–12; appears to act out of fear, 66, 70–71; birth, 9; drives cattle, 181, *184–85*, 197; in Dwārakā, 104; learns to walk, 32–34, 150, *160–62*; lifts Govardhana, 183, *191–92*, 198; name means "black," 8, 10, 108; raised among cowherds, 10; sexually precocious, 13, 95, *168*, 183, *188–89*; slays Kaṃsa, 194; sources for tale of, 10–11*n*; as spirit of mountain, 182, *189–90*; steals Gopīs' clothes, 183, *188*; swallows mud, 36, 166, *174*; tied to mortar, 107, 167–68, *178*; wants to play with moon, 166, *170*. *See also* Demons; Gopīs; Rādhā; Yaśodā
Kṛṣṇa, metaphysical aspect of: afloat on Sea, 150. as *avatāra* of Viṣṇu, 51–52; conceived from black hair of Viṣṇu, 8, 108; extraordinary potential for action, 32, 72, 150, *161*, *163*, 212*n7*; forgets own divinity, 39*n*,

99, 107-9, *161-62*, 166; identified with Śiva, 80-84, *208*; perceived by gods as threat to creation, 73, 150, 156-57, 212*n*7; reveals own divinity, 57, 166-67, *174*, *175*. *See also Brahmaṇ*; *Līlā*
*Kṛṣṇakarṇāmṛta*, 13, 54*n*
Kṣatriyas, destroyed by Paraśurāma, 173
Kṣīrasāgara, churned by gods and demons, 72-74, 85-89, 150, *161*, *162*, *163*, *165*, *172*
Kūrma, aids in churning Kṣīrasāgara, 53*n*, *62*, *72*, 73, 85, 86-87, 88-89, *93*, *99*, 100, *116*, *161*, *162*, *172*

Lakṣmaṇa: brother of Rāma, 16, *54*, *171*; in strategy of "bedtime story", 56-57
Laṅkā, *53*, *173*
*Laukika* and *alaukika*: contrasted, 34*n*, 51, 74, 111-12, 119-20, 123; mixture of viewed as impediment to *rasa*, 34*n*
*Līlā*: as child's game, 18; defined by Aurobindo, 11*n*; devotee's participation in, 2, 11-12, 21, 23; experience of characters in, 24; Kṛṣṇa himself deceived by, 107; mentioned in poems, *6*, *53*, *73*, *163*, *173*, *184*; nature of, 2, 11-12; Rādhā's role in, 14. *See also Sūr-līlā*
Limerick, as example of return to norm, 130
Line unit: as "frame," 74, 81-82, 99, 101-2; in translation, xv-xvi; versus couplet as unit of contrast, 119-20
Longing, of Gopīs for Kṛṣṇa, 194-95, *195-96*, *201-2*, *204*
Lotus, enmity with moon, 77

MacCaffrey, Isabel, on Milton's similes, 79
MacFie, J.M., claims Tulsīdās' Rāma is not completely believable, 69
*Mahābhārata*, Kṛṣna's role in, 10
*Mākhan-cor*. *See* Butter-thief
*Māna*, as subtype of *vipralambha*, 96
Mandara, Mount, used by gods as churning-stick, *52*, *72*, *73*, *87*, *89*, 116, *161*, *162*, *163*, *172*. *See also* Kūrma
Man-lion. *See* Narasiṃha

Mārkaṇḍeya, sees Kṛṣṇa afloat on banyan-leaf, 150
*Maryādā puruṣottama Rāma*, 61
Mathura, Kṛṣṇa departs for, 194
*Mātrā*, basis of *pada* meters, 125-26
Matsya, first *avatāra* of Viṣṇu, 13, 53*n*, *93*, *99*, 100, *161*, *172*
*Māyā*: deceives cowherds, 183; illusory power of Kṛṣṇa, 6, *206*; of *putrasneha*, 39
Metaphor: conventionalized in poems of longing, 194; and metonymy, 89-90; versus literal statement, 114*n*
Meter. *See* Prosody
Metonymy: and metaphor, 89-90, 137; as relational mode, 81, 111
Metrical norm, concept of, 132
Metrical parallelism: difficulty of explaining complex patterns of, 131-32; not treated in traditional prosody, 126, 127; plays major role in North Indian verse, 127; reinforced by alliteration, 128, 131; in Sūr's verse, 126-32; used as "focus," 129-30; used to strengthen closure, 127, 128, 130
Microcosm and macrocosm, correspondence between, 89, 123-24
Milky Ocean. *See* Kṣīrasāgara
Milton, John: on rhyme, 91*n*; similes of, 79, 80, 90; and Sūr both blind, 91
Mīrābāī, 94
Mischief, Kṛṣṇa's, 61. *See also* Butter-thief
Miśra, Gaurīśaṅkar, on Sūr's meters, 125
Moon: churned from Kṣīrasāgara, 73, 85-86, 88-89, 150, *165*; eclipsed by Rāhu, 84, *169*; enmity with lotus, 77; face commonly compared to, 84-87, 88-89, *162*, *165*, *169*, *179*; Kṛṣṇa wants to play with, 166, *170*; rests on Śiva's head, 80, *115*, 116, *164*
Mughals, Sūr's association with, x
Muslims, Sūr's apparent indifference to, 3
Mythology: as aspect of poetic convention, 40; audience knowledge of, 45-48; as "biography of gods," 60; of Kṛṣṇa in *Bhāgavata Purāṇa*, 35, 149; Vaiṣṇavite contrasted with

Western, 57, 59–60, 80–81; of Viṣṇu highly complex, 51–52

Nāgarī Pracāriṇī Sabhā, xii
"Naïve" structure, 94–95
*Nakha-śikha*, "head-to-toe" description, 97–98
Names: pun on Sūr's, 15*n*; of Rādha-Kṛṣṇa as joint entity, 109, 183, *187–88*; *sakhī* and *sakhā*, 2 and *n*; as strategy in "bedtime-story", 55–56
Nanda: color of, 108, *160*, *171*; courtyard of, 89, *111*, *159*, *160*; foster-father of Kṛṣṇa, 9; sees world in Kṛṣṇa's mouth, 167, *175*
Narasiṃha, man-lion *avatāra*, 16*n*, 53*n*, 100, 116, *161*, *163*, *172*
Nathan, Leonard: on "enumerative structure," 105; on unity in poetic structure, 41–42
*Neti*, *53*, *165*, *173*, *185*
*Nirguṇa* vs. *saguṇa*, 195, *203–4*, 219–20*n17*
Non-identity, essential in comparisons, 78
Nowottny, Winifred, on metaphor and simile, 86, 115*n*
Nursery rhymes, 43, 90–91, 93

Obscurity, in Thomas' poem is functional, 123
Oedipal irony. *See* Dramatic irony
Oedipus, 105, 106
Omniscience. *See* Audience, "omniscient"
Oral performance, importance of sequential perception in, 41
Oral tradition: in medieval India, xi; and paratactic structure, 91–92, 93–95, 104–5
Originality, in dealing with traditional material, 61

*Pada*: defined, 16*n*; number of in *Sūrsāgar*, xi, xii, 26
*Pada*, conventions of: *bhaṇitā*, 101; even number of lines, 67; "foot," 138; meter, 124–26; rhyme, 91, 101; *yati*, 125–26, 127
*Pāṃvoṃ-calnā-pada*, 32–34
*Pāṇḍavas*, *186*
*Parabrahma*. *See Brahmaṇ*
Paraśurāma, 53*n*, 100, *173*
Paratactic structure, 91–95, 104
Passion, *bhakti* as redirection of, 5
"Pastoral" quality of Sūr's verse, 140
Pathos, added to Kṛṣṇa-tale by Sūr, 69
Pecok, Bishop, 12
Penultimate line: and *bhaṇitā*, 67; preclosural cues in, 99, 102–4
Poem, as means occurring in time, 40
Poetry, as means to participation in *līlā*, 12
Prahlāda, *52*, *110*, *115*, *118*, *163*, *172*
Pralaya, "sea" of dissolution, 31*n*, 53*n*, 150, *154*, 212*n7*
Preclosural cue: alliteration as, 56; *bhaṇitā* as, 51, 57, 67; in penultimate line, 99, 102–4; shortening of unit of repetition as, 102
Prosody: conventions of in Hindi, 124–26; of Hindi compared with Greek and Latin, 125; Sūr's sophistication in use of, 138; in Sūr's verse, 124–33; used to structure argument, 74, 82–83, 87, 117–18; viewed as prescriptive system, 124–25, 132–33. *See also* Alliteration; Metrical parallelism; Rhyme
Pseudeo-simile: in poetry of Milton, 79; in poetry of Sūr, 79–90
"Psychology of information," 46
"Pūtanā" (poem), 48
Pūtanā, attempts to poison Kṛṣṇa, *48*, 48–51, 150, *152–53*

Queary, Lewis: on "contract," 43–44

Rādhā: as aspect of Kṛṣṇa, 14; fair in color, *187*; first meeting with Kṛṣṇa, 183, *187*; Kṛṣṇa in power of, *199*; love affair with Kṛṣṇa, 183, *187–88*, 194, *198–201*; marriage to Kṛṣṇa, 194; as paradigm for *madhura* mode of *bhakti*, 14, 110; as *śakti* of Kṛṣṇa, 109; taunted by mother, 109–10, 183, *187'88*; unaware of Kṛṣṇa's divinity, 110
Rāhu, 84
Rāma: breaks Śiva's bow, 205, *207–8*; as cult figure, 4, 14; Kabīr claims is *nirguṇa*, 14*n*; as paragon of *dharma*, 61; in poem by Kabīr, 93; story of, 16–17, *53–54*, 54–56, 61–65, 68–69, 85; worship of, 15. *See also Avatāra*

Ramanujan, A.K., on "spontaneity" in *bhakti* literature, 94-95, 136
*Rāmcaritmānas*, 15, 16-17, 61
*Rām-rājya*, 65
*Rasa*: and *bhava*, 22; impediments to, 34*n*; play on multiple meanings of, 218*n12*; as "soul of poetry," 22*n*; theory of, 21-22. *See also Bhāva*; *Sakhya*; *Sṛṅgāra*; *Vātsalya*
*Rāsa-līlā*, 6, 194, *199-200*
*Rāsa-maṇḍala*. *See Rāsa-līlā*
*Rasāsvādana*: and *brahmāsvādana*, 25*n*; impediments to, 34*n*
"Ratnākar," Jagannāth Dās, xi
Rāvaṇa, archenemy of Rama, 16, *53*, *54*, *62*, 75, *100*, *162*, *171*, *173*
"Rediscovered episode," strategy of the, 60-62, 68, 212*n7*
Reflection, as motif in Kṛṣṇa poetry, 87, 88-89, *159*, *162*, *166*, *170*, *175-76*, 216*n5*
Relative clause: and anticipation, 64, 65; in English and Hindi, 117, 121; figurative applications of, 115-24; given little recognition in poetics, 115, 121; has "poetic" and "prosaic" functions, 114-15; semantic function of, 117; and simile, 114-16, 118; used as "frame," 118-119, 112 and *n*; used to frame god and child, 116
Repetition: as contract, 102; cumulative effect of, 102; effect of interruption of, 29; of first word of poem, 56-57. *See also* Epanaphora
Return to norm: as closural strategy, 124, 130; limerick as example of, 130
Rhetoric of spontaneity, 138
Rhyme: in closural strategy, 49-50; common schemes in Hindi, 125; in conjunction with epanaphora, 74, 101-2, 119-20; as convention of *pada*, 101; effect of change in, 63; in Hindi tradition, 91; internal, 126; Milton on, 91; in translation, xv-xvi; used to structure argument, 74
Robinson, Edwin Arlington, "How Annandale Went Out," 46-47
Rohiṇī: Balarāma transplanted to womb of, 9; "mother" of Balarāma, 9, *111*, 111-12, *160*
Rūpa Goswāmin, on *bhāvas* of *bhakti*, 21, 22, 25

*Saguṇa*. *See Nirguṇa*
Said, Edward, on beginnings, 45
Sakaṭāsura: attempts to slay Kṛṣṇa, 150, *153-54*, 212*n7*
*Sakhya-bhāva*, 22, 68
*Śakti*: Rādhā as, 109
*Śakuntalā*, 106
Saṅkhāsura, *52*, *172*. *See also* Matsya
*Sants*, insist on *nirguṇa* nature of divine, 14*n*
Sanskrit: epiphany in, 40, 42; as language of elite, 4, 5; poetry in, 13, 40, 42, 54*n*; *subhāṣita*, 42
*Sāra*, most common *pada* meter, 125-26, 128-29, 132
Śarmā, Harbaṃślāl, on "whirlwind" poem, 31
Śarmā, Munśīrām: on *rasa*, 22*n*; on *tribhaṅga* poem, 97
Sequence: anatomical, mythological, 95; as aspect of poetic structure, 40-41, 93-94, 95-104; of *avatāras*, 52-53; and contract, 99. *See also Avatāra*.
Śeṣa: Balarāma incarnation of, 8; mentioned in poems, *62*, *154*, *157*, *165*, *172*, *179*; Viṣṇu reclines on, 53*n*
Siṃhikā, 85, *92*, *169*
Simile: couplets, 81-82, 87, 91, 118; of Milton, 91; most important figure in Sanskrit poetics, 76; has "poetic" and "prosaic" functions, 114-15; and relative clause, 114-16, 118; in Sūr's poetry, 76-90; Sūr's use of criticized, 76-77; as "syntactical form," 114
Sītā: concern for Rāma, 68-69; *svayaṃvara* of, 61-65, 68-69, 205, *207-8*; wife of Rāma, 16, *54*
Śiva: bow of in *Sītā-svayaṃvara*, 61-62, 64-65, 68-69, *207*; as cult figure, 4; as Destroyer, 8, 150; and Kṛṣṇa identified, 80-84, 150, *164*, *208*, 220*n5*; mentioned in poems, *62*, *93*, *118*, *154*, *156*, *163*, *165*, *178*, *185*
Smith, Barbara Herrnstein: on closure, 44-45; on paratactic structure, 93-94, 95; on "return to norm," 130; on "terminal modification," 50

Sontag, Susan, on arrogance of interpretation, 134–35
Spontaneity, attributed to *bhakti* poetry, 94–95, 104–5, 135–36; rhetoric of, 138
Śrīdāma, 66, *186*
Śrīdhara: Brahmin who attempts to kill Kṛṣṇa, 150, 155–160; may be Sūr's invention, 150
Śrīnāthjī: icon of, 182; temple of, x
*Sṛṅgāra-rasa*, 96, 97
*Sthāyi-bhāva. See Bhāva*
Strategy. *See* individual types (e.g., Closural strategy; Rediscovered episode strategy; etc.)
Structure. *See* individual types (e.g., Paratactic structure)
*Subhāṣitaratnakoṣa*, 13, 84
Śukla, Rāmcandra: compares Sūr and Tulsī, 17, 140; on Sūr's similes, 76–77, 79
Sūrdās:
life: association with sect of Vallabha, ix–xi; biographical sources, x; blindness, 1, 3, 91, 209; death scene, 209; meeting with Vallabha, 5–6; possible association with Akbar, x; questions of biography, 3, 5–6; as "Singer of Tales," xi
poetry: attitudes toward social norms, 17; compared with Tulsī's, 15–17, 61, 65, 68–69 and *n*, 140; English writings on, 22*n*; more complex than commonly supposed, 24; not self-contained narrative units, 45; in posture of sinner, 205–7; shows preference for metonymy over metaphor, 137; subtle sense of structure in, 95, 104–5, 114, 135, 136–38
*"Sūr-līlā,"* 18, 23
*Sūrsāgar*: attempts at critical edition of, xi, xii; and *Bhāgavata Purāṇa*, 211*n1*; Braj-bhāṣā language of, ix, 3–4; as collection of questionable authorship, ix–xiii; intended audience for, xiii; number of *padas* in, xi, xii, 26; printed editions, xii; ritual use by Vallabha sect, ix–x, xii
"Sūr tradition", xi–xiii
Symbols, and arrogance of interpretation, 135
Synecdoche: as rhetorical figure, 74, 89–90, 112; and simile, 137. *See also* Metonymy
Syntactic chiasmus, 83
Syntactic parallelism: effect of alteration in, 47; and paratactic structure, 138; in Sūr's verse, 28
Syntax, as element of poetic structure, 62–65, 82–83, 101–2, 114–24

Tagore, Rabindranath, 21
*Tāla*: defined, 219*n9*; and prosody, 133
Ṭaṇḍan, Premnārāyaṇ, 31, 33*n*
Tāṇḍava, *80*, 83
*Ṭeka*: defined, 33*n*; metrically short line, 125; as refrain, 101
Tense, effect of change in, 58, 62–63
Terminal modification, as closural strategy, 50–51
Thomas, Dylan, "The force that," 121–24
"Three bends". *See Tribhaṅga*
"Three Worlds," *118, 151, 156, 166, 169, 175, 184*
Time: as aspect of poetic structure, 40–41; "frightened" by Kṛṣṇa, *116*; and temporal disorientation in verse by Tulsī, 63
Tiwārī, Śaśi, 31
Tortoise. *See* Kūrma
Tradition, defined by Cunningham, 60. *See also* Sūr tradition
Tragedy, foreign to Sanskrit drama, 106
*Tribhaṅga*, 97, 98
*Trimūrti*, 7
Tripartite argument, 92–93, 104
Triple City, destroyed by Śiva, 61, 69, *80, 115, 164*
Tripurāri. *See* Triple City
Tṛṇāvarta, attacks Kṛṣṇa, *27*, 47–48, *157–58*
Tulsīdās: analysis of poem by, 61–65; author of *Rāmcaritmānas*, 15, 16–17, 61; author of *Vinaya Patrikā*, 94, 205; compared to Sūr, 15–17, 65, 68–69 and *n*, 140; uses metrical parallelism, 127
"Twin Trees", sons of Kubera freed by Kṛṣṇa, 167–68, *179–80, 191*

Uddhava, mission of to Gopīs, 76, 194–95, *202–4*

Ullmann, Stephen, on metaphor, 114*n*
Unit of repetition, shortening of as preclosural cue, 102. *See also* Couplet; Line
Unity, in poetic structure, 41–42, 95, 104–5
*Upamā*, 76, 78
*Utprekṣā*, 76

Vaiṣṇavism, includes worship of both Rāma and Kṛṣṇa, 14
Vallabha, sect of: and Govardhana, 182, 205; icon in, 89–90; Sūr's association with, ix–x, 5–6
Vālmīki *Rāmāyaṇa*, 75
Vāmana, dwarf *avatāra* of Viṣṇu, 53*n*, *93*, *99*, 100, *162*, *172*
Van Buitenen, J.A.B.: on *bhakti* literature, 94, 135; on Sūrdās, 140
Varāha, boar *avatāra* of Viṣṇu, 53*n*, *62*, *77*, *78*, *93*, *99*, 100, *161*, *164*, *172*
Variations on a theme, as structural principle, 92, 94, 105
Varmā, Brajeśvar, on connected narratives in *Sūrsāgar*, 211*n*1
Vasudeva, 8–9
Vāsuki, *72*, *73*, *117*, *162*, *163*
*Vātsalya bhāva*: contract for, 58; and mood of characters, 24; relation to *māyā* of *putrasneha*, 39; relationship to epiphany, 34–35, 71; in Rūpa Goswāmin's system, 22; sometimes saccharine, 141; Yaśodā as paradigm for, 110; in "Yaśodā daydreams" poem, 28, 29, 33*n*, 34
Vaudeville, Charlotte: characterizes Sūr's poems as "Pastorales," 140; on Sūr as "improvisateur," 135; on Sūr's life, x
Vedas: mentioned in poems, *99*, *116*, *153*, *161*, *165*, *173*, *185*, *207*; stolen by Saṅkhāsura, 172
Veṇugopāla, 96
Vibhīṣana, *199*, *162*
Vidyāpati, poetry of, 14–15, 84
*Vinaya-pada*, *205–8*
*Vipralambha*, 96
*Viraha*. *See* Longing
Viṣṇu: Brahmā born from navel of, *118*, *157*, *162*; Earth requests to become incarnate, *100*, 104; as Preserver, 7–8; reclines on Śeṣa, 53*n*. *See also Avatāra*; Vaiṣṇavism
*Viṣṇu Purāṇa*, as source for Kṛṣṇa-mythos, 10–11*n*
Viṭṭhalnāth, 209
Vṛndāvana. *See* Brindāban
Vṛṣabhānu, *109*, *188*, *190*

Wellek, Rene, and Austin Warren, on metonymy and metaphor, 89–90
Wimsatt, W.K., and Monroe Beardsley, on affective and intentional fallacies, 23*n*
White, Charles S.J., 31 and *n*
Wilson, H.H.: on Kabīr, ix

Yādavas: Kṛṣṇa born among, 8; relocate in Dwārakā, 10
Yamunā: banks as site of *rāsa-līlā*, 194, *200*; *-dah*, 67, 70, 181
Yaśodā: asserts authority over Kṛṣṇa, 110, 112, *116*, *118*, *163*; fair in color, 108, 160, *171*; favorite devotional role for Sūr, 12; foster-mother of Kṛṣṇa, 9–10, 108, 110–12; as paradigm for *vātsalya*, 110; punishes Kṛṣṇa, 37–38, 107, 167–68, *178–79*; sees universe in Kṛṣṇa's mouth, 36, 166, *166–67*, *174*; as "target" of dramatic irony, 110; unaware of Kṛṣṇa's divinity, 12, 37–38, 55, 58, 110–12
"Yaśodā daydreams" (poem), *27*
"Yaśodā delights" (poem), *32*
*Yati*: conventions of, 81*n*, 101, 117, 125–26, 127; divides line into "feet," 81*n*
Yeats, William Butler, "The Second Coming," 51
*Yugala*, union of god and *śakti*, 109

www.ingramcontent.com/pod-product-compliance
Lightning Source LLC
Chambersburg PA
CBHW021700230426
43668CB00008B/680
* 9 7 8 0 5 2 0 3 0 2 8 5 3 *